W9-CGN-391

Managing

FOR

DUMMIES®

3RD EDITION

Managing FOR DUMMIES®

3RD EDITION

**by Bob Nelson, PhD
and Peter Economy**

WILEY

Wiley Publishing, Inc.

Managing For Dummies® 3rd Edition

Published by
Wiley Publishing, Inc.
111 River St.
Hoboken, NJ 07030-5774
www.wiley.com

Copyright © 2010 by Wiley Publishing, Inc., Indianapolis, Indiana

Published simultaneously in Canada

No part of this publication may be reproduced, stored in a retrieval system or transmitted in any form or by any means, electronic, mechanical, photocopying, recording, scanning or otherwise, except as permitted under Sections 107 or 108 of the 1976 United States Copyright Act, without either the prior written permission of the Publisher, or authorization through payment of the appropriate per-copy fee to the Copyright Clearance Center, 222 Rosewood Drive, Danvers, MA 01923, (978) 750-8400, fax (978) 646-8600. Requests to the Publisher for permission should be addressed to the Permissions Department, John Wiley & Sons, Inc., 111 River Street, Hoboken, NJ 07030, (201) 748-6011, fax (201) 748-6008, or online at http://www.wiley.com/go/permissions.

Trademarks: Wiley, the Wiley Publishing logo, For Dummies, the Dummies Man logo, A Reference for the Rest of Us!, The Dummies Way, Dummies Daily, The Fun and Easy Way, Dummies.com, Making Everything Easier, and related trade dress are trademarks or registered trademarks of John Wiley & Sons, Inc. and/or its affiliates in the United States and other countries, and may not be used without written permission. All other trademarks are the property of their respective owners. Wiley Publishing, Inc., is not associated with any product or vendor mentioned in this book.

LIMIT OF LIABILITY/DISCLAIMER OF WARRANTY: THE PUBLISHER AND THE AUTHOR MAKE NO REPRESENTATIONS OR WARRANTIES WITH RESPECT TO THE ACCURACY OR COMPLETENESS OF THE CONTENTS OF THIS WORK AND SPECIFICALLY DISCLAIM ALL WARRANTIES, INCLUDING WITHOUT LIMITATION WARRANTIES OF FITNESS FOR A PARTICULAR PURPOSE. NO WARRANTY MAY BE CREATED OR EXTENDED BY SALES OR PROMOTIONAL MATERIALS. THE ADVICE AND STRATEGIES CONTAINED HEREIN MAY NOT BE SUITABLE FOR EVERY SITUATION. THIS WORK IS SOLD WITH THE UNDERSTANDING THAT THE PUBLISHER IS NOT ENGAGED IN RENDERING LEGAL, ACCOUNTING, OR OTHER PROFESSIONAL SERVICES. IF PROFESSIONAL ASSISTANCE IS REQUIRED, THE SERVICES OF A COMPETENT PROFESSIONAL PERSON SHOULD BE SOUGHT. NEITHER THE PUBLISHER NOR THE AUTHOR SHALL BE LIABLE FOR DAMAGES ARISING HEREFROM. THE FACT THAT AN ORGANIZATION OR WEBSITE IS REFERRED TO IN THIS WORK AS A CITATION AND/OR A POTENTIAL SOURCE OF FURTHER INFORMATION DOES NOT MEAN THAT THE AUTHOR OR THE PUBLISHER ENDORSES THE INFORMATION THE ORGANIZATION OR WEBSITE MAY PROVIDE OR RECOMMENDATIONS IT MAY MAKE. FURTHER, READERS SHOULD BE AWARE THAT INTERNET WEBSITES LISTED IN THIS WORK MAY HAVE CHANGED OR DISAPPEARED BETWEEN WHEN THIS WORK WAS WRITTEN AND WHEN IT IS READ.

For general information on our other products and services, please contact our Customer Care Department within the U.S. at 877-762-2974, outside the U.S. at 317-572-3993, or fax 317-572-4002.

For technical support, please visit www.wiley.com/techsupport.

Wiley also publishes its books in a variety of electronic formats. Some content that appears in print may not be available in electronic books.

Library of Congress Control Number: 2010929307

ISBN: 978-0-470-61813-4

Manufactured in the United States of America

10 9 8 7 6 5 4 3 2 1

WILEY

About the Authors

Bob Nelson, PhD: Dr. Nelson (San Diego, California) is president of Nelson Motivation Inc., a management training and consulting company that specializes in helping organizations improve their management practices, programs, and systems.

Dr. Nelson has sold more than 3.5 million books on management and motivation, which have been translated in more than 35 languages, including *1001 Ways to Reward Employees* (now in its 55th printing), *The 1001 Rewards & Recognition Fieldbook, 1001 Ways to Energize Employees, 1001 Ways to Take Initiative at Work, Keeping Up in a Down Economy, Ubuntu: An Inspiring Story of an African Principle of Teamwork and Collaboration,* and (with Peter Economy) *The Management Bible* and *Consulting For Dummies,* 2nd Edition.

He has appeared extensively in the media, including on CBS's *60 Minutes,* CNN, MSNBC, PBS, and National Public Radio, and has been featured in *The New York Times, The Wall Street Journal, The Washington Post, BusinessWeek, Fortune,* and *Inc.* magazines to discuss how to best motivate today's employees.

Dr. Nelson holds an MBA in organizational behavior from UC Berkeley and received his PhD in management with Dr. Peter F. Drucker at the Drucker Graduate Management School of Claremont Graduate University in suburban Los Angeles, where his doctoral dissertation was titled "Factors that Encourage or Inhibit the Use of Non-Monetary Recognition by U.S. Managers."

For more information about available products or services offered by Nelson Motivation Inc., including registration for Dr. Nelson's free Tip of the Week, visit www.nelson-motivation.com. For information about having Dr. Nelson present to or consult with your organization, association, or conference, contact Nelson Motivation Inc. at 800-575-5521 in the U.S., or Dr. Nelson directly at bobrewards@aol.com or by phone at 858-673-0690 PST.

Peter Economy: Peter Economy (La Jolla, California) is the associate editor for *Leader to Leader,* the Apex Award–winning publication of the Leader to Leader Institute. Peter is also the best-selling author of more than 50 books, including *Managing For Dummies, The Management Bible, The SAIC Solution: How We Built an $8 Billion Employee-Owned Technology Company,* and *Lessons from the Edge: Survival Skills for Starting and Growing a Company.* Peter was the home-based business expert for the AllBusiness.com, NBCi, McAfee.com, iVillage.com, and CNBC.com websites. He also was the staff management expert for *TIME* magazine's TIME Vista Boardroom Web site, along with such business luminaries as reengineering expert Michael Hammer and marketing gurus Michael Treacy and Jack Trout. Peter also penned a regular column on client relations for 1099.com, a Web site geared to the needs of independent professionals, and he has written articles for a number of magazines, including *Gallup Management Journal* and *Sailing World*. Peter earned his BA from Stanford University and his postgraduate certificate in business administration from Edinburgh Business School. Visit Peter at his Web site, www.petereconomy.com.

Dedication

To any manager who has struggled to do the job and every employee who has had to live with the consequences.

Authors' Acknowledgments

Bob recalls three influential mentors in his career: Jim Reller, a delegator par excellence in Bob's first corporate position at Control Data Corporation, often gave out assignments with a disclaimer such as, "I could probably do this task faster than you, but I believe you'll learn a lot from the process"; Dr. Ken Blanchard, co-author of *The One Minute Manager,* whom Bob worked with for more than ten years, demonstrated how to get the best efforts from people by using the softer side of management and never directly telling them what to do; and Dr. Peter F. Drucker, whom Bob worked with in his PhD studies at Claremont Graduate University, taught him that the best management principles were also the simplest ones.

These mentors taught more than just the technical skills of assigning work, conducting a performance appraisal, or disciplining an employee. They emphasized the people side of management: how to motivate employees by example, reward them when they exceed expectations, and make each person feel like he or she is the most important in the world.

Bob and Peter also appreciate everyone at Wiley Publishing, Inc., who has helped to make their books — and *Managing For Dummies,* 3rd Edition, in particular — be the best, including Stacy Kennedy, Elizabeth Rea, Krista Hansing, and Julie Cookson.

On the personal side, Bob would like to acknowledge the ongoing love and support of his parents, Helen and Edward; his wife, Jennifer; and his children, Daniel and Michelle. Peter acknowledges his wife, Jan, and his children, Peter J, Skylar Park, and Jackson Warren, for their everlasting love and for putting up with his crazy life. May the circle be unbroken.

Publisher's Acknowledgments

We're proud of this book; please send us your comments at http://dummies.custhelp.com. For other comments, please contact our Customer Care Department within the U.S. at 877-762-2974, outside the U.S. at 317-572-3993, or fax 317-572-4002.

Some of the people who helped bring this book to market include the following:

Acquisitions, Editorial, and Media Development

Project Editor: Elizabeth Rea
    (Previous Edition: Allyson Grove)

Acquisitions Editor: Stacy Kennedy

Copy Editor: Krista Hansing
    (Previous Edition: Chad R. Sievers)

Assistant Editor: Erin Calligan Mooney

Senior Editorial Assistant: David Lutton

Technical Editor: Julie B. Cookson, PHR

Editorial Manager: Michelle Hacker

Editorial Assistant: Jennette ElNaggar

Cover Photos: © Jupiter Images/Philip J. Brittan

Cartoons: Rich Tennant
    (www.the5thwave.com)

Composition Services

Project Coordinator: Katherine Crocker

Layout and Graphics: Christin Swinford

Proofreaders: Rebecca Denoncour,
    Nancy L. Reinhardt

Indexer: Potomac Indexing, LLC

Publishing and Editorial for Consumer Dummies

Diane Graves Steele, Vice President and Publisher, Consumer Dummies

Kristin Ferguson-Wagstaffe, Product Development Director, Consumer Dummies

Ensley Eikenburg, Associate Publisher, Travel

Kelly Regan, Editorial Director, Travel

Publishing for Technology Dummies

Andy Cummings, Vice President and Publisher, Dummies Technology/General User

Composition Services

Debbie Stailey, Director of Composition Services

Contents at a Glance

Table of Contents

Introduction

· ·

Congratulations! As a result of your astute choice of material, you're about to read a completely fresh approach to the topic of management. If you've already read other books about management, you've surely noticed that most of them fall into one of two categories: (1) deadly boring snooze-o-rama that makes a great paperweight; or (2) recycled platitudes glazed with a thin sugar coating of pop psychobabble, which sound great on paper but fail abysmally in the real world.

Managing For Dummies, 3rd Edition is different. First, this book is fun. Our approach reflects our strong belief and experience that management can be fun, too. You can get the job done and have fun in the process. We even help you maintain a sense of humor in the face of the seemingly insurmountable challenges that all managers have to deal with from time to time. On some days, you'll face challenges — perhaps pushing you to your limit or beyond. However, on many more days, the joys of managing — teaching a new skill to an employee, helping land a new customer, accomplishing an important assignment, and so on — can bring you a sense of fulfillment that you never imagined possible.

Second, the vast majority of popular business books seem to be here today and gone tomorrow. Like it or not, many managers (and the companies they work for) seem to be ruled by the business fad of the month. In *Managing For Dummies,* 3rd Edition, we buck the trend by concentrating on tried-and-true solutions to the most common situations that real supervisors and managers face. Our solutions stand up over time and work in even turbulent times. Since we published the first edition of *Managing For Dummies* in 1996, managers all around the world have bought more than half a million copies of this book, and it has been translated into more than 16 different languages. Long story short, you won't find any mumbo-jumbo here — just practical solutions to everyday problems that any manager will find of value.

Managing For Dummies, 3rd Edition breaks the rules by providing a comprehensive overview of the fundamentals of effective management, presented in a fun and interesting format. It doesn't put you to sleep, nor is it sugarcoated. We know from personal experience that managing can be an intimidating job. New managers — especially ones promoted into the position for their technical expertise — often have trouble knowing what they need to do. Don't worry. Relax. Help is at your fingertips.

About This Book

Managing For Dummies, 3rd Edition is perfect for all levels of management. If you're a new manager or a manager-to-be, you can find everything you need to know to be successful. If you're an experienced manager, we challenge you to shift your perspective and take a fresh look at your management philosophies and techniques. Despite the popular saying that you can't teach an old dog new tricks, you can always incorporate changes that make your job (and the jobs of your employees) easier, resulting in more fun and effectiveness.

Of course, even the most experienced manager can feel overwhelmed from time to time, new tricks or not.

For Bob, this moment came when he was giving an important business presentation to a group of international executives — only to have one of the executives point out that his pants were unzipped. Although Bob scored bonus points for getting his audience's attention with this novel fashion statement, he could've done so in a more strategic way.

For Peter, his overwhelming moment came when he reprimanded an employee for arriving late to work and later learned that the employee had been late because she had stopped at a bakery to buy Peter a cake in celebration of Boss's Day. Needless to say, the event wasn't quite as festive as it could've been!

Face it, whether you're new to the job or are facing a new task in your current job, all managers feel overwhelmed sometimes. The secret to dealing with stress is to discover what you can do better (or differently) to obtain your desired results. When you do make a mistake, pick yourself up, laugh it off, and learn from it. We wrote this book to make learning easier so that you won't have to make all the same mistakes and learn the hard way.

Conventions Used in This Book

When writing this book, we included some general conventions that all *For Dummies* books use. We use the following:

- ✔ We *italicize* any words you may not be familiar with and provide definitions.
- ✔ We **bold** all keywords in bulleted lists and the actual steps in numbered lists.
- ✔ All Web sites and e-mail addresses appear in `monofont`.

What You're Not to Read

Not surprisingly, we think every word in this book is worth your time. We know, however, that you may not want to read it all. With that understanding in mind, we make it easy for you to identify "skippable" material by placing it in sidebars. A sidebar is a gray box in each chapter that contains information that is interesting and related to the topic at hand, but not absolutely essential for your success as a manager.

Foolish Assumptions

As we wrote this book, we made a few assumptions about you, our readers. For example, we assumed that you're either a manager or a manager-to-be and that you're truly motivated to discover some new approaches to managing organizations and to leading people. We also assumed that you're ready, willing, and able to commit yourself to becoming a better manager.

How This Book Is Organized

Managing For Dummies, 3rd Edition is organized into five parts. Each part covers a major area of management practice, and the chapters within each part cover specific topics in detail. Following is a summary of what you'll find in each part.

Part I: Getting Started as a Manager

Becoming a successful manager means understanding and applying several basic skills. This part begins with a discussion of what managers are and what they do, and then looks at the most basic management skills: leading, inspiring, and engaging.

Part II: Mastering Key Management Duties

The heart of management boils down to a number of important management duties — tasks every manager needs to master to successfully get the job done. These duties include hiring new employees, setting goals, coaching and mentoring, working with teams, managing virtual employees, and monitoring performance and execution. We cover each of these duties in this part.

Part III: Tools and Techniques for Managing

To carry out their day-to-day duties, managers have a variety of tools and techniques at their disposal. We cover the most important of these management tools and techniques in this part, including delegating, communicating, evaluating performance, budgeting and accounting, harnessing technology, and applying corporate social responsibility.

Part IV: Tough Times for Tough Managers

As any manager can testify, management isn't all fun and games. In fact, managing can be downright challenging at times. In this part, we consider some of the toughest tasks of managing: managing change and disciplining and firing employees.

Part V: The Part of Tens

Finally, we include the Part of Tens: a quick-and-dirty collection of chapters, each of which gives you ten pieces of information that every manager needs to know. You'll find common management mistakes, advice for new managers, and strategies for maintaining your work-life balance. Look to these chapters when you need a quick refresher on managing strategies and techniques.

Icons Used in This Book

To guide you along the way and point out the information you really need to know, this book uses icons along its left margins. You'll see the following icons in this book:

This icon points to tips and tricks that make managing easier.

If you don't heed the advice next to these icons, the situation may blow up in your face. Watch out!

Remember these important points of information, and you'll be a much better manager.

This icon points out wise sayings and other kernels of wisdom that you can take with you on your journey to becoming a better manager.

These anecdotes from Bob and Peter and other real-life managers show you the right — and sometimes wrong — ways to be a manager.

Where to Go from Here

This book is unique because you can read each chapter without having to read what comes before or after. Or you can read the book backward or forward. Or you can just carry it around with you to impress your friends.

If you're a new or aspiring manager and you want a crash course in management, you may want to start at the beginning and work your way through to the end. Forget about going back to school to get your MBA — you can save your money and take a trip to Hawaii instead. Simply turn the page and take your first step into the world of management.

If you're already a manager and are short on time (and what manager isn't short on time?), you may want to turn to a particular topic, such as delegating tasks or hiring employees, to address a specific need or question. The table of contents and index can direct you to the answers you seek.

Enjoy your journey!

Part I
Getting Started as a Manager

The 5th Wave   By Rich Tennant

"It's not the bootlickers or nitpickers that bother me; it's the wall-walkers and carpet-divers that get on my nerves."

In this part . . .

Before you can become an effective manager, you need to master some basic skills. In this part, you find out what you're expected to do as a manager and the challenges you may face. Then we cover some of the most important managing skills that will take you far in your position, including becoming a leader, inspiring employees through support and rewards, and creating an engaged workforce through communication and autonomy.

Chapter 1

You're a Manager — Now What?

Managing is truly a calling — one that, during our long tenures as managers, we authors are proud to have answered. *We're the few. The proud. The managers.* In the world of business, no other place allows you to have such a direct, dramatic, and positive impact on the lives of others and on the ultimate success of your enterprise. This chapter provides an overview of the challenging and ever-changing world of management. Whether you're a manager or a manager-to-be, you can benefit from our inside look into the kinds of management techniques that can help you get the best from your employees every day of the week.

Identifying the Different Styles of Management

One definition describes *management* as "getting things done through others." Another definition more specifically defines management as "making something planned happen within a specific area through the use of available resources." Seems simple enough. So why do so many bright, industrious people have trouble managing well? And why do so many companies today seem to offer a flavor-of-the-month training program that changes each time some new management fad blows through the business scene?

Unfortunately, good management is a scarce commodity, both precious and fleeting. Despite years of changing management theory and countless management fads, many workers — and managers, for that matter — have developed a distorted view of management and its practice. Managers often don't know the right approach to take or exactly what to do. And as the saying goes, "If it's foggy in the pulpit, it'll be cloudy in the pew."

Do you ever hear any of the following remarks at your office or place of business?

- ✔ "We don't have the authority to make that decision."

- ✔ "She's in charge of the department — fixing the problem is her responsibility, not ours."

- ✔ "Why do they keep asking us what we think when they never use anything we say?"

- ✔ "I'm sorry, but that's our policy. We're not allowed to make exceptions."

- ✔ "If my manager doesn't care, I don't, either."

- ✔ "It doesn't matter how hard you work; no one's going to notice anyway."

- ✔ "You can't trust those employees — they just want to goof off."

When you hear remarks like these at work, red lights should be flashing before your eyes, and alarm bells should be ringing loudly in your ears. Remarks like these indicate that managers and employees aren't communicating effectively — that managers don't trust their employees, and that employees lack confidence in their managers. If you're lucky, you find out about these kinds of problems while you still have a chance to do something about them. If you're not so lucky and you miss the clues, you may be stuck repeatedly making the same mistakes.

The expectations and commitments that employees carry with them on the job are largely a product of the way their managers treat them. Following are the most commonly adopted styles of management. Do you recognize your management style?

Tough guy (or gal) management

What's the best way to make something planned happen? Everyone seems to have a different answer to this question. Some people see management as something you do *to* people — not *with* them. Does this type of manager sound familiar? "We're going to do it my way. Understand?" Or perhaps the ever-popular threat: "It had better be on my desk by the end of the day — or else!" If worse comes to worst, a manager can unveil the ultimate weapon: "Mess up one more time, and you're out of here!"

This type of management is often known as *Theory X management,* which assumes that people are inherently lazy and need to be driven to perform. Managing by fear and intimidation is always guaranteed to get a response. The question is, do you get the kind of response you really want? When you closely monitor your employees' work, you usually end up with only short-term compliance. In other words, you never get the best from others by lighting a fire under them — you have to find a way to build a fire within them.

Sometimes managers have to take command of the situation. If a proposal has to be shipped out in an hour and your customer just sent you some important changes, take charge of the situation to ensure that the right people are on the task. When you have to act quickly with perhaps not as much discussion as you'd like, however, it's important to apologize in advance and let people know why you're acting the way you are. Remember that the majority of employees leave their positions because of the actions (or lack thereof) of their direct supervisor or manager. So make sure you move quickly but with clear communication and respect for your staff.

Nice guy (or gal) management

At the other end of the spectrum, some people see management as a "nice guy" or "nice gal" kind of idea. *Theory Y management* assumes that people basically want to do a good job. In the extreme interpretation of this theory, managers are supposed to be sensitive to their employees' feelings and avoid disturbing their employees' tranquility and sense of self-worth. This approach may come across like this: "Uh, there's this little problem with your report; none of the numbers are correct. Now, don't take this personally, but we need to consider our alternatives for taking a more careful look at these figures in the future." This scenario also plays out when someone from the peer group is promoted into a management position. He sometimes can't easily transition from being a buddy into being the manager.

Again, managers may get a response with this approach (or they may choose to do the work themselves!), but are they likely to get the best possible response? No, the employees are likely to take advantage of the managers.

The right kind of management

Good managers realize that they don't have to be tough all the time — and that nice guys and gals often finish first. If your employees are diligently performing their assigned tasks and no business emergency requires your immediate intervention, you can step back and let them do their jobs. Not only do your employees learn to be responsible, but you also can concentrate your efforts on what is most important to the bottom-line success of your organization.

A manager's real job is to inspire employees to do their best and establish a working environment that allows them to reach their goals. The best managers make every possible effort to remove the organizational obstacles that prevent employees from doing their jobs and to obtain the resources and training that employees need to do their jobs effectively. All other goals — no matter how lofty or pressing — must take a back seat.

Bad systems, bad policies, bad procedures, and poor treatment of others are organizational weaknesses that managers must identify and repair or replace. Build a strong organizational foundation for your employees. Support your people, and they will support you. When given the opportunity to achieve, workers in all kinds of businesses, from factories to venture capital firms, have proven this rule to be true. If you haven't seen it at your place of business, you may be mistaking your employees for problems. Quit squeezing them and start squeezing your organization. The result is employees who want to succeed and a business that flourishes right along with them. Who knows? Your employees may even stop hiding when they see you coming their way!

Squeezing employees may be easier than fighting the convoluted systems and cutting through the bureaucratic barnacles that have grown on your organization. You may be tempted to yell, "It's your fault that our department didn't achieve its goals!" Yes, blaming your employees for the organization's problems may be tempting, but doing so isn't going to solve the problems. Sure, you may get a quick, short-lived response when you push your people, but ultimately, you're failing to deal with the organization's real problems.

Everyone wants to "win." The difficult challenge of management is to define "winning" in such a way that it feels like winning for everyone in the organization. People are often competing with co-workers for a "piece of the pie" instead of trying to make the pie bigger. It's your job to help make a bigger pie.

Meeting the Management Challenge

When you're assigned a task in a nonmanagement position, completing it by yourself is fairly simple and straightforward. Your immediate results are in direct response to your effort. To accomplish your task, first you review the task, then you decide how best to accomplish it, and then you set schedules and milestones for its successful completion. Assuming that you have access to the tools and resources necessary to accomplish your task, you can probably do it yourself quickly and easily. You're an expert doer — a bright, get-things-done type of person.

However, if you hold a management position, you were probably selected because you're skilled in the areas you're now responsible for managing. For example, Peter's friend John was a member of a team of software programmers developing a complex application for portable computers. When he was a team member, everything was fine. He came to work in a T-shirt and jeans — just like the rest of his teammates — and often spent time with his programmer friends after hours. The bond that the team shared changed, however, when John became the team's manager.

In his new role of manager, John first changed offices. Instead of sharing an open bay with the other programmers, he moved into his own office — one with four walls and a window looking out over the parking lot. A secretary guarded his door. Of course, the jeans and T-shirt had to go — they were replaced with a business suit and tie. Instead of having fun programming, John was suddenly concerned about more serious topics, such as cost over-runs, schedule delays, percent direct, and days receivable. As John's role changed, so did John. And as John changed, so did his relationship with his co-workers. He was no longer a co-worker; he was The Boss. To achieve his goals, John quickly had to make the transition from a doer to a manager of doers.

When you want to get a task done through someone else, you employ a different set of skills than when you do the task yourself. This simple decision to pass the responsibility of completing a task to someone else introduces an interpersonal element into your equation. Being good technically at your job is no longer enough, no matter how good your technical skills are. Now you must have good planning, organization, leadership, and follow-up skills.

In other words, in addition to being a good doer, you have to be a good manager of doers. If you need some help in this area, discuss outside training opportunities (Management 101) with your supervisor or manager so you are equipped immediately. There's no time to waste!

Skipping quick fixes that don't stick

Despite what many people want you to believe, management isn't always a shoot-from-the-hip proposition. Sure, some managers may make decisions too quickly from time to time, but the most effective ones take the time they need to consider their options before making a decision. Being a manager isn't easy. Yes, the best management solutions tend to be common sense; however, turning common sense into common practice is often difficult.

Management is an attitude, a way of life. Management is a very real desire to work with people and help them succeed, as well as a desire to help your organization succeed. Management is a life-long learning process that doesn't end when you walk out of a one-hour seminar or finish viewing a 25-minute video. Management is like the old story about the unhappy homeowner who was shocked to receive a bill for $100 to fix a leaky faucet. When asked to explain the basis for this seemingly high charge, the plumber said, "Tightening the nut cost you $5. Knowing which nut to tighten cost you $95!"

Management is a people job. If you're not up to the task of working with people — helping them, listening to them, encouraging them, and guiding them — then you shouldn't be a manager.

Because management is such a challenge, an entire management training industry has sprung up, ready to help managers learn how to solve their problems. Unfortunately, trainers often focus on creating instant gratification among course attendees, many of whom have spent hundreds and even thousands of dollars to be there.

Once Peter went to one of those touchy-feely offsite management meetings meant to build teamwork and communication among the members of the group. Picture this: Just after lunch, a big tray of leftover veggies, bagels, fruit, and such was sitting on a table at the side of the room. The facilitator rose from his chair, faced the group, and said, "Your next task is to split yourselves into four groups and construct a model of the perfect manager by using only the items on that tray of leftovers." A collective groan filled the room. "I don't want to hear any complaints," the trainer said. "I just want to see happy people doing happy things for the next half-hour."

The teams feverishly went about their task of building the perfect manager. With some managers barely throttling the temptation to engage each other in a massive food fight, the little figures began to take shape. A banana here, a carrot stick there . . . and, voilá! After a brief competition for dominance, the winners were crowned. The result? We thought you'd never ask. Check out Figure 1-1.

We have to admit that the result was kind of cute (and kind of tasty, too), but did it really make a difference in the way these managers managed their employees when they returned to the office the next day? We don't think so. Was the seminar a nice break from the day-to-day office routine? Yes. Was it a meaningful teaching tool with lasting impact? No.

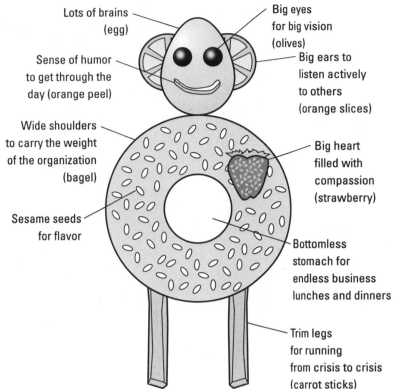

Lots of brains
(egg)

Big eyes
for big vision
(olives)

Sense of humor
to get through the
day (orange peel)

Big ears to
listen actively
to others
(orange slices)

Wide shoulders
to carry the weight
of the organization
(bagel)

Big heart
filled with
compassion
(strawberry)

Sesame seeds
for flavor

Bottomless
stomach for
endless business
lunches and dinners

Figure 1-1:
The veggie
manager.

Trim legs
for running
from crisis to crisis
(carrot sticks)

Partnering with your employees

If this challenge isn't already enough, managers today face yet another challenge — one that has shaken the foundations of modern business. The new reality is partnering managers and workers in the workplace.

Originally, management meant dividing the company's work into discrete tasks, assigning the work to individual workers, and then closely monitoring the workers' performance and steering them in the right direction to accomplish their tasks on time and within budget. The old reality of management often relied on fear, intimidation, and power over people to accomplish goals. If things weren't going according to management's plan, management simply commanded its way out of the problem: "I don't care what you have to do to get it done — just get it done. Now!" The line between managers and workers was drawn clearly and drawn often.

Watch out! Technology explosion ahead!

In the new world of information technology, the old ways of doing business are being turned on their sides. With the presence of computer networks, e-mail, and voice mail, the walls that divide individuals, departments, and organizational units have come crashing down. In the words of Frederick Kovac, former vice president of planning for the Goodyear Tire and Rubber Company, "It used to be, if you wanted information, you had to go up, over, and down through the organization. Now you just tap in. Everybody can know as much about the company as the chairman of the board."

In the new business environment, what's going on inside the organization is a reflection of what's going on outside the organization. The following factors are creating rapid and constant change in today's new business environment:

- A surge of global competition
- New technology and innovation
- The flattening of organizational hierarchies
- A global economic downturn, with widespread cost cutting and layoffs
- The rise of small business
- The changing values of today's workers
- The increasing demands for better customer service

Sure, managers still have to divide and assign work, but workers are taking on more of that responsibility. Most important, managers are finding out that they can't command their employees' best work — they have to create an environment that fosters their employees' desire to do their best work. In short, the new reality is the partnership of managers and workers in the workplace.

The landscape of business worldwide has changed dramatically during the past few decades. If you don't change with it, you're going to be left far behind your competitors. You may think that you can get away with treating your employees like "human assets" or children, but you can't. You can't, because your competitors are discovering how to unleash the hidden power of their employees. They're no longer just talking about it; they're doing it!

Being open to new ideas and procedures

A few years ago, Bob made a presentation to a group of high-tech managers. As he was wrapping up his presentation, he opened the floor to questions. A hand shot up. "With all the downsizing and layoffs we've endured, people are lucky to get a paycheck, much less anything else. Why do we have to bother to empower and reward employees?" Before Bob had a chance to respond, another manager in the audience shot back, "Because it's a new army."

This response really sums it all up. In business, times are changing. Now that employees have tasted the sweet nectar of empowerment, you can't turn back. Companies that stick with the old way of doing business — the hierarchical, highly centralized model — will lose employees and customers to companies that make the new ways of doing business a part of their corporate culture. The best employees will leave the old-model companies in droves, seeking employers who will treat them with respect and who are willing to grant them greater autonomy and responsibility.

That leaves you with the employees who don't want to take risks or rock the boat. You get the yes-men and yes-women. No one will challenge your ideas because they're afraid to. No one will suggest better or more efficient ways to do business because they know that you won't listen or care anyway. Your employees won't bother to go out of their way to help a customer because you don't trust them to make the most basic decisions — the ones that can make the biggest difference to the satisfaction, or the lack thereof, of your precious customers.

Imagine the difference between an employee who tells your key customer, "Sorry, my hands are tied. I am not allowed to make any exceptions to our policies," and the employee who tells that customer, "Sure, I'll do everything in my power to get you your order by your deadline." Which type of employee do you think your customers prefer to do business with? Which type of employee do you prefer to do business with?

Managers used to rent behavior. Some workers were even called "hired hands." Today hiring your hands isn't good enough. You must find a way to engage their souls and bring their best efforts to the workplace each day.

Establishing two-way trust

Companies that provide exceptional customer service unleash their employees from the constraints of an overly controlling hierarchy and allow front-line workers to serve their customers directly and efficiently. For many years, Nordstrom, Inc. devoted exactly one page to its manual, shown in Figure 1-2.

> **We're glad to have you with our Company. Our number one goal is to provide outstanding customer service.**
>
> **Set both your personal and professional goals high.**
>
> **Nordstrom Rules:**
>
> **Rule #1: Use your good judgement in all situations.**
>
> **There will be no additional rules. Please feel free to ask your department manager, store manager, or division general manager any question at any time.**

Figure 1-2: Nordstrom's rules show an exceptional amount of trust in employees.

Source: *Business and Society Review, Spring 1993, n85*

Today employees also receive a standard employee handbook — the company's legal environment has changed considerably over the past decade — but this one page still guides most employee behavior at the company. You may think that a *small* company with five or ten employees can get away with a similar policy, but certainly not a big company like yours. However, Nordstrom isn't a small business, by any stretch of the imagination — unless you consider a company with 52,000 or so employees and more than $8.5 billion in annual sales small.

How does management at a large business like Nordstrom get away with such a policy? They do it through trust.

First, Nordstrom hires good people. Second, the company gives them the training and tools to do their jobs well. Then management gets out of the way and lets the employees do their work. Nordstrom knows that it can trust its employees to make the right decisions because the company knows that it has hired the right people for the job and has trained them well.

We're not saying that Nordstrom doesn't have problems — every company does. But Nordstrom has taken a proactive stance in creating the environment that employees most need and want.

Can you say the same for your organization?

When you trust your employees, they respond by being trustworthy. When you recognize them for being independent and responsive to their customers, they continue to be independent and responsive to their customers. And when you give them the freedom to make their own decisions, they more often than not make good ones. With a little training and a lot of support, these decisions back up the best interests of the company because the right people at the right level of the organization make them.

Mastering the New Functions of Management

Remember the four "classic" functions of management — plan, organize, lead, and control — that you learned in school? (Yeah, we were asleep in that class, too.) These management functions form the foundation from which every manager works. Although these basic functions are fine for taking care of most of your day-to-day management duties, they fail to reflect the new reality of the workplace and the new partnership of managers and workers. What's needed is a new set of management functions that builds upon the four classic functions of management. You're in luck. The sections that follow describe the functions of the new manager in the 21st-century workplace.

Energize

Today's managers are masters of making things happen — starting with themselves. As the saying goes, "If it's to be, it's to begin with me." Think of the best managers you know. What one quality sets them apart from the rest? Is it their organizational skills, their fairness, or their technical ability? Perhaps their ability to delegate or the long hours they keep sets them apart.

All these traits may be important to a manager's success, but we haven't yet named the unique quality that makes a good manager great. The most important management function is to get people excited and inspired — that is, to *energize* them.

Great managers create far more energy than they consume. The best managers are organizational catalysts. Instead of taking energy from an organization, they channel and amplify it to the organization. In every interaction, effective managers add to the natural energy of their employees and leave the employees in a higher energy state than when they started the interaction. Management becomes a process of transmitting the excitement that you feel about your organization and its goals to your employees in terms that they can understand and appreciate. And certainly get their ideas and, where appropriate, their buy-in for even more success! Before you know it, your employees will be as excited about the organization as you are, and you can simply allow their energy to carry you forward.

A picture is worth a thousand words. This statement is as true for the pictures that you paint in the minds of others as for the pictures that people paint on canvas or print on the pages of magazines and books. Imagine taking a vacation with your family or friends. As the big day draws near, you keep the goal exciting and fresh in the minds of your family or friends by creating a vision of the journey that awaits you. Vivid descriptions of white-sand beaches, towering redwoods, glittering skylines, secluded lakes, hot food, and indoor plumbing paint pictures in the minds of each of your fellow travelers. With this vision in mind, everyone works toward a common goal of a successful vacation.

Successful managers create compelling visions — pictures of a future organization that inspire and compel employees to bring out their best performance.

Empower

Have you ever worked for someone who didn't let you do your job without questioning your every decision? Maybe you spent all weekend working on a special project, only to have your boss casually discard it. "What were you thinking when you did this, Elizabeth? Our customers will never buy into that approach!" Or maybe you went out of your way to help a customer, accepting a return shipment of an item against company policy. "Why do you think we have policies — because we enjoy killing trees? No! If we made exceptions for everyone, we'd go out of business!" How did it feel to have your sincere efforts at doing a great job disparaged? What was your reaction? Chances are, you won't bother making the extra effort again.

Despite rumors to the contrary, when you empower your employees, you don't stop managing. What changes is the way you manage. Managers still provide vision, establish organizational goals, and determine shared values. However, managers must establish a corporate infrastructure — skills training, teams, and so on — that supports empowerment. And although all your employees may not want to be empowered, you still have to provide an environment that supports employees who are eager for a taste of the freedom to apply their personal creativity and expertise to your organization.

What managers really do

With tongue planted firmly in cheek, we universally agree that all managers perform five functions in an organization:

✔ **Eat:** Management clearly has its rewards, one of which is an expense account and all the company-paid lunches and dinners you can get away with. And if those yo-yos in accounting dare to question the business purpose of your meals, you can always threaten to leave them off your list of invitees.

✔ **Meet:** Meetings are truly a perk of management. The higher you rise in an organization, the more time you spend in meetings. Instead of doing productive work, you spend more time than ever listening to presentations that have no relevance to your department, drinking three-day-old coffee, and keeping close tabs on your watch as your meeting drags on well past its scheduled ending time.

✔ **Punish:** With so many wayward employees, the best managers learn to punish early and punish often. What better way to show your employees that you care? Punishment also sends a welcome signal to upper management that you don't put up with any nonsense from your underlings.

✔ **Obstruct:** When you ask managers what single achievement makes them proudest, they are likely to bring out policies as thick as the Yellow Pages that were carefully drafted over many years. A close look at the policy may reveal a package of deftly written red tape that does more to prevent good customer service than it does to support it.

✔ **Obscure:** Managers are masters of the art of miscommunication. No one knows better than a manager that information is power: The people who have it wield the power, and the people who don't are lost. With potential enemies all around, why give anyone else a chance to get an advantage over you? "Hey! That information is on a need-to-know basis only!" And for heaven's sake, why let your employees in on the inner workings of the organization? They wouldn't appreciate or understand it anyway, right?

Actually, this *isn't* the list of the functions of management. Although the list may ring true in many cases, we're just pulling your leg.

 Great managers allow their employees to do great work. This role is a vital function of management, for even the greatest managers in the world can't succeed all by themselves. To achieve the organizations' goals, managers depend on their employees' skills. Effective management means leveraging the efforts of every member of a work unit to focus on a common purpose. If you're constantly doing your employees' work for them, not only have you lost the advantage of the leverage your employees can provide you, but you're also putting yourself on the path to stress, ulcers, and worse.

However, far worse than the personal loss that you suffer when you don't empower employees is that everyone in your organization loses. Your employees lose because you aren't allowing them to stretch themselves or to show creativity or initiative. Your organization loses the insights that its creative workforce brings with it. Finally, your customers lose because your employees are afraid to provide them with exceptional service. Why should they, if they're constantly worried that you will punish them for taking initiative or for pushing the limits of the organization to better serve your customers?

As William McKnight, former CEO of manufacturing giant 3M, put it, "The mistakes people make are of much less importance than the mistakes management makes if it tells people exactly what to do."

Support

A manager's job is no longer that of a watchdog, police officer, or executioner. Increasingly, managers must be coaches, colleagues, and cheerleaders for the employees they support. The main concern of today's managers needs to be shaping a more supportive work environment that enables each employee to feel valued and be more productive.

When the going gets tough, managers support their employees. Now, this doesn't mean that you do everything for your employees or make their decisions for them. It does mean that you give your employees the training, resources, and authority to do their jobs, and then you get out of the way. You're always there for your employees to help pick up the pieces if they fall, but fall they must if they're going to learn. The idea is the same as in learning to skate: If you're not falling, you're not learning.

The key to creating a supportive environment is establishing trust or *openness* throughout an organization. In an open environment, employees can bring up questions and concerns. In fact, they're encouraged to do so. When the environment is truly open, an individual can express concerns without fear of retribution. Hidden agendas don't exist, and people feel free to make the same remarks in business meetings that they'd say after work. When employees see that their managers are receptive to new ideas, they're more likely to feel invested in the organization and to think of more and better ways to improve systems, solve problems, save money, and better serve customers.

Managers also support each other. Guarding personal fiefdoms, fighting between departments, and withholding information have no place in the modern organization; companies cannot afford to support these dysfunctional behaviors. All members of the organization, from top to bottom, must realize that they play on the same team. To win, team members must support each other and keep their co-workers apprised of the latest information. Which team are you on?

Communicate

Without a doubt, communication is the lifeblood of any organization, and managers are the common element that connects different levels of employees. We have seen firsthand the positive effects on a business and its employees when managers communicate, and the negative effects when managers don't.

Managers who don't communicate effectively are missing out on a vital role of management.

Communication is a key function for managers today. Information is power, and as the speed of business accelerates, information must be communicated to employees faster than ever. Constant change and increasing turbulence in the business environment necessitate more communication, not less. Who's going to be around in five years? The manager who has mastered this function or the one who has not?

With the proliferation of e-mail, voice mail, text messages, tweets, and the other new means of communication in modern business, managers simply have no excuse not to communicate with their employees. You can even use the telephone or try a little old-fashioned face-to-face talk with your employees and co-workers.

To meet the expectations you set for them, your employees have to be aware of your expectations. A goal is great on paper, but if you don't communicate it to employees and don't keep them up-to-date on their progress toward achieving that goal, how can you expect them to reach it? Simply, you can't. It's like training for the Olympics but never getting feedback on how you're doing against the competition.

Employees often appreciate the little things — an invitation to an upcoming meeting, praise for a job well done, or an insight into the organization's finances. Not only does sharing this kind of information make a business run better, but it also creates tremendous goodwill and cements the trust that bonds your employees to the organization and to the successful completion of the organization's goals.

Taking the First Steps toward Becoming a Manager

Believe it or not, many managers are never formally trained to be managers. For many of you, management is just something that's added to your job description. One day you may be a computer programmer working on a hot new Web browser, and the next day you may be in charge of the new development team. Before, you were expected only to show up to work and create a product. Now you're expected to lead and motivate a group of workers toward a common goal. Sure, you may get paid more to do the job, but the only training you may get for the task is in the school of hard knocks.

Managers (or managers-to-be) can easily discover how to become good managers by following the recommendations in the sections that follow. No one way is absolutely right or absolutely wrong; each has its pluses and minuses.

Look and listen

If you're fortunate enough to have had a skilled teacher or mentor during the course of your career, you've been treated to an education in management that's equal to or better than any MBA program. You've learned firsthand the right and wrong ways to manage people. You've learned what it takes to get things done in your organization, and you've learned that customer satisfaction involves more than simply giving your customers lip service.

Unfortunately, any organization with good management also has living, breathing examples of the wrong way to manage employees. You know the people we're talking about: the manager who refuses to make decisions, leaving employees and customers hanging. Or the boss who refuses to delegate even the simplest decision to employees. Or the supervisor who insists on managing every single aspect of a department, no matter how small or inconsequential. Examples of the right way to manage employees are, regrettably, still few and far between.

You can benefit from the behaviors that poor managers model. When you find a manager who refuses to make decisions, for example, carefully note the impact that the management style has on workers, other managers, and customers. You feel your own frustration. Make a mental note: "I'll never, ever demotivate another person like that." Indecision at the top inevitably leads to indecision within all ranks of an organization — especially when employees are punished for filling the vacuum left by indecisive managers. Employees become confused, and customers become concerned as the organization drifts aimlessly.

I meet, you meet, we all meet

According to the experts, managers are attending more meetings than ever. The average businessperson spends more than 25 percent of his or her time in meetings, but middle managers spend 40 percent of their time in meetings — worse, executives spend up to a staggering 80 percent of their time in meetings. Even more shocking is that about half of every hour spent in meetings is wasted by the participants' inefficiency and ineffectiveness.

Observe the manager who depends on fear and intimidation to get results. What are the real results of this style of management? Do employees look forward to coming to the office every day? Are they all pulling for a common vision and goal? Are they extending themselves to bring innovation to work processes and procedures? Or are they more concerned with just getting through the day without being yelled at? Think about what you would do differently to get the results you want.

You can always learn something from other managers, whether they're good managers or bad ones.

Do and learn

Perhaps you're familiar with this old saying (attributed to Lao Tze):

> Give a man a fish, and he eats for a day,
>
> Teach a man to fish, and he eats for a lifetime.

Such is the nature of managing employees. If you make all the decisions, do the work your employees are able to do when given the chance, and try to carry the entire organization on your own shoulders, you're harming your employees and your organization far more than you can imagine. Your employees never find out how to succeed on their own, and after a while, they quit trying. In your sincere efforts to bring success to your organization, you stunt your employees' growth and make your organization less effective and vital.

Top five management Web sites

Wondering where to find the best information on the Web about the topics addressed in this chapter? Here are our top five favorites:

- ✔ Harvard Business School Working Knowledge: hbswk.hbs.edu

- ✔ *Leader to Leader* magazine: www.pfdf. org/knowledgecenter/journal. aspx

- ✔ *Fast Company* magazine: www.fast company.com

- ✔ *MIT Sloan Management Review:* sloan review.mit.edu

- ✔ The McKinsey Quarterly: www. mckinseyquarterly.com

Simply reading a book (even this one) or watching someone else manage — or fail to manage — isn't enough. To take advantage of the lessons you learn, you have to put them into practice. Keep these key steps in mind:

1. **Take the time to assess your organization's problems.** Which parts of your organization work and which don't? Why or why not? You can't focus on all your problems at once. Concentrate on a few problems that are the most important, and solve them before you move on to the rest. If issues exist across client or business groups, schedule time to discuss them with key stakeholders and idea-share to resolve problems.

2. **Take a close look at yourself.** What do you do to help or hinder your employees when they try to do their jobs? Do you give them the authority to make decisions? Just as important, do you support them when they go out on a limb for the organization? Study your personal interactions throughout your business day. Do they result in positive or negative outcomes? If you haven't had a personality/management assessment done, consider it. If you decide to move forward with one, then budget for it and schedule a follow-up meeting after it is conducted to discuss the results.

3. **Try out the techniques that you learn from reading or from observing other managers at work.** Go ahead! Nothing changes if you don't change first. "If it's to be, it's to begin with me."

4. **Step back and watch what happens.** We promise that you'll see a difference in the way you get tasks done and the way your customers and employees respond to your organization's needs and goals.

Chapter 2

Lead, Follow, or Get Out of the Way

· ·

In This Chapter

▶ Comparing leadership and management

▶ Becoming a leader

▶ Zeroing in on key leadership traits

▶ Leading collaboratively

· ·

*W*hat makes a leader? Experts have written countless books, produced endless videos, and taught interminable seminars on the topic of leadership. Yet despite all the discussion on this important topic, the quality of leadership eludes many who seek it.

Studies show that all effective leaders have two primary traits in common: a positive outlook and forward thinking. They're sure of themselves and their ability to influence others and impact the future. Although leadership and management are similar, leadership goes above and beyond management. According to management visionary Peter Drucker, leadership is the most basic — and scarcest — resource in any business enterprise. Good leadership is thus particularly valuable to an organization, as well as to those who work within it.

Everyone in an organization wants to work for a great leader, yet a leader means many things to many people. In this chapter, we discuss the key skills and attributes that make good managers into great leaders. Leadership requires applying a wide variety of skills; no single trait suddenly makes you an effective leader. However, you may notice that some of the leadership skills this chapter details are also key functions of management — ones that we review in Chapter 1. This similarity is no coincidence. By the way, for an in-depth look at leadership, check out *Leadership For Dummies* (Wiley), by Marshall Loeb and Stephen Kindel.

Understanding the Difference between Management and Leadership

Being a good manager is quite an accomplishment. Management is by no means an easy task, and mastering the wide range of varied skills required can take many years. The best managers get their jobs done efficiently and effectively, with a minimum of muss and fuss. Similar to the people behind the scenes of a great sports match or theater performance, the best managers are often the employees whom you notice the least.

Great managers are experts at optimizing their current organizations to accomplish their goals and get their jobs done. By necessity, they focus on the here and now, not on the tremendous potential the future can bring. Managers are expected to make things happen now, not at some indefinite, fuzzy point in the future. "Don't tell me what you're going to do for me next year or the year after that! I want results, and I want them now!" However, having good managers in an organization isn't enough.

Great organizations need great management. However, great management doesn't necessarily make a great organization. For an organization to be great, it must also have great leadership.

A manager can be organized and accomplish tasks efficiently without being a leader — someone who inspires others to achieve their best. For that matter, someone can be an inspiring leader but fall short when it comes to mastering the processes required to run an organization. In general, managers manage processes; they lead people.

Employees want the men and women they work for to exhibit leadership. "I wish my boss would just make a decision — I'm just spinning my wheels until she does. I guess I'll just wait here until she lets me know what she wants me to do." And wait they do — until the boss finally notices that the project is two months behind.

Top executives also want the men and women who work for them to exhibit leadership. "You need to take responsibility for your department and pull the numbers into the black before the end of the fiscal year!" And employees want their peers to show leadership. "If he's not going to straighten out that billing process, I'll just have to work around it myself!"

Leaders have vision. They look beyond the here and now to see the vast potential of their organizations. And although great leaders can effectively get things done in their organizations, they accomplish their goals differently from managers. How so? Managers use values, policies, procedures, schedules, milestones, incentives, discipline, and other mechanisms to *push* their employees to achieve the organization's goals. Leaders, on the other hand, challenge their employees to achieve the organization's goals by creating a compelling vision of the future — a vision that *pulls* employees to achieve those goals — and then unlocking their employees' potential.

Think about some great leaders. President John F. Kennedy challenged the American people to land a man on the moon. We did. Jack Welch of General Electric challenged his workers to help the company attain first or second place in every business it owned. They did. Alan G. (A. G.) Lafley challenged the management and workers of Procter & Gamble (P&G) to pull the company out of its serious financial and product doldrums, restoring P&G's industry leadership in profits and innovative new products. They did.

All these leaders share a common trait: They painted compelling visions that grabbed their followers' imagination and then challenged them to achieve these visions. They also acknowledged the hard work and contributions of their employees. Without the vision leaders provide and the contributions of their followers' hard work, energy, and innovation, the United States would never have landed a man on the moon, General Electric wouldn't be the hugely successful firm it is today, and the name Procter & Gamble would have been eclipsed by the competition.

Figuring Out What Leaders Do

The skills you need to be a leader are no secret; some managers have figured out how to use the skills and others haven't. And although some people seem to be born leaders, anyone can discover what leaders do and how to apply those skills.

Inspire action

Most workers want to feel pride in their organization and, when given the chance, happily give their all to a cause they believe in. Every organization has a tremendous well of creativity and energy just waiting to be tapped. Leaders use this knowledge to inspire their employees to take action and achieve greatness. Leaders know the value of employees and their critical importance in achieving the company's goals. Do the managers in your company know the importance of their employees? Check out what these managers had to say in Bob Nelson's *1001 Ways to Reward Employees:*

✔ Former chairman and CEO of the Ford Motor Company Harold A. Poling said, "One of the stepping stones to a world-class operation is to tap into the creative and intellectual power of each and every employee."

✔ According to Paul M. Cook, founder and former CEO of Raychem Corporation, "Most people, whether they're engineers, business managers, or machine operators, want to be creative. They want to identify with the success of their profession and their organization. They want to contribute to giving society more comfort, better health, [and] more excitement."

✔ Hewlett-Packard cofounder Bill Hewlett said, "Men and women want to do a good job, a creative job, and if they are provided the proper environment, they will do so."

Unfortunately, few managers reward their employees for being creative or going beyond the boundaries of their job descriptions. Too many managers search for workers who do exactly what they are told — and little else. This practice is a tremendous waste of worker creativity, ideas, and motivation.

Leaders are different. They unleash the natural energy within all employees by clearing roadblocks to creativity and pride and by creating a compelling vision for their employees to strive for. Leaders help employees tap into energy and initiative that they didn't know they had.

Use your influence as a manager to help your employees create energy in their jobs instead of draining it from them with bureaucracy, red tape, policies, and an emphasis on avoiding mistakes. Create a compelling vision for your employees and then clear away the roadblocks to creativity and pride. Your vision must be a stretch to achieve, but not so much of a stretch that they can't reach it.

Communicate

Leaders make a commitment to communicate with their employees and to keep them informed about the organization. Employees want to be an integral part of their organizations and want their opinions and suggestions to be heard. Great leaders earn the commitment of their workers by building communication links throughout the organization — from the top to the bottom, from the bottom to the top, and from side to side.

So how do you build communication links in your organization? Consider the experiences of the following business leaders as listed in Bob's *1001 Ways to Reward Employees:*

- ✔ According to Donald Petersen, former president and CEO of Ford Motor Company, "When I started visiting the plants and meeting with employees, what was reassuring was the tremendous, positive energy in our conversations. One man said he'd been with Ford for 25 years and hated every minute of it — until he was asked for his opinion. He said that question transformed his job."

- ✔ Andrea Nieman, administrative assistant with the Rolm Corporation, summarized her company's commitment to communication like this: "Rolm recognizes that people are the greatest asset. There is no 'us' and 'them' attitude here; everyone is important. Upper management is visible and accessible. There is always time to talk, to find solutions, and to implement changes."

- ✔ Said Robert Hauptfuhrer, former chairman and CEO of Oryx Energy, "Give people a chance not just to do a job but to have some impact, and they'll really respond, get on their roller skates, and race around to make sure it happens."

When many years ago coauthor Bob became a department manager at Blanchard Training and Development (now the Ken Blanchard Companies), he made a commitment to his team of employees to communicate with them. To make his commitment real, Bob added specifics: He promised that he would report the results of every executive team meeting within 24 hours. Bob's department valued his team briefings because, through this communication, he treated all individuals as colleagues, not as underlings.

Great leaders know that leadership isn't a one-way street. Leadership today is a two-way interchange of ideas in which leaders create a vision and workers throughout an organization develop and communicate ideas of how best to reach the vision. The old one-way, command-and-control model of management doesn't work anymore — certainly not as a daily means of managing a company. Most employees aren't willing to simply take orders and be directed all day long. If you think your employees want to be ordered around, you're only fooling yourself.

Support and facilitate

Great leaders create environments in which employees are safe to speak up, tell the truth, and take risks. Incredibly, many managers punish their employees for pointing out problems, disagreeing with the conventional wisdom of management, or merely saying what's on their minds. Even more incredible, many managers punish their employees for taking risks and losing, instead of helping their employees win the next time around.

Great leaders support their employees and facilitate their ability to reach their goals. The head of an organization where coauthor Peter once worked did just the opposite. Instead of leading his employees with vision and inspiration, he pushed them with the twin cattle prods of fear and intimidation. Management team members lived in constant fear of his temper, which exploded without warning and seemingly without reason. More than a few managers wore the psychological bruises and scars of his often-public outbursts. Instead of contributing to the good of the organization, some managers simply withdrew into their shells and said as little as possible in this leader's presence.

Consider these managers' statements in *1001 Ways to Reward Employees:*

- ✔ Catherine Meek, former president of compensation consulting firm Meek and Associates, and now executive director of School on Wheels, says, "In the 20 years I have been doing this and the thousands of employees I have interviewed in hundreds of companies, if I had to pick one thing that comes through loud and clear, it is that organizations do a lousy job of recognizing people's contributions. That is the number one thing employees say to us. 'We don't even care about the money; if my boss would just acknowledge that I exist. The only time I ever hear anything is when I screw up. I never hear when I do a good job.'"

- ✔ According to Lonnie Blittle, an assembly line worker for Nissan Motor Manufacturing Corporation U.S.A., "There was none of the hush-hush atmosphere with management behind closed doors and everybody else waiting until they drop the boom on us. They are right down pitching in, not standing around with their hands on their hips."

- ✔ James Berdahl, vice president, Technology Solutions Group for BI, says, "People want to feel empowered to find better ways to do things and to take responsibility for their own environment. Allowing them to do this has had a big impact on how they do their jobs, as well as on their satisfaction with the company."

Instead of abandoning their employees to the sharks, great leaders throw their followers life preservers when the going gets particularly rough. Although leaders give their employees free rein in how they achieve their organizations' goals, leaders are always there in the background ready to assist and support workers whenever necessary. With the added security of this safety net, employees are more willing to stretch themselves and take chances that can create enormous payoffs for their organizations.

Leaders may also take time to get to know their employees — learning about their employees' interests, families, personal triumphs, and tragedies. By personalizing the experience, they get great buy-in from employees. The leaders also share their human side with their employees, which makes them more approachable while building bridges of understanding and trust.

Surveying Leading Leadership Traits

Today's new business environment features unrelenting change — all the time and in every conceivable way. About the only constant you can be sure of anymore is that everything will change. And after it changes, it will change again and again.

Business will continue to transform in the foreseeable future, but great leadership remains steadfast, like a sturdy rock standing up to the storms of change. Numerous traits of great leaders have remained the same over the years and are still highly valued. The following sections discuss the leading leadership traits.

Optimism

Great leaders always see the future as a wonderful place. They may encounter much adversity and hard work on the way to achieving their goals, but leaders always look forward to the future optimistically. This optimism becomes a glow that radiates from all great leaders and touches the employees who come into contact with them.

People want to feel good about themselves and their futures, and they want to work for winners. Workers thus naturally flock to people who are optimistic instead of pessimistic. Who wants to work for someone who simply spouts doom and gloom about the future of a business? Negative managers only demotivate their employees and co-workers, inspiring them to spend more time polishing their resumes than improving their organizations.

Optimism is infectious. Before long, a great leader can turn an organization full of naysayers into one that's overflowing with positive excitement for the future. This excitement results in greater worker productivity and an improved organizational environment. Morale increases, and so does the organization's bottom line.

Be an optimist. Let your excitement rub off on the people around you.

Confidence

Great leaders have no doubt — at least, not in public — that they and their talented team of employees can accomplish any task they set their minds to.

Confident leaders make for confident followers, which is why organizations led by confident leaders are unstoppable. An organization's employees mirror the behavior of their leaders. When leaders are tentative and unsure of themselves, so are workers (and the bottom-line results of the organization). When leaders display self-confidence, workers follow suit, and the results can be astounding.

 Be a confident leader. You've put in years of training, hard work, and dedicated service to get to where you are now. Your skills, talent, and leadership ability paved your path. Your example and vision inspire your employees to perform their best and give them more confidence in their abilities.

Integrity

One trait that sets great leaders apart from the rest of the pack is integrity — ethical behavior, values, and a sense of fair play. Honest people want to follow honest leaders. In a recent survey, integrity was the trait that employees most wanted from their leaders. When an organization's leaders conduct themselves with integrity, the organization can make a very real and positive difference in the lives of its employees, its customers, and others who come in contact with it. Employees then develop even more positive feelings about the organization.

Most workers devote a third (or more) of their waking hours to their jobs. Whether the organization makes light fixtures, disposes of radioactive waste, develops virtual reality software, or delivers pizzas, people want to be part of an organization that makes a positive difference in people's lives. Sure, money is important — people have to make car payments and buy baby shoes — but few count this *external* reward a secondary consideration to the *internal* rewards they derive from their work.

Decisiveness

The best leaders are decisive; they aren't afraid to make the necessary decisions to keep their organizations moving forward. Employees repeatedly complain that their bosses don't make decisions. Managers are hired to make decisions, yet more than a few are afraid to risk making a wrong decision. Many so-called leaders instead prefer to indefinitely postpone making a decision so they can appear to seek more information, alternatives, and opinions from others. Maybe they hope that future events cancel out the need to make the decision, or perhaps they want someone else to decide for them.

Great leaders make decisions. However, not every decision is created equal. Some decisions have little impact on the company and its employees and customers. These decisions can and should be made quickly. Other decisions are strategic and have a great, long-term impact on the company and its employees and customers. These decisions require much deliberation and information gathering and analysis and should never be made in a shoot-from-the-hip fashion. Yet other decisions lie somewhere in between these two extremes.

Match your decision-making style to the nature of the decision to be made. When you have the information you need to make a quality decision, make it. Don't waffle or equivocate. Making decisions is one of your key jobs as a manager.

Sharing Leadership Roles with Employees

A new kind of leadership is gaining traction in an increasing number of organizations: *collaborative leadership.* When leaders lead collaboratively, they share leadership with others in the organization — and not just with other managers and supervisors. They share leadership with employees at all levels, from the shop floor to the front line.

What does collaborative leadership look like in the workplace? Consider a few examples:

- ✔ To encourage collaborative leadership, banking powerhouse JPMorgan Chase maintains a flat organization with only four levels of employees worldwide: managing director, vice president, associate, and analyst. With fewer lines of reporting, every employee has the opportunity — and the responsibility — to play a greater role in leading and making decisions.

- ✔ W.L. Gore and Associates — manufacturer of a variety of products, including Gore-Tex — is famous for its unique lattice organizational structure that encourages collaborative leadership. W.L. Gore and Associates has no formal hierarchy of ranks, titles, and layers of management. The company has only *sponsors* and *associates.* Sponsors must attract and engage a sufficient number of associates to get their projects off the ground.

- ✔ To achieve its ultimate goal of "the genuine care of and comfort of our guests," management of the Ritz-Carlton Hotel Company promotes lateral service, a philosophy that encourages employees to handle whatever problem comes their way without consulting higher-ups, regardless of their place on the organizational chart.

✔ Aside from Chairman and President Carol Sturman, employees of Colorado-based Sturman Industries don't have titles. The organization is flat, and Carol encourages all employees to play an active role in decision making. Employees even vigorously discuss and debate high-level corporate policies, such as the company's drug-free workplace policy and the company's at-will employment policy, before the company adopts them.

In his book *Leadership Ensemble: Lessons in Collaborative Management from the World's Only Conductorless Orchestra,* Peter takes a close look at the unique brand of collaborative leadership that New York City's Orpheus Chamber Orchestra practices. One of the world's greatest orchestras, Orpheus also is one of the few to perform without a conductor. Most orchestras are identified not by the musicians who play the music, but by their conductors, who are often visionary, charismatic (and autocratic) leaders. The conductor calls all the shots when it comes to the notes that an orchestra's musicians play, and how and when they play them.

By forgoing the traditional model of a conducted orchestra — one leader and many followers — Orpheus fosters a culture of collaboration in which every musician actively shapes the group's final product: its music. Does this system work? Yes. Orpheus's performances have been acclaimed throughout the world, and the group has numerous Grammy-winning albums and other awards to its credit.

At the heart of the Orpheus Process — the system of collaborative leadership that has brought the group great success over its three-decade history — are eight principles:

✔ **Put power in the hands of the people doing the work.** The employees closest to the customers are in the best position to understand the customers' needs and make decisions that directly impact the customers.

✔ **Encourage individual responsibility for product and quality.** Putting power in the hands of the people doing the work also requires employees to take responsibility for the quality of their work. When employees play an active role in the organization's leadership, they naturally respond by taking a personal interest in the quality of their work.

✔ **Create clarity of roles.** Before employees can comfortably and effectively share leadership duties with others, they need clearly defined roles indicating what each person is responsible for.

✔ **Foster horizontal teamwork.** No single person has all the answers to every question, so effective organizations rely on horizontal teams — both formal and informal — that reach across department and other organizational boundaries. These teams obtain input, solve problems, act on opportunities, and make decisions.

Top five leadership Web sites

Wondering where to find the best information on the Web about the topics addressed in this chapter? Here are our top five favorites:

✔ *Leader to Leader* magazine: `www.leadertoleader.org/knowledgecenter/journal.aspx`

✔ *Fast Company* magazine: `www.fastcompany.com`

✔ Leadervalues: `www.leader-values.com`

✔ Center for Leadership and Change Management: `leadership.wharton.upenn.edu`

✔ The Leadership Network: `www.tbs-sct.gc.ca/chro-dprh/dev-eng.asp`

✔ **Share and rotate leadership.** Moving people in and out of positions of leadership (depending on the particular talents and interests of the individuals) helps organizations tap the leadership potential within every employee, even employees who aren't part of the formal leadership hierarchy.

✔ **Discover how to listen and how to talk.** Effective leaders don't just listen; effective leaders talk — and they know the right (and wrong) times to make their views known. Effective organizations encourage employees to speak their minds and to contribute their ideas and opinions, regardless of whether others agree with what they have to say.

✔ **Seek consensus (and build creative systems that favor consensus).** One of the best ways to involve others in the leadership process is to invite them to play a role in the discussions and debates involved in important organizational decisions. Seeking consensus requires a high level of participation and trust, and it results in more democratic organizations.

✔ **Dedicate passionately to your mission.** When people feel passion for their organizations, they care more about them and their performance. They express this caring in increased participation and leadership.

Collaborative leadership is growing in popularity in all kinds of organizations, in all kinds of places. Why? Organizations today can't afford to limit leadership to just a few individuals at the top. To survive and prosper, today's organizations need to get the most out of every employee. All employees need to take a leadership role in their organizations, to make decisions, serve customers, support colleagues, and improve systems and procedures. Employees — and leaders — who can't meet this challenge may find themselves left behind by others who can.

Chapter 3

Recognizing and Rewarding High Performance

- -

In This Chapter

▶ Emphasizing positive consequences

▶ Finding the right motivation for today's employees

▶ Being generous with praise

▶ Strategizing recognition and rewards

▶ Rewarding employees as individuals and as a team

- -

*T*he question of how to motivate employees has always loomed large over managers. Most of management comes down to mastering skills and techniques for motivating people — to make them better, more-productive employees who love their jobs more than anything else in the world. (Okay, maybe you'd be happy if they just liked their jobs and didn't complain so much.)

You can motivate employees in two ways: rewards and punishments. If employees do what you want them to do, thank them with *positive consequences* such as recognition, awards, money, promotions, and rewards. Alternatively, if employees don't do what you want, punish them with *negative consequences* such as warnings, reprimands, demotions, firings, and so on. By nature, employees seek positive consequences and shy away from negative consequences.

This chapter deals with the positive side of employee motivation, especially recognition and rewards. (We cover the punishment side in Chapter 18.)

Managing Positive Consequences

Research shows that you can improve employee performance more effectively by using positive consequences than negative ones. We aren't saying that negative consequences don't have a place; sometimes you have no choice but to punish, reprimand, or even terminate employees. However, first give your employees the benefit of the doubt and assume that they want to do a good job. Then acknowledge them when they do. This chapter helps you use positive recognition, praise, and rewards to encourage the behaviors you seek and catch people doing things right. You'll motivate your employees to excel in their jobs, you'll improve performance and morale, you'll be more successful, and your company will evolve into a better place to work.

By leading with *positive reinforcers,* not only do you inspire your employees to do what you want, but you also develop happier, more productive employees in the process — and that combination is tough to beat!

The most proven driver of desired behavior and performance known to mankind is positive reinforcement, which can be simply summarized in the phrase "You get what you reward." As a manager in any organization, you'll get more of the desired performance from your employees by taking the time to notice, recognize, and reward them when they excel in their work than anything else you could possibly do.

Consequences drive performance of any kind, and positive consequences such as employee recognition are needed to systematically reinforce successes and desired behavior when they occur.

This seems like a common-sense notion, yet in practice, positive reinforcement often doesn't happen. Consider this example. You have two employees: Employee A is incredibly talented, and Employee B is a marginal performer. You give similar assignments to both employees. Employee A completes the assignment before the due date and turns it in with no errors. Because Employee A is already done, you give him two additional assignments. Meanwhile, Employee B not only runs late, but when he finally turns in the report you requested, it is full of errors. Because you're now under a time crunch, you accept Employee B's report and correct it yourself.

What's wrong with this picture? You've shown Employee B that submitting substandard work behind schedule is okay. Furthermore, he sees that you'll personally fix it! You've rewarded an employee who clearly doesn't deserve it.

On the other hand, you've given Employee A more work for being a diligent, outstanding worker, so you're actually punishing him. You may think nothing of assigning more work to Employee A, but he knows the score. When Employee A sees that all he gets for being an outstanding performer is more work (while you let Employee B get away with doing less work), he's not going to like it. And if you end up giving both employees basically the same raise (and don't think they won't find out), you make the problem worse. You will lose Employee A, either literally, when he takes another job, or in spirit, when he stops working so hard.

Turkeys for the holidays

Here's an example of how an intended positive consequence can and does go wrong. Bob has a great story about a large California aerospace manufacturer that decided to thank all its employees at Christmas with a turkey for the holidays. Sounds good so far, doesn't it? However, some employees noticed that their turkeys were smaller than their co-workers' turkeys. Soon the complaints reached the executive suites — employees with smaller turkeys thought they were being punished for poor performance.

Naturally, management couldn't overlook this misconception. The following year, management instructed the supplier of the Christmas turkeys to supply turkeys of the same weight. The turkey supplier responded that all turkeys were not created equal. Supplying thousands of identical-weight turkeys would be impossible. Faced with this dilemma, management did what only management could do: It attached a printed note to each turkey stating, "The weight of your turkey does not necessarily reflect your performance over the last year."

Complaints continued, and the situation only worsened. Some employees wanted a choice between turkey and ham; others wanted a fruit basket, and so on. As the years went by, management found it necessary to hire a full-time turkey administrator! Finally, the annual Christmas turkey program came to a crashing halt when management discovered that certain employees were so disillusioned that they were dumping the turkeys out of their boxes, filling the boxes with company-owned tools, and sneaking them past security.

Did the company achieve its goal of equal reward for all? Obviously not. The program didn't boost employee performance or morale; it only caused a new set of management problems.

If you never take the time to thank and appreciate your employees for a job well done, all your top performers will eventually realize that doing their best work is not in their best interest. They'll leave to find an organization that values their contribution, or they'll simply kick back and forget about doing their best work because no one (that means you, the manager) seems to care anyway!

Nothing is as unfair at work as the equal treatment of unequal performers. Before you set up a system to recognize and reward your employees, make sure you know exactly what behaviors you want to reward and check periodically to see that what you set up is working. (See the later section "Creating a Recognition and Rewards System" for more guidance in setting up a system to motivate employees.)

Positive consequences bring about positive results, and what you do doesn't have to cost a lot of money to be effective. When cash flows freely, many companies don't hold back on the rewards, incentives, and perks for employees.

During the good times, such rewards are often an essential retention and motivation strategy. However, in tough and challenging times, many companies have found that they can't afford to reward employees as they did before, but they also can't afford *not* to reward them as well. Research by Accountemps found that 19 percent, the second highest category, reported that "recognition programs" served as one of the best remedies for low employee morale, and 13 percent of executives reported that offering financial rewards was an important aspect for improving employee morale in tough times; 11 percent of executives felt that "unexpected rewards" helped to improve morale.

According to a recent survey by incentive company Maritz, employees who work at recognition-oriented companies are

- Five times more likely to feel valued
- Seven times more likely to stay with the company
- Six times more likely to invest in the company
- Eleven times more likely to feel completely committed

Every company needs this commitment and effort from employees, especially in difficult times. A recent Tower Perrins study reports that committed employees deliver 57 percent more effort than uncommitted ones.

Figuring Out What Motivates Today's Employees

Studies show that what managers believe their employees most want from their jobs differs considerably from what employees report as being most desirable. Nonmonetary forms of recognition are generally more effective motivators than monetary ones — including cash. Although simple forms of recognition such as verbal praise and written thank-you notes are proven to work as motivation, many employees report that they seldom receive such incentives during the course of their careers; it's an enormous opportunity lost for countless organizations.

Using a variety of motivating incentives

According to Dr. Gerald Graham of Wichita State University, the most motivating incentives (as reported by employees today) are

- **Manager-initiated incentives:** Instead of coming from some nebulous ad-hoc committee or corporate bigwig, or appearing completely out of the blue, the most valuable recognition comes directly from one's supervisor or manager.

- **Performance-based incentives:** Employees want to be recognized for the jobs they're hired to do. The most effective incentives are based on job performance, not on non-performance-related factors such as attendance, attire, or a lucky number drawn out of a hat at the monthly sales meeting.

For employees, the most motivating incentives are initiated by managers instead of the organization and are contingent on performance instead of provided just for showing up to work. Recognition is most meaningful when it's given as soon as possible after the desired behavior or performance.

Don't reserve recognition for special occasions only — and don't just use it with the top performers. All employees need to be recognized when they do good work in their jobs. Your employees are doing good things that you want them to do every day. Catch them doing something right, and recognize their successes regularly and often!

The following incentives are simple to execute and take little time, yet they're the most motivating for employees:

- Give an employee personal or written congratulations for a job well done. Do it timely, often, and sincerely.

- Acknowledge employees in a public setting such as a company newsletter or department staff meeting, for maximum value.

- Offer time off or flexibility in working hours.

- Take the time to meet with and listen to employees — as much as they need or want.

- Give employees specific and frequent feedback about their performance. Support them in improving performance.

- Publicly recognize, reward, and promote top performers; deal with low and marginal performers so that they improve or leave (see Chapters 17 and 18 for guidance in these situations).

- Provide information on how the company makes and loses money, details on upcoming products, and specifics on services and strategies for competing. Explain the employee's role in the overall plan.

- Involve employees in decisions, especially decisions that affect them. Involvement equals commitment.

✔ Give employees a chance to grow and develop new skills; encourage them to be their best. Show them how you can help them meet their goals while achieving the organization's goals. Create a partnership with each employee.

✔ Give employees a sense of ownership in their work and their work environment. This ownership may be symbolic — for example, business cards for all employees, regardless of whether they need them to do their jobs.

✔ Strive to create a work environment that's open, trusting, and fun. Encourage new ideas, suggestions, and initiative. Help employees learn from mistakes; don't punish them for their missteps.

✔ Celebrate the successes of the company, the department, and the individuals within. Take time for team- and morale-building meetings and activities. Be creative and fresh.

For comprehensive listings of incentive ideas that really work, check out Bob's best-selling books *1001 Ways to Reward Employees, 1001 Ways to Energize Employees, The 1001 Rewards & Recognition Fieldbook,* and *1001 Ways to Take Initiative at Work,* available from www.nelson-motivation.com.

Creating a supportive work environment

Employee motivation is a moving target that's constantly changing with today's employees. The incredible speed and acceleration of change in business coupled with the impact of technology and expanded global competitive forces has placed pressure on managers to get the most from each employee. With these forces pressing in from all sides, managers can have difficulty keeping up with what employees need to do, much less figure out what to tell them to do. Inspiring managers must embrace these changing business forces and management trends. Instead of using the power of their positions to motivate workers, managers must use the power of their ideas. Instead of using threats and intimidation to get things done, managers must create environments that support their employees and allow creativity to flourish.

As a manager, you can create a supportive workplace in the following ways:

✔ **Build and maintain trust and respect.** Employees stay motivated to perform their best if their managers trust and respect them. By including employees in the decision-making process, managers get better ideas (that are easier to implement) and, at the same time, improve employee morale, loyalty, and commitment.

✔ **Open the channels of communication.** All your employees must communicate openly and honestly with one another. Quick and efficient communication throughout your organization may be the factor that differentiates you from your competition. Encourage your employees to speak up, offer suggestions, and break down organizational barriers such as rampant departmentalization turf wars that separate them from one another. A collaborative environment will foster group success and build team respect and engagement.

✔ **Make your employees feel safe.** Can your employees tell you bad news as comfortably as they can good news? If not, you haven't created a safe environment for your employees. Everyone makes mistakes; people discover valuable lessons from them. If you want motivated employees, let them take chances and share the bad along with the good. Avoid the urge to punish them when they make a mistake.

✔ **Develop your greatest asset — your employees.** The job of managing has shifted drastically from telling people what to do to finding out what best motivates employees and getting the work done through those motivations. Along the way, you can challenge your employees to improve their skills and knowledge, and give them the support and training they need to do so. Acknowledge their contributions and continually work with them on what they want and need. Concentrate on the positive progress employees make, and recognize and reward their successes whenever possible. Above all, be honest with them and always show integrity; after all, they're watching you!

Realizing that you hold the key to your employees' motivation

In our experience, most managers believe that their employees determine how motivated they choose to be. Managers tend to think that some employees naturally have good attitudes, that others naturally have bad attitudes, and that they (as managers) can't do much to change these attitudes. "If only we could unleash the same passion and energy people have for their families and hobbies," these managers think. "Then we could really get something done around here!"

As convenient as blaming your employees for their bad attitudes may be, looking in a mirror may be a more honest approach. Studies show that, for the most part, you determine how motivated (and unmotivated) your employees are. Managers create a motivating environment that makes it easier for employees to be motivated. When the time comes, recognize and reward them fairly and equitably for the work they do well.

A day at the spa

Instead of issuing bonuses, the owner of Swanky Bubbles Restaurant and Champagne Bar in Philadelphia gave his employees gift cards to an upscale spa and salon. He saved thousands of dollars, and employees still felt rewarded. Employees also had the opportunity to spend time together outside of work — something many simply aren't able to do — which resulted in a greater sense of teamwork and camaraderie.

When you give out rewards, keep in mind that employees don't want handouts, and they hate favoritism. Don't give recognition when none is warranted. Don't give recognition just to be nice or with the hope that people will like you better. Provide rewards for performance that helps you be mutually successful. Giving rewards inappropriately not only cheapens the value of the incentives, but it also lowers your credibility in the eyes of your other employees. Trust and credibility with your employees are two of the most important qualities you can build in your relationship with your employees; if you lose these qualities, you risk losing the employees.

The following recommendations can help you seek out the positive in your employees and reinforce the behaviors you want:

- **Have high expectations for your employees' abilities:** If you believe that your employees can be outstanding, soon they will believe it, too. When Peter was growing up, his parents rarely needed to punish him when he did something wrong. He needed only the words "We know that you can do better" to get him back on course.

- **Give your employees the benefit of the doubt:** Do you really think your employees want to do a bad job? Unless they're consciously trying to sabotage your firm, no one wants to do a bad job. Your job is to figure out what you can do to help employees succeed. Additional training, encouragement, and support should be among your first choices — not reprimands and punishment.

- **Catch your employees doing things right:** Although most employees do a good job in most of their work, managers naturally tend to focus on what employees do wrong. Instead of constantly catching your employees doing things wrong, catch them doing things right. Not only can you reinforce the behaviors you want, but you can also make your employees feel good about working for you and for your firm.

Recognizing the limitations of money as a motivator

Most people don't come to work just for money. We're not saying that money isn't important; clearly, it is. We all need money to pay our bills and live in the manner to which we are accustomed. We're also not saying that money has no motivational value; clearly, it does. And the strength of that motivation varies during one's life. For example, if you're about to buy a new home, you have some unexpected medical bills, or you have children in college, you're more keenly aware of your monetary needs and are much more motivated by cash.

But for most people, most of the time, when you're able to comfortably pay your monthly bills, your self-esteem quickly and inevitably turns to other factors that have much greater significance: feeling that you're making a contribution, having a manager who tells you when you do a good job, having the respect of your peers and colleagues, feeling like a valued part of a team, being involved and informed about what's going on in the company, and doing meaningful and interesting work.

The money employees are paid is *compensation*. That money is a product of your company's compensation philosophy and policies, its market, and its geographic considerations. *Recognition* is not compensation; it's what you offer employees above and beyond compensation to get the best effort from them.

According to management theorist Frederick Herzberg, a fair salary is considered a *hygiene* factor — something employees need to do the job they're hired to do. Hygiene factors include other basic needs, such as adequate workspace, sufficient lighting, and a comfortable environment. Hygiene factors enable employees to do their jobs — but not their *best* jobs possible. Getting people to do their best jobs is the function of what Herzberg calls *motivators*. Motivators include praise and recognition, challenging work, and growth and development opportunities. In essence, there's a huge difference between getting people to come to work in the first place and getting them to do their best work.

Unfortunately, many people correlate the amount of money they earn with their perceived worth to the organization. Higher pay indicates higher worth, and lower pay means lower worth. Avoid responding just to employees who constantly ask for more money. Why? Because you want to reinforce *results,* not requests. You'll never get the best effort from employees just by paying them more. Employees who only want more money will never be satisfied with what they're paid. Their expectations will always rise with each salary increase.

When incentives become entitlements

Employees who receive annual bonuses and other periodic, money-based rewards quickly come to consider them part of their basic pay. Money becomes an expectation and then an entitlement for many, if not most, workers.

Peter once worked at a company where he received an annual bonus that amounted to approximately 10 percent of his annual pay. The first time he received the bonus, he was excited by it. His motivation skyrocketed, and he pledged his eternal loyalty to the firm.

However, after Peter realized that receiving the bonus was going to be an annual event, he quickly took it for granted. In his mind, he converted the reward (for work above and beyond his basic job description) into a part of his basic compensation package. As far as Peter was concerned, his annual salary was really the amount of his base pay plus the annual bonus. He even based his holiday spending plans on the assumption that the bonus would arrive on or about a certain date — and it always did. Of course, if one year he hadn't received the bonus, disappointment and open hostility would have erupted in its absence.

But since money is a basic need, don't you sometimes have to pay people well first, *before* the other factors we've discussed come into play? This question came up at a conference keynote presentation Bob was giving, and he was delighted to have another member of the audience stand up and say, "Not necessarily! I've found that, using positive reinforcement, I was able to increase the level of performance of my employees, which led to increased sales revenues, which ultimately made it *possible* to pay people better." In other words, nonmonetary incentives became the catalyst for improving employee productivity, enabling everyone to gain financially in the process.

You have to make employees feel valued so that they want to do their best work on a daily basis, to consistently act in the best interests of the organization. If you truly want your company to be competitive in today's fast-moving, global marketplace, you need to obtain extraordinary results from ordinary people. You can get such results from your employees by focusing your attention on how you treat them. For the best results, pay employees fairly but treat them superbly.

As a busy manager, you may like the convenience of cash rewards because you simply fill out a check request once a year to take care of all your motivation for the year. Manager-initiated rewards based on performance may sound like a lot of work. To be frank, running an effective rewards program does take more work than running a simple but ineffective one. But as we show you in this chapter, the best rewards can be quite simple. When you get the hang of using them, you can easily integrate them into your daily routine and management practice.

When it comes to rewards, far too many managers believe that their employees want only more money. Certainly, money can be an important way of letting employees know their worth to the organization, but it tends not to be a sustaining motivational factor to most individuals. Cash rewards such as salary, bonuses, and merit increases are important, but seldom are they the only motivators that spark employees to apply their best efforts on the job.

A recent study by Maritz revealed the following anomalies about cash rewards:

- Rewards that are strictly monetary are not as effective as non-cash-based items. Monetary rewards tend to be less personal, so they hinder the opportunity to develop and grow interpersonal relationships.

- Monetary rewards do little to establish a link between the behavior and the incentive. Instead of furthering company values, money alone can diminish core values.

Cash rewards involve one more problem. In most organizations, performance reviews — and corresponding salary increases — occur only once a year (or even less often if salaries are frozen). The most effective motivators are typically recent events within the immediate work group, such as being thanked for doing a good job, gaining a manager's support, and being praised before others. To motivate employees, you need to recognize and reward achievements and progress toward goals on a daily basis.

Creating a Recognition and Rewards System

Motivated employees don't emerge miraculously. You need a plan to reinforce the behavior you want:

1. **Create a supportive environment for your employees by first finding out what they most value.**

2. **Design ways to implement recognition to thank and acknowledge employees when they do good work. Act on recognition opportunities as they arise, realizing that what motivates some employees doesn't motivate others.**

3. **Acknowledge employees' contributions and continually work with them on what they want and need. But be honest with them and always show integrity; after all, they're watching you.**

4. **Stick with your recognition plan over time, but be prepared to make changes to your plan based on what works and what doesn't.**

In general, employees are more strongly motivated by the potential to earn rewards than they are by fear of punishment. Clearly, a well-constructed and well-planned rewards system is important in creating a motivated, effective workforce. Consider some simple guidelines when setting up a system of low-cost rewards in your organization:

✔ **Link rewards to organizational goals.** To be effective, rewards need to reinforce the behavior that leads to an organization's goals. Use rewards to increase the frequency of desired behavior and decrease the frequency of undesired behavior. For example, find ways to recognize the organization's core values or most pressing strategic objectives for the current quarter.

✔ **Define parameters and mechanics.** After you identify the behaviors you want to reinforce, develop the specifics of your rewards system. Establish clear and easily understandable rules. Make the targets attainable and ensure that all employees have a chance to obtain rewards. For example, all employees should have an opportunity to be recognized for achievements of their positions, not just salespeople for sales.

✔ **Obtain commitment and support.** To get the best results, plan and implement your rewards program with direct involvement from both your employees and your managers. You need to market your program throughout the organization on an ongoing basis, reminding everyone of the importance of recognition, past successes, available tools, and benefits to the organization.

✔ **Monitor effectiveness.** Is your rewards system getting the results you want? If not, take another look at the behaviors you want to reinforce and make sure that your rewards are closely linked. Even the most successful rewards programs tend to lose their effectiveness over time as employees begin to take them for granted. Keep your program fresh by discontinuing rewards that have lost their luster and bringing in new ones from time to time.

Using Praise and Recognition to Everyone's Advantage

A common misconception about using rewards and recognition to motivate employees is that it costs a company too much money — money that should be devoted to other purposes, especially when budgets are tight. This misconception is problematic enough in times of high economic growth and prosperity, but it's particularly damaging in down economic times. Rewards, recognition, and praise don't need to be lavish or expensive to be effective. The most motivating and meaningful forms of recognition, as reported by today's employees, typically cost little or nothing.

Including four types of praise

Bob's research has found that simple praise for doing good work takes four of the top ten spots of desired employee motivators:

- ✓ **Personal praise:** Face-to-face thanks and acknowledgment for a job well done
- ✓ **Written praise:** A written note or formal letter of thanks
- ✓ **Electronic praise:** Personal thanks and acknowledgment via e-mail or voice mail
- ✓ **Public praise:** Recognition in front of one or more other people, in a public forum such as a meeting or broad form of communication such as a newsletter or newspaper

At first glance, these different forms of praise may all seem like a single dimension — employee praise — but they aren't. Each of these dimensions is mutually exclusive and provides a different and distinct value and meaning to individual employees. All these forms of praise are important to employees.

At meetings, allocate some time to recognize outstanding effort or share success stories. Ending meetings on a high note, especially when the agenda is laden with less-than-happy items, is a great way to remind employees that, even in downtimes, positive things are still happening.

Using elements of a good praising

In the workplace, praise is priceless, yet it costs nothing. In one recent poll, workers named personal praise from their manager for doing a good job as the most motivating incentive, yet almost 60 percent of employees say they seldom, if ever, receive such praise from their manager. Although giving effective praise may seem like common sense, many people have never learned how to do it.

Use the acronym ASAP[3] to remember the essential elements of good praise:

✔ **As soon:** Timing is important when using positive reinforcement. Praise employees as soon as they complete an achievement or display a desired behavior. The sooner you notice and reinforce desired behavior, the more likely the employee and others in the workplace are to repeat that behavior. You may even interrupt someone in a meeting to provide a quick word of praise, until you're able to discuss the achievement at greater length.

✔ **As sincere:** Words alone can fall flat if you aren't sincere in why you're praising. Offer praise because you're truly appreciative and excited about the other person's success; otherwise, your efforts may come across as a manipulative tactic (something you do only when you want an employee to work late, for example).

✔ **As specific:** Avoid generalities in favor of details of the achievement. "You really turned that angry customer around. You let him unload all his emotions and then focused on what you *could* do for him." Specifics give credibility to your praising and also serve a practical purpose of stating exactly what was good about a behavior or achievement.

✔ **As personal:** A key to conveying your message is praising in person, face-to-face, whenever possible. This shows that you value the activity enough to put aside everything else you have to do and just focus on the other person. Because everyone has limited time, taking time to interact personally indicates that this activity has a higher value to you.

✔ **As positive:** Too many managers undercut praise with a concluding note of criticism. When you say something like "You did a great job on this report, but there were quite a few typos," the *but* verbally erases everything that came before. Save the corrective feedback for an employee development discussion.

✔ **As proactive:** Most managers need to take the time and effort to praise more frequently. Look for opportunities to praise whenever positive news arises, such as in staff meetings; use praising tools such as thank-you note cards, voice mail, or notations on your planning calendar. Lead with the positive and by catching people doing things right, or you'll tend to be reactive in your interactions with others and will primarily focus on mistakes.

You can praise an employee directly or in front of others. You can even praise employees when they aren't around, knowing that your remarks will more than likely make their way back to them.

Covering key aspects of effective recognition

Even more important than money to today's employees is getting recognition for the job they're doing, especially when they're doing it well. Bob's research has found that, almost universally (more than 99 percent of the time), today's employees want and expect to be recognized when they do good work. However, only 12 percent of employees report that they're consistently recognized in ways that are important to them; three times as many employees (36 percent) report that they're definitely not recognized in meaningful ways, and most employees (85 percent) say they feel overworked and underappreciated.

When done well, the act of recognizing an employee should take into account the following considerations:

- **Contingency:** Contingency relates to how closely the recognition is tied to the behavior recognized. Contingent recognition is given only when an employee exhibits some sort of desired behavior or performance, such as when an employee handles a difficult customer request or completes a project on time. Noncontingent recognition is generalized; it may be given, for example, when an organization holds a company picnic for all employees or celebrates an employee's birthday.

- **Timing:** Recognition is most meaningful when it's given as soon as possible after the desired behavior or performance. Recognition loses meaning (or can even become alienating to the recipient) when it's not timely, which means that saving up individual recognition for an annual performance appraisal or rewards banquet can be counterproductive.

- **Frequency:** Positive reinforcement is most effective in shaping desired behavior or performance when it's frequent, at least until the behavior becomes established. For recognition to reinforce performance, the recognition itself has to be reinforced. Frequency should always be considered when designing a rewards and recognition program.

  Organizations typically use nonmonetary recognition on a formal yet infrequent basis around specific events, such as when celebrating a record sales quarter. If a company wants to institutionalize nonmonetary recognition, it often establishes programs, such as an employee-of-the-month program or a safety awards program. Or it can go further, making this kind of recognition a daily part of management practices, such as with daily feedback on performance, personal one-on-one praise, and frequent thank-you notes.

- **Formality:** A formal reward is one that stems from a planned and agreed-upon program of incentives. Examples of formal rewards include employee-of-the-month programs, years-of-service awards, and attendance awards. An informal reward is more spontaneous and flexible, often stemming from the relationship between the parties involved. Examples of informal rewards include a personal word of thanks for a job well done or recognition in a staff meeting for excellent customer service. Formality leads to a pattern of defined behaviors, whereas informality leads to a pattern of interacting roles.

✔ **Recognition setting and context:** Recognition can be given to an employee privately or in front of some or all of the company's personnel. Everyone likes a spontaneous personal word of thanks, but recipients tend to value formal praise more highly — although shy individuals (perhaps 20 percent of the population) usually prefer private and less formal displays of gratitude. Make sure you take into account your employee's personal nature. You can present recognition impersonally, such as by mail, or in a personal manner, even anecdotally and emotionally. Most employees prefer recognition presented with a personal touch, regardless of the size of the audience.

✔ **Significance of the provider:** In general, employees highly value manager-initiated recognition, but who should provide the recognition: the individual with the most status or the one with a special relationship to the recipient? There's a trade-off when the person with the most emotional significance to the recipient doesn't also have power within the organization hierarchy.

✔ **Value to the recipient:** Recognition is more meaningful when the recipient highly values the form it takes. One individual may value rewards that relate to the job, such as a specialized work tool, a software upgrade, or an educational opportunity; another individual may value rewards that relate to his personal and family life and that he can share with others. Such rewards might include dinner out with a significant other, a weekend getaway, a barbecue set, or tickets to a sporting event. Customize rewards and recognition for the recipient.

Consider whether the recipient would most value tangible recognition, intangible recognition, or both. Tangible recognition might be a trophy or plaque. Intangible or symbolic recognition includes ceremonies, public announcements, time off, or the gift of more responsibility or more space, as in a corner office.

The best managers may have always been skilled at providing recognition to employees, but organizations today need *every* manager to be rewards-and-recognition savvy and to create the kind of workplace where we all want to work.

Incentives at Google and why they work

Employees of Google save both time and money by staying onsite to eat. Beyond enjoying three free meals each day, employees who eat at the company cafeteria interact with each other, creating a sense of community and idea sharing. They can also take advantage of onsite car washes and oil changes so that they don't have to spend their lunch hours or other work time taking care of these routine tasks. The added benefit of checking one more task off their personal to-do list also makes employees more productive and less distracted.

Making an impact with a simple "Thanks"

It all starts with a thank-you. And sometimes that's all it takes. Most employees don't just need to be thanked for something they've done well — they *expect* it. And they expect it to be done immediately or soon after their good performance. Waiting too long shows indifference and implies that the praise is more of an afterthought or something you've put off. Even affirmation from co-workers can change employees' attitudes and give them a greater sense of meaning and purpose.

Employees need to feel as though their efforts are well spent, even if the results can realistically be classified as only baby steps. Focusing on accomplishments gives your employees the encouragement they may need to keep moving forward in a difficult time. If they feel as though they're consistently giving their all, only to hear that the effort isn't enough, even the most enthusiastic employees will be undermined.

Although recognition of success is important to include in regular communication and meetings, unexpected celebrations can also be effective. Systematically taking the time to point out your employees' strengths and successes can help overcome the cloud of negative energy that befalls an organization during the downtimes.

As we note at the beginning of this chapter, you're more likely to lead your employees to great results by focusing on their positive accomplishments than by finding fault with their negative outcomes. Despite this fact, many managers' primary mode of operation is correcting employees' mistakes instead of complimenting their successes.

In one study, 58 percent of employees ranked a personal thank-you from their managers as their most motivating incentive, yet those same employees reported that they seldom received such thanks. The employees ranked written thanks for doing a good job as motivating incentive number two, yet 76 percent said they seldom received thanks from their managers. Perhaps these statistics show why a lack of praise and recognition is one of the leading reasons people leave their jobs.

Years of psychological research have clearly shown that positive reinforcement works better than negative reinforcement, for a couple reasons:

✔ It increases the frequency of the desired behavior.

✔ It creates good feelings within employees.

On the other hand, negative reinforcement may decrease the frequency of undesired behavior, but it doesn't necessarily result in the desired behavior.

Instead of being motivated to do better, employees who receive only criticism from their managers eventually just avoid their managers whenever possible. Furthermore, negative reinforcement (particularly when manifested in ways that degrade employees and their personal sense of worth) can create tremendously bad feelings with employees. And employees who are unhappy with their employers have a much more difficult time doing a good job than contented employees.

Making a big deal about little things

Should you reward your employees for their little day-to-day successes, or should you save up rewards for when they accomplish something major? The answer to this question lies in the way most people get their work done on a daily basis.

For most people in business, work isn't a string of dazzling successes that come one after another without fail. Instead, the majority of work consists of routine activities. Employees perform most of these duties quietly and with little fanfare. For example, a typical workday may consist of an hour or two of reading memos and e-mail messages, listening to voice-mail messages, and talking to others on the phone. The manager may spend another couple hours in meetings and perhaps another hour in one-on-one discussions with staff members and co-workers, much of which involves dealing with problems as they occur. With additional time spent on preparing reports or filling out forms, the manager devotes precious little time to decision making — the activity that has the greatest impact on an organization.

For an hourly or line worker, this dearth of opportunities for dazzling success is even more pronounced. If the employee's job is assembling lawnmower engines all day (and she does a good, steady job), when does she have an opportunity to be outstanding in the eyes of her supervisor?

American Express recognizes great performers

If you could increase your organization's net income by 500 percent in a decade, would you take the time to recognize your great performers? The Travel Related Services division of American Express did by creating its Great Performers program to recognize and reward exceptional employee performance. The program accepted nominations from employees, supervisors, and even customers. Winners of the Great Performers award were eligible for selection by a worldwide governing committee to become Grand Award recipients. In addition to an all-expenses-paid trip for two to New York City, Grand Award winners received $4,000 in American Express traveler's checks, a platinum award pin, and a certificate.

Disney does it right even in the busiest times

One of the biggest challenges in recognizing others is doing it in the midst of the daily operations of your business — that is, when you and your employees are the busiest. The Walt Disney World Dolphin Resort in Orlando, Florida, is an excellent example of how to provide recognition under pressure. Instead of viewing "being busy" as an executive excuse for not recognizing employees, they focus their energies on new and creative ways to increase recognition. For example:

✔ When surveyed, Dolphin employees reported that managers weren't around much during busiest times. As a result, management initiated "Five-Minute Chats," in which all managers were assigned ten employees who didn't report to them. Their assignment was to check in with each employee for five minutes over the span of 30 days.

✔ During busy days when employees simultaneously checked in and out more than 1,000 people, supervisors set up refreshments and balloons in the employee area behind the hotel check-in counter. Supervisors were there to cheer employees on and to jump in during employee breaks.

✔ Dolphin management started using "Wow!" cards, trifolded wallet cards made from different-colored construction paper in which employees and managers could write quick thank-you notes to others who "wowed" a customer or another employee. "Captain Wow," their very own superhero, dropped by regularly to thank them and acknowledge their work.

No matter what business you're in, look for the times when you and your employees are most under pressure and develop ways to thank, acknowledge, and recognize employees during those times. Doing so can be the best pressure-relief valve you'll ever have.

Major accomplishments are usually few and far between, regardless of your place in the organizational chart. Work is a series of small accomplishments that eventually add up to big ones. If you wait to reward your employees for their big successes, you may be waiting a long time.

Reward your employees for their small successes as well as their big ones. You may set a lofty goal for your employees to achieve — one that stretches their abilities and tests their resolve — but remember that praising your employees' progress toward the goal is perhaps more important than praising them when they finally reach it.

Finding power in peer-initiated recognition

All employees like to be recognized for a job well done, but recognition from one's peers carries special significance. Perhaps this is because such awards are seldom expected. Perhaps it's because everyone knows that managerial favoritism played no part in the selection. Whatever the reason, you can be assured that the recognition is well earned and sincere when employees single out someone from their ranks for recognition and praise.

Tom Tate, program manager for the Office of Personnel Management in the Personnel and Management Training Division of the U.S. government, shares a story of the Wingspread Award, an engraved trophy that the division head presents to the division's special performer. One year, the recipient wanted to also recognize a deserving colleague. The employee passed the award on to that employee, who later wanted to recognize yet another peer. Over time, the award took on great value and prestige because it came from one's peers. Each recipient could keep it as long as desired until another special performer was discovered. When a recipient was ready to pass it on, a ceremony and lunch was scheduled. Consider these other examples of peer-initiated awards:

- ✔ Employees at the Angus Barn Restaurant in Raleigh, North Carolina, vote on The People's Choice award to recognize a model employee.

- ✔ At ICI Pharmaceuticals Group in Wilmington, Delaware, a peer can nominate a fellow employee for the Performance Excellence Award for any idea that helps the business (saves money, increases productivity, and the like) or any action that goes above and beyond the call of duty.

- ✔ At Meridian Travel Inc. in Cleveland, Ohio, CEO Cynthia Bender has the company's 62 employees write in their votes for Employee of the Month. "Managers always have their favorites, but the employees know who pitches in and helps out," says Bender. "This makes employees notice others more and develops camaraderie."

You can easily encourage employees to recognize other employees, but it's most likely to happen if you initiate a program in your workplace. At The Ken Blanchard Companies, in Escondido, California, employees use the Eagle Award to recognize other employees for acts of extraordinary service. Whenever an employee performs a work-related favor, another employee can give her a "hatchling" — a sticker of an egg plus a write-up about what that employee did and why it was significant. When an employee receives 16 hatchlings, a group of employees gives her an Eagle Award plaque during a brief ceremony at her desk. An employee may also get an Eagle Award for a single outstanding event. The program was announced and explained at a company meeting, and a small committee of volunteers administers the mechanics of the program. Employee reception to the program has been strong, and the benefits to the company have been significant.

Give employees some time to recharge

The Corcoran Group, a top real estate agency in Manhattan, takes a unique approach to policies during slow times. Founder Barbara Corcoran instituted a practice of giving salespeople an extra few weeks of vacation when sales are down. With not much going on, it's easier to be short staffed and give employees some time to restore morale and alleviate stress. So far, this practice has been effective: Salespeople return refreshed, with a renewed and positive attitude.

Rewarding Employees without Breaking the Bank

Showing appreciation sends the message that the company values employees and wouldn't be able to operate without them. Involving employees in the reward process promotes a sense of teamwork and helpfulness.

Sometimes the money simply isn't available for cash rewards or big-ticket items. But you still have options for showing employees that the company values and appreciates their time and work. Even something as simple as an ice cream social, a company-sponsored lunch, or morning donuts can make employees feel valued.

The Business Journal recognized Core Creative, in Milwaukee, Wisconsin, as one of the "Best Places to Work." At the end of every summer, the company sets aside time to find a creative way to recognize exceptional employees, both employees who are simply performing well and employees who have gone above and beyond for clients. Another company in the Midwest consistently distributes personal notes from vice presidents and managers and highlights outstanding employees through feature articles on the intranet. Many such effective recognition and reward items have little or no cost.

Consider a few categories when you next want to thank your employees:

- ✔ **Low-end rewards:** This can include items like gift cards from Starbucks or Amazon.com; gas cards; car wash or discount restaurant coupons; gift certificates; or treats such as a pizza, donuts, or even a bouquet of flowers.

Jeanette Pagliaro, co-owner of Visiting Angels, an elder-care service that operates throughout the United States, often gets positive feedback from clients or supervisors about her employees. Employees who garner such pointed recognition receive Angel Bucks, which they can use to buy prizes at a company-sponsored auction.

- ✔ **Symbolic recognition:** This recognition can take the form of tokens, pins, ribbons, a certificate, or a plaque that has special meaning.

Busch Gardens in Tampa, Florida, supplies tokens to all supervisors to give to employees to reinforce core values. Employees can redeem the tokens in their paychecks for $10, but most employees who receive the tokens prefer to keep them and forgo the money.

- ✔ **Time off:** Use time as an award itself by providing a voucher for a long lunch, a free afternoon, or an additional day off.

At Greenough Communications in Boston, Massachusetts, high-performing employees are awarded by being able to leave at 3 p.m. on Friday. JS Communications in Los Angeles, California, recently gave employees two free "I Don't Want to Get Out of Bed" days to use in the forthcoming year.

✔ **Employee perks:** You can make simple, low-cost benefits available to all employees. Soft drinks, fresh coffee, bottled water, snacks, and the use of a company fitness room are great for company morale.

Best, Best and Krieger has held fast to simple employee perks such as "Bagel and Donut Friday" and an annual holiday party as a way to bring employees together in a social setting. Employees at California-based Kiner Communications, a public relations firm, enjoy baskets of fresh fruit and attend a company-sponsored holiday party each year.

If it's important that your employees work together as a team, you need to recognize the team, teamwork, and team successes when they occur. You can do so through simple celebrations when team goals are achieved or milestones are met. Or you can give the team the opportunity to decide how best to celebrate their successes.

Teambuilding activities are another way to reward the team that can serve a dual purpose. They help unite employees and create an improved sense of community, and they also can be a nice break from the monotony of work, something that's much needed in a time when morale and spirits are low. As an added benefit to the company and employees alike, such activities promote working together by creating a positive atmosphere in which employees tend to work harder and more efficiently.

Teambuilding with a twist

After General Mills acquired Pillsbury, division leaders came together and organized the Spirit Team. The sole purpose of this group was to organize activities that brought everyone together and sparked positive attitudes. The Spirit Team organized volunteer days at a nonprofit organization, building on the idea that teambuilding can't be fully accomplished with just one event. Now the group organizes between eight and ten events at the same organization each year. Positive feedback on employee surveys cites a connection to the volunteer program and employees' good feelings about both their jobs and the company.

Top five motivation Web sites

Wondering where to find the best information on the Web about the topics addressed in this chapter? Here are our top five favorites:

- Nelson Motivation, Inc.: `www.nelson-motivation.com`

- Recognition Professionals International: `www.recognition.org`

- Aubrey Daniels International: `www.aubreydaniels.com`

- Towers Watson: `www.towerswatson.com`

- Maritz: `www.maritz.com`

Chapter 4

Creating an Engaged Workforce

Almost every organization claims that its people are the most valued asset, but few companies systematically follow through on that belief in ways that can truly empower employees to make a difference. By being proactive, positive, focused, and forward-looking, managers can inspire employees — and employees can inspire themselves and their co-workers — in practical ways that obtain real results and allow their companies to become stronger, more profitable, and more competitive in even the most difficult marketplace.

Taking control of their circumstances helps employees take control of their jobs — and their lives — and makes positive things happen where only negatives existed before. Redefining circumstances in this way puts employees in the driver's seat. This chapter shows you how to create a framework for managing employees in positive and practical ways to overcome negative times and circumstances. It offers a strategy, process, and critical success factors to focus on, all supported with examples, techniques, and case studies of how other managers have succeeded in fostering more engaged employees.

Understanding the Power of Employee Engagement

Employees are motivated to do a good job where they work (we've yet to meet an employee who gets up in the morning hoping to make a mess of things at work!). They want to help the organization as best they can to be successful and to keep their jobs. But they can't do this in a vacuum. They need the leadership and support of management where they work to help create the context for their success.

The problem of employees who aren't engaged in their jobs has a devastating impact on many organizations. The Gallup Organization, which tracks more than 3.8 million workers around the world, looked into employee engagement, and the results weren't pretty. According to Gallup's survey of American companies, only 29 percent of workers — less than one-third — are engaged in their jobs. These employees feel a profound connection to their company and are passionate about their work. However, most workers — 54 percent — aren't engaged in their jobs at all. These employees show up at work and punch the clock, but they pour neither energy nor passion into their work. Believe it or not, the statistics get worse. Fully 17 percent of American workers — almost one in five — are actively disengaged. These unhappy employees get little or no work done. Why? Because they often fearful of change and of being accountable for their own futures.

Envision for a moment raising the engagement level of your workforce — transforming both the average 54 percent of workers who aren't engaged in their jobs and the 17 percent of workers who are actively disengaged at work. Imagine the power, energy, creativity, efficiency, innovation, and customer service you could unleash.

This is the power of employee engagement, and it's why you, as a manager, need to find ways to tap it.

Creating a Clear and Compelling Direction

The starting point of any effort to improve employee engagement is to give employees a clear and compelling vision. If employees don't know — or aren't inspired by — what the organization is trying to do, they'll find it more difficult to summon the motivation to succeed, especially in tough times. Frances Hesselbein, president of the Leader to Leader Institute, once put it this way: "No matter what business you're in, everyone in the organization needs to know why."

People who perform well feel good about themselves. When personal or company goals are being reached or surpassed, the level of engagement among employees is typically at its highest, which then affects other areas of performance as well. If this spills over to better customer service or higher-quality products and services, it can have a direct impact on customer loyalty. Increased customer loyalty can positively impact sales and revenue as well.

Attaining or maintaining high levels of engagement and motivation among employees is decidedly more difficult in challenging economic times. If employees spend most of their time fretting over the financial state of the company (which has a direct impact on their personal financial state), they spend less time on their work, causing productivity as well as customer service to suffer. For advice on dealing with economic challenges and other hard times in your business, turn to the later section "Communicating bad news and dealing with rumors."

Assessing employees' understanding of mission and purpose

Do a reality check: Ask employees what the mission and purpose of the organization is and what their role is in reaching that purpose. If you get a different answer from each person you ask, it's a good indication that the message has drifted or — perhaps hasn't been clear for some time. Use this opportunity to revisit the purpose of your business group or function.

To gain clarity about the organization's mission, management guru Peter Drucker recommends that you ask five questions to get at the core of your business. These questions help connect what your organization is trying to achieve with your customers in the marketplace:

- ✔ What is our mission?
- ✔ Who is our customer?
- ✔ What does the customer value?
- ✔ What are our results?
- ✔ What is our plan?

Clarifying the vision is a useful starting point in deciding what is most important for the organization (or department) to focus on to be successful. The result needs to be a compelling purpose that can inspire everyone. "A vision is not just a picture of what could be — it is an appeal to our better selves, a call to become something more," says Harvard professor Rosabeth Moss Kanter. From that vision, you can shape your *unique competitive advantages* — that is, the aspects that you can offer your customers and that your competition cannot. These advantages represent your strengths in the marketplace that you most need to capitalize on to succeed. In changing times, the unique advantages you have to offer and the needs of your customers can shift drastically, so looking at this frequently makes sense.

A company adapts to changing times

One computer equipment and software company based in San Diego saw its future orders drop significantly. Its sales representatives reported that customers' capital budgets were being frozen, so customers no longer had the funds to purchase capital equipment. (The firm's business model required customers to purchase both hardware and software, which they would completely own, and then pay ongoing maintenance fees to have the firm service both the equipment and the software that ran that equipment.)

The firm laid off about 10 percent of its employees and froze salaries, but management knew that was just a short-term fix for a declining cash flow. More importantly, top management met with the firm's sales representatives and brainstormed what could be done to address the situation and what the competition was doing in response to the situation. As a result, the company launched revised strategies, including the following:

✔ A change in the pricing model to include new options for payment, such as a "per-use" leasing payment model that didn't require the customer to purchase expensive equipment.

✔ A new, software-only solution that, for the first time, allowed customers to run needed applications on existing computers that they owned or equipment that they wanted to purchase from other vendors.

✔ New financing options in which the company financed the purchase of its customers' equipment. This allowed clients to begin using the company's product without having to initially tap into resources from their capital budget.

✔ The targeting of new markets, such as the federal government (which had more available funds), which the company had never focused on.

All these changes required everyone in the organization to think through implications for the business and make adjustments accordingly. As a result, the firm was able to attract new clients with their revised offerings. Some of the strategies are longer term and, hence, are still being developed, but overall the approach has helped the firm generate new sales revenue from new clients during a difficult financial time.

Modifying strategies to meet goals

When you've clarified your vision for your group and started to reassess and revitalize your goals, analyze what's currently working — and what's not — for the business. For example, established customers may be cutting back on using the services of your firm, but what new clients have recently started to invest with you? What do those new clients have in common and how can you approach similar clients in the marketplace? Changing times call for changing strategies to meet your company's goals. Engage employees to help with these changes by seeking their input and ideas for improving business operations, saving the company money, or better serving customers.

Opening Lines of Communication

The need to know what's going on in one's job is pervasive. People want to know not just the necessary information to do the work they're assigned, but also what their co-workers are doing and how successful the organization is. Management needs to communicate information to employees about the organization's mission and purpose, its products and services, its strategies for success in the marketplace, and even what's going on with the competition.

In our research, the highest-ranking variable that 65 percent of employees want most from their managers is ample information at work. This statistic has a degree of significance that places it in a category of its own. These research findings correlate with recent research from Accountemps that found communication to be the leading variable that 48 percent of executives reported could best impact low morale in their organization.

One of the most common errors many organizations and managers make is to not share adequate information with employees. In some instances, top management doesn't share information because managers themselves are uncertain about the constantly changing economic landscape. In other instances, managers feel that sharing information with employees decreases their power and status. Management also may try to "protect" employees from fears surrounding a potential job loss or the ability of senior management to effectively handle a pending crisis. More often, these well-intended actions backfire; closed-door meetings and hushed hallway conversations create a sense of unease among employees and lead to speculation, heightened fear, and worst-case-scenario rumors.

Employees want and need to know what's going on within the organization, even if the information isn't always positive. Nothing is wrong with being honest with employees when the firm is struggling. Doing so can lead to an increase in teamwork and dedication, especially if you use the bad news as an opportunity to brainstorm and communicate with employees about ideas and plans for turning things around. Bringing employees into the loop during the downtimes can instill in them a greater sense of involvement and responsibility, which ultimately leads to increased employee feelings of value and trust.

Employing direct, two-way communication

To maximize employee engagement, keeping employees abreast of management's goals and ensuing plans is imperative. Something as simple as a company-wide meeting that presents the state of the organization to all employees and clearly addresses goals (both financial and nonfinancial) can make a world of difference in easing employee tensions and fears.

When discussing major issues like organizational changes, communication should come in the form of a dialogue instead of a lecture, and management should encourage questions. Such key updates should also be shared in advance of information that is made public, as in a press release. Employees must be made to feel as though they have the freedom to express their fears and concerns, and receive honest and informative responses. Feedback sessions, departmental meetings, and company-wide gatherings should ideally serve two purposes: to gather feedback and to provide information.

Exploring communication techniques

Methods for communicating with employees depend on the situation. Group settings require different interaction than one-on-one communication. Following are some suggestions for best communicating with individuals and groups:

- ✔ **Individuals**

  - Engage in periodic one-on-one meetings with each employee.

  - Offer personal support and reassurances, especially for your most valued employees.

  - Provide open-door accessibility to management.

  - Invite employees to write anonymous letters to top management about their concerns.

- ✔ **Groups**

  - Conduct town hall meetings.

  - Host CEO-led breakfasts or brown-bag lunches.

  - Maintain a 24-hour "news desk" on the company intranet.

  - Provide periodic "state-of-the-union" updates on the business.

  - Be open and honest in explaining the situation and challenges going forward.

  - Allow questions and provide answers.

    Take questions in advance of the meeting or allow written questions to be submitted anonymously.

  - Record meetings and distribute the proceedings to employees who are unable to attend.

You can also communicate outside the structure of a meeting. Create a question-and-answer section in your internal newsletter or on your company Web site. Or set up a blog site for your CEO (especially if your company has satellite offices or employees who travel frequently) to gather immediate feedback concerning key issues and updates. Have key contacts from your human resources, public relations, and legal departments on hand to support the CEO in answering specific questions from those areas.

Communicating bad news and dealing with rumors

One of the most important points to remember is that employees aren't looking for a sugar-coated delivery of information. The best way to explain the state of an organization is in a clear, concise, and honest manner. If sales are declining at a rapid or steady pace, every member of the staff has to know. Sharing this information emphasizes to all employees the collective ownership of the organization's performance. From front-line staff to mid- and upper-level management, everyone shares a portion of the responsibility for an organization's revenue, performance, and future.

By including each employee in an honest, behind-the-scenes look at the fiscal landscape of an organization and the approach or plan to resolve the crisis, you send the underlying message that every single person is a critical part of the whole. That message, in turn, creates a greater sense of accountability. Feeling as though they're part of the solution instead of the problem gives employees the confidence they need to buckle down and do their part to pull the organization through a time of crisis.

Establishing open lines of communication across the company can put an end to one of the most detrimental viruses that spreads throughout an organization: rumors. Human nature dictates that it's easier to believe negative statements than positive ones. Because most rumors are clothed in a shroud of negativity, it's crucial to stop them at the source, if possible, even openly asking employees about rumors they've heard.

Withholding information is a great way to give birth to rumors that spread like wildfire. Merely talking to employees can ease uncertainty and let them know that you're there to provide information, not keep it from them. Gathering the departments and giving each of them an opportunity to share brings the entire organization together. Most important, employees receive information based on fact, not fiction, and are better equipped to move forward and make well-informed decisions.

Involving Employees and Encouraging Initiative

Communicating better with employees is the first step in empowering them to act in the best interests of the organization. But that's just the beginning.

When employees are armed with more frequent and relevant information, they're more likely to act on that information in ways that can best help the organization. The act of honest and open communication shows that managers have both trust and respect for their employees. Adding the explicit request and encouragement for employees to get involved in helping the company can lead to profound results, from improved daily operations to a better bottom line.

According to a survey we conducted of employees in a variety of industries, 50 percent of employees want their managers to ask for their opinions and ideas at work, and more than 50 percent want their managers to involve them in decisions made at work. This section explores ways for you to become a more engaged manager, with engaged employees who share their ideas and have some input in decision making.

Guiding employee focus

Managers and workers are entering into a new kind of partnership in the workplace. Today's managers are discovering that they have to create an environment that encourages employees to *contribute* their best ideas and work, to help seek out new opportunities (such as new sources of revenue), and to overcome obstacles facing the company (such as rising costs), wherever possible. Workers are discovering that if they expect to survive the constant waves of change sweeping across the global business marketplace, as well as hold on to their current job, they have to join together with other employees to contribute to their organizations in ways they've never been called upon to do. Managers need to discuss the following questions with their employees:

- **Employee impact:** Are employees aware of how they impact the company's bottom line — that is, how their jobs financially impact the organization?

- **Revenue-generating ideas:** How can the company generate additional income? Whether it's new fees, cross-selling, or up-selling, what new ideas can the company try?

- **Cost-saving suggestions:** How can the company trim, delay, or eliminate costs? Which expenses are critical, and which are optional or can temporarily be cut?

- **Process improvements:** What steps in the organization's processes can be streamlined, to save time, resources, and money?

- **Customer needs and requests:** How can employees help others in the company who are focused on customer needs and requests? How can the company further explore customers' needs?

- **New products or services:** What ideas exist for new products or services? How can those ideas be better developed and implemented?

✔ **Morale and teambuilding:** Who's interested in helping to improve employee teamwork and morale? How can this be done at little cost?

✔ **Telecommuter integration:** How can the organization better use and integrate virtual employees?

Asking employees for their input and ideas

We haven't yet found an organization that doesn't have an "open door" policy encouraging employees to speak to their manager about any concerns, ideas, or suggestions. But in practice, this policy doesn't work well. In the typical U.S. company today, the average employee makes 1.1 suggestions per year at work. Contrast that employee with the typical Japanese worker, who offers an average of 167 suggestions a year, and you see the potential opportunity for improvement.

Soliciting ideas needs to be a constant and expanding strategy. Anonymous surveys and casual questions at the end of a meeting aren't enough to accomplish the task. After initial cost-saving measures are put into place, it's time to talk seriously about how best to move forward in an economical yet productive manner to make the changes stick. The company needs to revise policies and procedures, reinforcing its effort to do things smarter, cheaper, and better.

To maximize buy-in and motivation, challenge your employees to identify ways to improve. Employees must understand that you need their efforts now more than ever. After communicating this, you need to create new mechanisms that inspire ongoing employee involvement.

Do you want more ideas from your employees — ideas for saving money, improving customer service, streamlining processes, and so forth? What business manager or owner doesn't?

We're convinced that all employees have at least one $50,000 idea on the tip of their tongue. The trick is to find a way to let it out. (See the strategies that Boardroom, Inc., uses in the nearby sidebar for ideas.) Yet we find that most companies do little, if anything, to get ideas from their employees. If they do decide to take action, it's in the form of a "suggestion box" placed in the lunchroom with (for some reason) a lock on it. The first dozen or so employees who submit suggestions, if they hear back at all, often get a form letter months later that more or less states, "Here's why we're not using your silly idea. . . ."

The result? The suggestion program grinds to a halt. We even recently heard of one company that ended its dead suggestion program because, it announced, *the company had already gotten all the ideas.* How convenient.

Management doesn't feel that's the case at AT&T Universal Card Services in Jacksonville, Florida, where the company gets some 1,200 ideas *per month* from employees, month after month. Nor does management feel that way at Valeo — in a recent year, the French automaker received 250,000 ideas for improvement from employees.

Taking initiative at Boardroom

Boardroom, Inc., a newsletter and book publisher based in Greenwich, Connecticut, expects every employee — from receptionist to chairman — to submit at least two ideas each week for improvements. The company credits the "I Power" program, initially established to encourage cost savings, with a five-fold increase in revenue and untold benefit to employee morale, energy, and retention. Each employee is asked to turn in two suggestions every week, which an employee volunteer evaluates the same week. For many suggestions, the evaluator responds with "What a great idea!" and then returns the idea to the person who suggested it, with implicit permission to proceed with implementing the idea.

As Martin Edelston, chairman and CEO of Boardroom, says, "Sometimes the best idea can come from the newest, least experienced person on your staff." In one example, an hourly paid shipping clerk suggested that the company trim the paper size of one of its books to meet the requirements for the more affordable 4-pound shipping rate. The company made the change and saved half a million dollars the first year and several years since. Explains Marty, "I had been working in mail order for over 20 years and never realized there was a 4-pound shipping rate. But the person who was doing the job knew it, as most employees know how their jobs can be improved."

The first year, the program limited suggestions to one's own job, until employees understood that the intention was less to complain than it was to think of ways to improve. The company now has group meetings just to brainstorm and share ideas about specific issues or functions.

The benefits of the suggestions aren't limited to saving money, either. Says Antoinette Baugh, director of personnel, "People love working here because they know they can be part of a system where they can make a contribution." Adds Lisa Castonguay, renewals and billing manager, "My first couple weeks, I was kind of taken aback because everyone was smiling and everyone was open." She recalls her first day of work, when she was pulled into a group meeting and, within 30 minutes of walking in the front door, was asked, "What do you think we should do about this problem?"

Lisa almost fell on the floor. She had just left a company after eight years and had never been asked for an opinion there. When she got over the initial shock, she felt good having her opinions and ideas valued by the people she worked with. As a result, it was easy for her to want to think of additional ways to help the company.

The impact is both positive and contagious. "People became agents of their own change," says Marty. "There's so much inside all of us, and we don't even know it's there until someone asks about it. And in the process it just builds and builds." Adds Brian Kurtz, vice president of marketing, "It's a constant flow of communication. People are not sitting in a cubicle, totally insulated from one another."

Involving employees in decision making

Most decisions regarding reductions or changes come from the top down, but is that really the best direction? No one knows jobs or departments better than the people who live and breathe them every day, so it makes sense to start there.

For example, if a reporting process is ineffective or costly, talk to the individual responsible for managing the process. Consider the example of a receptionist at Champion Solutions Group in Florida who received expense reports from field sales representatives via overnight delivery. When her suggestion that the reports be faxed instead of shipped was implemented, the company saw a 40 percent reduction in postage costs. This led company leaders to seek employee advice for ways to realize cost savings.

When employees believe they have a hand in decision making, company-wide buy-in and participation is much easier to obtain. If the general consensus among staff is that decisions will be made with or without their input, the likelihood of anyone providing open and honest feedback is quite small. Asking employees for their input shows that you respect and trust them and will likely increase the quality of the decisions being made. But ultimately, the responsibility for any decisions remains with the manager, so collecting input from employees doesn't mean you're obligated to use what's shared in every instance.

Employees who offer solutions that result in cost savings must not go unrecognized. Incentives such as bonuses, trips, or gift cards not only reward the employee, but also inspire others to develop cost-saving ideas of their own. Make the process fun and rewarding. Hold contests, departmental competitions, or other organized events to increase employee involvement and interaction. Ask employees what type of incentives they value; they may want an extra vacation day or time to volunteer at a favorite charity.

You can't secure support for change without involving employees, so you need to ensure that employees have the opportunity to be involved in the decision-making process. Some simple ways to include employees follow:

- Ask for their opinions on matters important to the department.
- Invite them to actively participate in setting objectives and revising goals for the department.
- Establish task forces made up of employees whose objective is to identify better ways to work.

Increasing Employee Autonomy, Flexibility, and Support

All employees need to have a say in how they do their work, to make it more meaningful. When employees find their work meaningful, they become more engaged and effective. In tough times, the need for fully engaged employees is amplified. It's critical that they go beyond their job descriptions to do whatever they can to make a difference not only in their jobs, but also for the greater good of the company.

After employees have been enlisted to get involved and make suggestions and improvements, they need to be encouraged to run with their ideas, take responsibility, and champion those ideas through to closure and completion. Managers can encourage this increase in autonomy by

✔ Allowing employees to approach anyone they need for help

✔ Giving them the authority to use resources

✔ Permitting them to take necessary actions to get the work done

In our research on employee preferences at work, "autonomy and authority" and "flexibility of working hours" were two of the top motivators for today's employees. Providing these motivators greatly increases employee morale and performance and prompts them to do their best work possible.

Giving employees a say in their own work

No one likes to be micromanaged, and most employees prefer to determine how they work best. In other words, they prefer to be assigned a task and given the freedom to develop a work plan that suits them. Roles and responsibilities may already be defined, but they're customized based on the individual who occupies the position. Truly knowing your employees becomes important here: Understanding their strengths and weaknesses allows you to properly assign projects and tasks. Take it a step further by allowing employees to pick and choose the projects and responsibilities they can work on.

Allowing flexible work schedules

Based on our research, most employees cite increased flexibility in employee work schedules as a top motivator. Furthermore, depending on the type of work, a flexible schedule can increase efficiency in getting the work done.

For example, Bob once managed a work group that experimented with having employees work from home on certain projects. Everyone logged their hours and was available as needed to discuss work issues. Not counting the saved commute time, employees were twice as efficient in the work they could accomplish. With less socializing and fewer interruptions, employees were better able to focus on the work at hand.

Many employees struggle with how to effectively maintain a balance between their work and personal lives without compromising their success as employees, parents, or spouses. (We provide tips for keeping this balance in Chapter 22.) Research has shown that involvement in activities outside of work can serve as a stress reducer and create better, well-rounded employees. Your company can help employees achieve a better balance in their lives by implementing policies that promote a life outside of the workplace. Among the many options for increasing flexibility are the following:

- ✔ Alternate hours (arriving early and leaving early or vice versa)
- ✔ Four-day work weeks, with longer hours worked on fewer days
- ✔ Telecommuting (see Chapter 9)
- ✔ Job sharing
- ✔ Permission to leave work early, when necessary, or to take time off to compensate for extra hours worked

Flexibility shouldn't be limited to just the times when employees are struggling. Many companies have found that giving employees the options of a flexible schedule or telecommuting increases morale and productivity. Some employees appreciate the decreased amount of time they have to spend in the car each week and the money saved on gas or mileage. Other employees value limited childcare expenses or simply like the opportunity to spend more time with their children. Whatever the motivation, employees appreciate having some control over their own schedules and, as a result, feel as though the company has their best interest in mind.

Clearly determine and communicate your company's point of view regarding flexible schedules (as well as your department's viewpoint), and work with employees to make it happen where possible.

Making the most of technology for working remotely

Times have changed drastically over the decades, partly because of continuous technological advances. As such, the way in which business is conducted has also changed. Operating on a global scale has become much easier and more streamlined, thanks to new methods of communication that have aided decision making, smoothed operations, and eased expansion. Fortunately, technology has also opened up new possibilities for how employees work.

Gone are the days of communication limited to fax and phone lines or face-to-face meetings. These days, some businesses operate entirely on a virtual platform, with employees scattered throughout the country or even the world. Although not every company is able to operate this way, a large percentage of jobs can be done outside the typical 9-to-5 in the office. As a result, many companies have experimented with flexible schedules or telecommuting options in recent years.

Although it's tough for some managers or business owners to welcome the option of employees working remotely, remembering that employees are adults and should be treated as though they're responsible is important. Most employees perform better if they feel empowered and trusted. Consider these statistics:

- ✔ Eighty-six percent of employees today wish they had more time to spend with their families.

- ✔ In the last five years, nearly 30 percent of workers have voluntarily made career changes that resulted in a salary reduction, in an effort to lead a more balanced life.

- ✔ Almost 50 percent of employees value the option of flexible or work-from-home hours.

- ✔ Fifty-four percent of employees appreciate the option to leave work early to tend to family or child issues.

- ✔ A large percentage of workers would take a reduction in pay if doing so gave them more time for personal interests or allowed them to spend more time with family.

- ✔ More than 60 percent of workers feel that their jobs are part of their identity instead of simply a means to a paycheck.

A sense of balance between the personal and work aspects of life tops the list of most employees when asked what they need to feel good about their work. Not to be mistaken with just a desire to "work from home," the definition of *balance* to employees is, for the most part, the ability to retain a sense of self-identity. Even though a large percentage of employees feel as though their jobs constitute their identity, that's not necessarily the way they want it to be. Encouraging employees to explore interests outside their daily roles or expressing interest in their lives outside the office can convey a dedication to ensuring a good balance.

Providing managerial accessibility and support

When employees are encouraged to have more autonomy, independence, and flexibility in their jobs, management needs to support them in those roles. For example, in one survey Gallup conducted, 66 percent of respondents said their managers had asked them to get involved in decision making, but only 14 percent felt they'd been empowered to make those decisions. When changes occur within an organization as the result of a financial setback, employees are likely to feel a bit lost. Even with solid communication plans, an air of uncertainty and worry can still permeate. Managers can set an example by involving employees in the transition process, providing recommendations for working with the changes, and providing adequate resources for problem solving.

Investing in people at Edward Jones

Edward Jones makes every effort to make its employees feel valued, and the results are evident in the longevity and positive attitude of nearly every employee. A survey of Edward Jones employees conducted by *Fortune* magazine revealed that 96 percent of employees considered the company a friendly place to work, and more than 89 percent felt that managers followed through on what they said or promised. But the most telling statistic is that 83 percent of employees have every intention of working at Edward Jones until they retire.

The vast majority of employees cited their reason for holding the company in such high regard as a sense of truly being cared for. And even though the company has grown rapidly over the years, the culture has remained the same. Employees who have been with the company for decades feel as though principles and values have remained intact throughout all the growing pains.

The personal and professional growth of their employees is of utmost importance to managers at Edward Jones. Employees are encouraged to explore new opportunities within the company, which combats the threat of employees growing bored and looking for new experiences outside the company. Some employees are asked to lead or participate in new ventures, ranging from moving around within the office where they're based to traveling overseas to launch new departments, projects, or offices. The philosophy behind this practice is rooted in the Edward Jones culture, which strives to develop initiative and drive in all employees. Employees have the autonomy to forge ahead with new roles or projects that they identify, assuming that the fit is right. If employees come up short in a few key areas, they're provided with the training necessary to effectively move into the desired role.

To help employees sustain necessary levels of motivation, work with them to identify potential barriers to their success. Don't simply assume that no obstacles exist or that all the obstacles are evident. Look to employees for guidance and input, and allow them to point out barriers to accomplishing a task, completing a project, or merely going about their daily duties.

Establishing effective lines of communication that involve and support *all* employees is especially imperative if managerial or other staff changes occur — for example, if new managers are put in place, project groups are reassigned, or departments are downsized. No matter how small the changes, employees will feel as though they've lost some sort of control over their situation.

Consider some guidelines for building rapport with and supporting your employees:

- ✔ **Take time with employees.** Everything comes back to communication: Getting out and talking to employees, spending time with front-line staff, and making an effort to truly listen to employees can open your eyes to seemingly small accomplishments that may otherwise go unnoticed. No matter how small, the roles and responsibilities of every employee are a critical factor in the overall success of an organization.

- ✔ **Ask employees what they want and need.** Don't assume that you or your management team knows automatically. And don't assume that employees who have been with you for several years want the same thing today that they did five years ago. Encourage open and honest dialogue.

- ✔ **Be available for questions from employees.** Best, Best and Krieger — a large law firm in Southern California — promotes an open-door policy in which anyone who has questions or concerns regarding personal or professional security is free to discuss those worries with the firm's managing partner. Employees are facing some very real fears, and ignoring them only makes them worse.

- ✔ **Show understanding and empathy.** All employees need to feel that their managers are on their side, rooting for their success and helping them succeed in any way possible. When employees face life changes, tragedies, or circumstances that demand more of their time than usual, employees need to feel comfortable discussing their situation with their managers or employers. If they're met with understanding and a willingness to help, they won't ever forget it. And the happier and more stable your employees are, the better your business will fare.

✔ **Support employees when they make mistakes.** Employees need their manager's support more than ever when they make a mistake. It's easy to find fault and openly criticize employees, perhaps even in front of their peers. But if you take that approach, your employees will lose a degree of self-esteem, as well as the willingness to act independently and use their best judgment — and may never get those qualities back.

To get the best of what employees have to offer the organization, managers must tap into their employees' talents, interests, and skills. Getting to know employees on a personal level and asking for their input, help, and ideas is a great starting point for any manager. In most cases, giving employees the autonomy and authority to act in the best interests of the organization and offering words of encouragement and praise along the way work wonders. Encouraging employees to pursue their ideas and supporting them in that process are also important for yielding positive results in the workplace.

Regardless of the approaches you ultimately decide to take in your efforts to increase employee engagement, remember these tips:

✔ Encouraging initiative starts with taking initiative. Everyone has an idea that can improve his or her job, department, or overall company. Find a way to get those ideas out. Do something different, experiment, and learn along the way.

✔ The system is more important than any single idea. Set up a system that is simple, doable, and fun. If the suggestion program becomes a boring burden, it isn't likely to continue for long.

✔ Stick with it. The best idea may not always be the first one, but the process of valuing your employees' ideas will lead to more and better ones.

Part II
Mastering Key Management Duties

The 5th Wave   By Rich Tennant

"Very good answer! Now let me ask you another question..."

In this part . . .

All managers are responsible for a variety of duties — that's why they're managers. In this part, we show you how to hire great employees, set goals, coach and mentor employees, work with teams, manage virtual employees, and monitor performance and execution.

Chapter 5

Hiring: The Million-Dollar Decision

In This Chapter

▶ Determining your needs

▶ Recruiting new employees

▶ Following interviewing do's and don'ts

▶ Evaluating your candidates

▶ Making the big decision

*F*inding and hiring the best candidate for a job has never been easy. The good news about all the streamlining, downsizing, and rightsizing going on in business nowadays is that a lot of people are looking for work. The bad news, however, is that few of them have the exact qualifications you're looking for.

Added to that, the Baby Boom generation that has dominated most organizations for the past couple decades is beginning to retire. During the next ten years, 32 million jobs will be vacated and 20 million new jobs will be created. This means 52 million jobs in the United States will need to be filled; however, the projected available labor force will be only 29 million. This leaves a gap of 23 million jobs — and a huge impact on recruiting, training, succession planning, transfer of knowledge, retaining, and leading. Three conditions — an aging workforce, a shrinking labor pool, and a projected population peak — are converging to create one of the most competitive marketplaces ever. It's up to managers and other business leaders to address these issues soon or risk falling behind the competition.

Your challenge as a manager is to figure out how to not just find the best candidates for your job openings, but also convince them that your company is the best place to work. This chapter guides you through both sides of that challenge. The lifetime earnings of the average American worker are calculated at approximately $1 million, so hiring really is a million-dollar decision!

Starting with a Clear Job Description

Is the position new, or are you filling an existing one? In either case, before you start the recruiting process, you need to ask yourself some questions. Do you know exactly what standards you're going to use to measure your candidates? Does your company require department head approval? Do you have a designated pay range for this position? The clearer you are about what you need and the boundaries you need to work within, the easier and less arbitrary your selection process becomes.

If you're filling an existing position, you probably already have a detailed job description available. Review it closely and make changes where necessary. Again, ensure that the job description reflects exactly the tasks and requirements of the position. When you hire someone new to fill an existing position, you start with a clean slate. For example, you may have had a difficult time getting a former employee to accept certain new tasks — say, taking minutes at staff meetings or filing travel vouchers. By adding these new duties to the job description before you open recruitment, you make the expectations clear and you don't have to struggle with your new hire to do the job.

If the job is new, now is your opportunity to design your ideal candidate. Draft a job description that fully describes all the tasks and responsibilities of the position and the minimum necessary qualifications and experience. If the job requires expertise in addition and subtraction, for example, say so. You're not going to fill the position with the right hire if you don't make certain qualifications a key part of the job description. The more work you put into the job description now, the less work you have to do after you bring in your new hire.

Finally, before you start recruiting, use the latest-and-greatest job description to outline the most important qualities you're seeking in your new hire. Consult and compare notes with other managers on your team to get input on your descriptions, and ask employees for their feedback as well. Use this outline to guide you in the interview process. Keep in mind, however, that job descriptions may give you the skills you want, but they don't automatically give you the kind of employee you want — finding the right person is much more difficult (and the reason you spend so much time recruiting in the first place).

Making an interview outline carries an additional benefit: You can easily document why you didn't hire the candidates who didn't qualify for your positions. Pay close attention here. If a disgruntled job candidate ever sues you for not hiring him — and such lawsuits are more common than you may suspect — you'll be eternally thankful that you did your homework in this area of the hiring process. One more thing: Don't make notes on the résumé — your comments could be used in a lawsuit.

Defining the Characteristics of Desirable Candidates

Employers look for many qualities in candidates. The following list gives you an idea of the qualities employers consider most important when hiring new employees. Other characteristics may be particularly important to you, your company, and the job you're looking to fill, and this list gives you a good start in identifying them.

- **Hard working:** Hard work can often overcome a lack of experience or training. You want to hire people who are willing to do whatever it takes to get the job done. Conversely, no amount of skill can make up for a lack of initiative or work ethic. Although you won't know for sure until you make your hire, carefully questioning candidates can give you some idea of their work ethic (or, at least, what they want you to believe about their work ethic). Of course, hard work alone isn't always the end-all, be-all of hiring. People can generate a lot of work, but if the work doesn't align with your company's strategies or isn't within the true scope of their role, then it's wasted effort. Be careful to note the difference as you assess your candidates.

- **Good attitude:** Although what constitutes a "good" attitude differs for each person, a positive, friendly, willing-to-help perspective makes life at the office much more enjoyable and makes everyone's job easier. When you interview candidates, consider what they'll be like to work with for the next five or ten years. Skills are important, but attitude is even more important. This is the mantra for the success of Southwest Airlines: "Hire for attitude, train for success."

- **Experienced:** When Peter graduated from Stanford University, he naively thought that he'd be hired immediately based on the weight of his institution's diploma. However, Peter lacked a critical element that's so important in the hiring process: experience. An interview gives you the opportunity to ask pointed questions that require your candidates to demonstrate that they can do the job.

- **Self-starter:** Candidates need to demonstrate an ability to take initiative to get work done. In an Internet survey Bob conducted for his book *1001 Ways to Take Initiative at Work,* initiative ranked as the top reason employees were able to get ahead where they work.

- **Team player:** Teamwork is critical to the success of today's organizations that must do far more with far fewer resources than their predecessors. The ability to work with others and to collaborate effectively is a definite must for employees today.

✔ **Smart:** Smart people can often find better and quicker solutions to the problems that confront them. In the world of business, work smarts are more important than book smarts (although books like *this* one can help!).

✔ **Responsible:** You want to hire people who are willing to take on the responsibilities of their positions. Questions about the kinds of projects your candidates have been responsible for and the exact roles those projects played in their success can help you determine this important quality. Finer points, like showing up for the interview and remembering the name of the company they're interviewing for, can also be key indicators of your candidates' sense of responsibility.

✔ **Flexible/resilient:** Employees who are able to multitask and switch direction if necessary in a seamless manner are real assets to any organization in today's fast-changing world.

✔ **Cultural fit:** Every business has its own unique culture and set of values. The ability to fit into this culture and values is key to whether candidates can succeed within a particular company (assuming that they already have the technical skills).

✔ **Stable:** You don't want to hire someone today and then find out he's already looking for the next position tomorrow. No company can afford the expense of hiring and training a new employee, only to have that person leave six months later. You can get some indication of a person's potential stability (or lack thereof) by asking pointed questions about how long candidates worked with a previous employer and why they left. Be especially thorough and methodical as you probe this particular area.

Hiring the right people is one of the most important tasks managers face. You can't have a great organization without great people. Unfortunately, managers traditionally give short shrift to this task, devoting as little time as possible to preparation and the actual interview process. As in much of the rest of your life, the results you get from the hiring process are usually in direct proportion to the amount of time you devote to it.

Finding Good People

People are the heart of every business. The better people you hire, the better business you have. Some people are just meant to be in their jobs. You may know such individuals — someone who thrives as a receptionist or someone who lives to sell. Think about how great your organization would be if you staffed every position with people who lived for their jobs.

Likewise, bad hires can make working for an organization an incredibly miserable experience. The negative impacts of hiring the wrong candidate can reverberate both inside and outside an organization for years. If you, as a manager, ignore the problem, you put yourself in danger of losing your good employees — and clients, business partners, and vendors. We can't overemphasize the importance of hiring the right people. Do you want to spend a few extra hours up front to find the best candidates, or do you later want to devote countless hours trying to straighten out a problem employee?

Of course, as important as the interview process is to selecting the best candidates for your jobs, you won't have anyone to interview if you don't have a good system for finding good candidates. So where can you find the best candidates for your jobs? The simple answer is *everywhere*.

Bob recalls that his best experience with hiring always came when he took a long-term view of the hire: a broad search and long hiring cycle that involved other employees in the process. The short-term, "We've gotta have somebody right away" approach often results in selecting an applicant who is the lesser of a number of evils — and whose weaknesses soon become problems for the organization.

Going through traditional recruiting channels

Your job is to develop a recruitment campaign that helps you find the kinds of people you want to hire. Don't rely solely on your human resources department to develop this campaign for you; you probably have a better understanding of where to find the people you need than they do (no offense to you folks in the human resources department!). Finally, make sure your input is heeded.

The following list presents some of the best ways to find candidates for your positions:

- ✔ **Internal candidates:** In most organizations, the first place to look for candidates is within the organization. If you do your job training and developing employees, you probably have plenty of candidates to consider for your job openings. Only after you exhaust your internal candidates should you look outside your organization. Not only is hiring people this way less expensive and easier, but you also get happier employees, improved morale, and new hires who are already familiar with your organization.

✔ **Personal referrals:** Whether from co-workers, professional colleagues, friends, relatives, or neighbors, you can often find great candidates through referrals. Who better to present a candidate than someone whose opinion you already value and trust? You get far more insight about the candidates' strengths and weaknesses from the people who refer them than you ever get from résumés alone. Not only that, but research shows that people hired through current employees tend to work out better, stay with the company longer, and act happier. When you're getting ready to fill a position, make sure you let people know about it. Your employees and co-workers may well mount their own Twitter and Facebook campaigns for you, getting the word out to a wide audience.

✔ **Temporary agencies:** Hiring *temps,* or temporary employees, has become routine for many companies. When you simply have to fill a critical position for a short period of time, temporary agencies are the way to go — no muss, no fuss. And the best part is that when you hire temps, you get the opportunity to try out employees before you buy them. If you don't like the temps you get, no problem. Simply call the agency, and they send replacements before you know it. But if you like your temps, most agencies allow you to hire them at a nominal fee or after a minimum time commitment. Either way, you win. One more point: If you're using temps, you can complete your organization's necessary work while you continue looking for the right full-time employee. This buys you more time to find the best person for the job without feeling pressure to hire someone who doesn't really meet all your needs.

✔ **Professional associations:** Most professions have their accompanying associations that look out for their interests. Whether you're a doctor (and belong to the American Medical Association) or a truck driver (and belong to the Teamster's Union), you can likely find an affiliated association for whatever you do for a living. Associations even have their own associations. Association newsletters, magazines, Web sites, blogs, and social networking sites are great places to advertise your openings when you're looking for specific expertise, because your audience is already prescreened for you.

✔ **Employment agencies:** If you're filling a particularly specialized position, are recruiting in a small market, or simply prefer to have someone else take care of recruiting and screening your applicants, employment agencies are a good, albeit pricey (with a cost of up to a third of the employee's first-year salary, or more), alternative. Although employment agencies can usually locate qualified candidates in lower-level or administrative positions, you may need help from an executive search firm or *headhunter* (someone who specializes in recruiting key employees away from one firm to place in a client's firm) for your higher-level positions.

> ✔ **Want ads:** Want ads can be relatively expensive, but they're an easy way to get your message out to a large cross-section of potential candidates. You can choose to advertise in your local paper, in nationally distributed publications such as *The Wall Street Journal,* or on popular Web sites such as craigslist (www.craigslist.com). On the downside, you may find yourself sorting through hundreds or even thousands of unqualified candidates to find a few great ones.

As a manager, it is in your interest to work with your human resources team to develop an ongoing talent pipeline for key and hard-to-fill positions, or where there is high turnover such as in sales roles.

Leveraging the power of the Internet

Every day, more companies discover the benefits of using the Internet as a hiring tool. The proliferation of corporate Web pages and online employment agencies and job banks has brought about an entirely new dimension in recruiting. Web pages let you present almost unlimited amounts and kinds of information about your firm and your job openings — in text, audio, graphic, and video formats. Your pages work for you 24 hours a day, 7 days a week.

Consider a few of the best ways to leverage the power of the Internet in your own hiring efforts:

> ✔ **Web sites and blogs:** If you don't already have a great recruiting page on your company Web site, you should. In addition to this baseline item, also consider setting up company blogs where employees can describe what they do and how they do it. This gives prospective job candidates insight into your organization, helping them decide for themselves whether yours is the kind of organization they want to actively pursue. Be sure to include a function where people can supply their e-mail address or sign up for an RSS feed to be updated as new positions open. Prices to set up a Web site or blog vary from free to a few thousand dollars a year, depending on how many bells and whistles you require.

> For an example of a particularly effective recruiting Web site, point your browser to www.qualcomm.com and click on the Careers tab.

> ✔ **E-mail campaigns:** If you set up the e-mail function on your Web site that we just mentioned, you'll soon collect a large number of addresses from potential job candidates. Don't just sit there — use them! Be sure to e-mail an announcement to everyone on your list every time you have a job opening. Even if the people who receive your e-mail message aren't interested, they may know someone who is and may forward your announcement.

- **Social networking sites:** Although many social networking sites exist, a small handful have risen to the top of the heap. Two, in particular, deserve your attention if you hope to broaden your search for good candidates: Facebook (`www.facebook.com`) and LinkedIn (`www.linkedin.com`). Many millions of people have established accounts at both of these sites; however, LinkedIn was specifically designed to help job seekers network with one another to find new job opportunities. This makes it a particularly effective way for you to get the word out about your open positions. Although Facebook isn't specifically set up for job networking, you can set up a fan page there and use it as an effective recruiting platform. There's no charge to set up and use a Facebook or LinkedIn account.

- **Twitter:** Many organizations today are using Twitter (`www.twitter.com`) as a real-time platform for getting out information to anyone interested in getting it. This includes prospective job applicants. The variety of information you can send out to the world is limited only by your imagination — and by the 140-character limit for individual tweets. There's no charge to set up and use your Twitter account.

- **Traditional job-hunting sites:** A number of job-hunting sites have become popular with people looking for new positions. This makes them good platforms from which to pitch your own job openings. Some of the most popular include CareerBuilder.com (`www.careerbuilder.com`), Monster.com (`www.monster.com`), and Beyond.com (`www.beyond.com`). You'll likely have to pay to post your jobs on these sites — prices vary.

Becoming a Great Interviewer

After you narrow the field to the top three or five applicants, the next step is to start interviewing. What kind of interviewer are you? Do you spend several hours preparing for interviews — reviewing résumés, looking over job descriptions, writing and rewriting questions until each one is as finely honed as a razor blade? Or are you the kind of interviewer who, busy as you already are, starts preparing for the interview when you get the call from your receptionist that your candidate has arrived?

Here's a hint: The secret to becoming a great interviewer is to be thoroughly prepared for your interviews. Remember how much time you spent preparing to be interviewed for your current job? You didn't just walk in the door, sit down, and get offered the job, did you? You probably spent hours researching the company, its products and services, its financials, its market, and other business information. You probably brushed up on your interviewing skills and may have even done some role-playing with a friend or in front of a mirror. Don't you think you should spend at least as much time getting ready for the interview as the people you're going to interview?

Asking the right questions

More than anything else, the heart of the interview process is the questions you ask and the answers you get in response. You get the best answers when you ask the best questions. Lousy questions often result in lousy answers that don't really tell you whether the candidate is right for the job.

A great interviewer asks great questions. According to Richard Nelson Bolles, author of the perennially popular job-hunting guide *What Color Is Your Parachute?*, you can categorize all interview questions under one of the following four headings:

- **Why are you here?** Why is the person sitting across from you going to the trouble of interviewing with you today? You have just one way to find out — ask. You may assume that the answer is because he or she wants a job with your firm, but what you find may surprise you.

  Consider the story of the interviewee who forgot that he was interviewing for a job with Hewlett-Packard. During the entire interview, the applicant referred to Hewlett-Packard by the name of one of its competitors. He didn't get the job.

- **What can you do for us?** Always an important consideration! Of course, your candidates are all going to dazzle you with their incredible personalities, experience, work ethic, and love of teamwork — that almost goes without saying. However, despite what many job seekers seem to believe, the question is not, "What can your firm do for me?" — at least, not from your perspective. The question that you want an answer to is, "What can you do for us?"

  One recruiter shares a story about the job applicant who slammed his hand on her desk and demanded a signing bonus. And this was before the interview had even started! We're not surprised that this particular candidate landed neither the job nor the bonus!

- **What kind of person are you?** Few of your candidates will be absolute angels or demons, but don't forget that you'll spend a lot of time with the person you hire. You want to hire someone you'll enjoy being with during the many work hours, weeks, and years that stretch before you — and the holiday parties, company picnics, and countless other events you're expected to attend. You also want to confirm a few other issues: Are your candidates honest and ethical? Do they share your views regarding work hours, responsibility, and so forth? Are they responsible and dependable employees? Would they work well in your company culture? Of course, all your candidates will answer in the affirmative to mom-and-apple-pie questions like these. So how do you find the real answers?

When Bob recruited, he tried to "project" applicants into a typical, real-life scenario and then see how they'd think it through. For example, he may have asked the prospect what she would do if a client called at 5 p.m. with an emergency order that needed to be delivered by 9 a.m. the next morning. This way, there's no "right" answer and candidates are forced to expose their thinking process: what questions they'd ask, what strategies they'd consider, which people they'd involve, and so forth. Ask open-ended questions and let your candidates do most of the talking!

✔ **Can we afford you?** It does you no good to find the perfect candidate but, at the end of the interview, discover that you're so far apart in pay range that you're nearly in a different state. Keep in mind that the actual wage you pay to workers is only part of an overall compensation package. You may not be able to pull together more money for wages for particularly good candidates, but you may be able to offer them better benefits, a nicer office, a more impressive title, or a key to the executive sauna.

Following interviewing do's

So what can you do to prepare for your interviews? The following handy-dandy checklist gives you ideas on where to start:

✔ **Review the résumés of each interviewee the morning before interviews start.** Not only is it extremely poor form to wait to read your interviewees' résumés during the interview, but you miss out on the opportunity to tailor your questions to those little surprises you invariably discover in the résumés.

✔ **Become intimately familiar with the job description.** Are you familiar with all the duties and requirements of the job? Surprising new hires with duties that you didn't tell them about — especially when they're major duties — isn't a pathway to new-hire success.

✔ **Draft your questions before the interview.** Make a checklist of the key experience, skills, and qualities that you seek in your candidates, and use it to guide your questions. Of course, one of your questions may trigger other questions that you didn't anticipate. Go ahead with such questions, as long as they give you additional insights into your candidate and help illuminate the information you're seeking with your checklist.

✔ **Select a comfortable environment for both of you.** Your interviewee will likely be uncomfortable regardless of what you do. You don't need to be uncomfortable, too. Make sure that the interview environment is well ventilated, private, and protected from interruptions. You definitely don't want your phone ringing off the hook or employees barging in during your interviews. You get the best performance from your interviewees when they aren't thrown off track by distractions.

✔ **Avoid playing power trips during the course of the interview.** Forget the old games of asking trick questions, turning up the heat, or cutting the legs off their chairs (yes, some managers still do this game playing!) to gain an artificial advantage over your candidates. Get real — it's the 21st century, for heaven's sake!

✔ **Take lots of notes.** Don't rely on your memory when it comes to interviewing candidates for your job. If you interview more than a couple people, you can easily forget who said exactly what, as well as what your impressions were of their performances. Not only are your written notes a great way to remember who's who, but they're an important tool to have when you're evaluating your candidates.

As you have no doubt gathered by now, interview questions are one of your best tools for determining whether a candidate is right for your company. Although some amount of small talk is appropriate to help relax your candidates, the heart of your interviews should focus on answering the questions just listed. Above all, don't give up! Keep asking questions until you're satisfied that you have all the information you need to make your decision.

Don't forget to take lots of notes as you interview your candidates. Try to avoid the temptation to draw pictures of little smiley faces or that new car you've been lusting after. Write the key points of your candidates' responses and their reactions to your questions. For example, if you ask why your candidate left her previous job, and she starts getting really nervous, make a note about this reaction. Finally, note your own impressions of the candidates:

✔ Top-notch performer — the star of her class.

✔ Fantastic experience with developing applications in a client/server environment. The best candidate yet.

✔ Geez, was this one interviewing for the right job?

Avoiding interviewing don'ts

The topic of interviewing don'ts is probably worth a chapter of its own. If you've been a manager for any time at all, you know that you can run into tricky situations during an interview and that certain questions can land you in major hot water if you make the mistake of asking them.

Five steps to better interviewing

Every interview consists of five key steps:

1. **Welcome the applicant.** Greet your candidates warmly and chat with them informally to help loosen them up. Questions about the weather, the difficulty of finding your offices, or how they found out about your position are old standbys.

2. **Summarize the position.** Briefly describe the job, the kind of person you're looking for, and the interview process you use.

3. **Ask your questions (and then listen!).** Questions should be relevant to the position and should cover the applicant's work experience, education, and other related topics. Limit the amount of talking you do as an interviewer. Many interviewers end up trying to sell the job to an applicant instead of probing whether a candidate is a good fit.

4. **Probe experience and discover the candidate's strengths and weaknesses.** The best predictor of future behavior is past behavior, which is why exploring applicants' past experience can be so helpful to see what they did and how they did it! And although asking your candidates to name their strengths and weaknesses may seem clichéd, the answers can be very revealing.

5. **Conclude the interview.** Allow your candidates the opportunity to offer any further information that they feel is necessary for you to make a decision, and to ask questions about your firm or the job. Thank them for their interest and let them know when they can expect your firm to contact them.

Some interviewing don'ts are merely good business practice. For example, accepting an applicant's invitation for a date is probably not a good idea. Believe it or not, it happens. After a particularly drawn-out interview at a well-known high-tech manufacturer, a male candidate asked out a female interviewer. The interviewer considered her options and declined the date; she also declined to make Prince Charming a job offer.

Then you have the blunders of the major legal type — the kind that can land you and your firm in court. Interviewing is one area of particular concern in the hiring process as it pertains to possible discrimination. For example, although you can ask applicants whether they are able to fulfill job functions, in the United States, you can't ask them whether they are disabled. Because of the critical nature of the interview process, you must know the questions that you absolutely should never ask a job candidate. Here is a brief summary of the kinds of topics that may get you and your firm into trouble, depending on the exact circumstances:

- Age
- Arrest and conviction record
- Debts

✔ Disability

✔ Height and weight

✔ Marital status

✔ National origin

✔ Race or skin color

✔ Religion (or lack thereof)

✔ Sex

✔ Sexual orientation

Legal or illegal, the point is that none of the preceding topics is necessary to determine applicants' ability to perform their jobs. Therefore, ask questions that directly relate to the candidates' ability to perform the tasks required. To do otherwise can put you at definite legal risk. In other words, what *does* count is job-related criteria — that is, information that's directly pertinent to the candidate's ability to do the job (you clearly need to decide this *prior* to interviewing!).

Evaluating Your Candidates

Now comes the really fun part of the hiring process — evaluating your candidates. If you've done your homework, then you already have an amazing selection of candidates to choose from, you've narrowed your search to the ones showing the best potential to excel in your position, and you've interviewed them to see whether they can live up to the promises they made in their résumés. Before you make your final decision, you need a bit more information.

Checking references

Wow! What a résumé! What an interview! What a candidate! Would you be surprised to find out that this shining employee-to-be didn't really go to Yale? Or that he really wasn't the account manager on that nationwide marketing campaign? Or that his last supervisor wasn't particularly impressed with his analytical skills?

A résumé and interview are great tools, but a reference check is probably the only chance you have to find out before you make a hiring decision whether your candidates are actually who they say they are. Depending on your organization, you may be expected to do reference checks. Or maybe your human resources department takes care of that task. Whichever the case, don't hire new employees without first doing an exhaustive check of their backgrounds.

The twin goals of checking references are to verify the information that your candidates have provided and to gain some candid insight into who your candidates really are and how they behave in the workplace. When you contact a candidate's references, limit your questions to topics related to the work to be done. As in the interview process, asking questions that can be considered discriminatory to your candidates isn't appropriate.

Here are some of the best ways to do your reference checking:

- ✔ **Check academic references.** A surprising number of people exaggerate or tell outright lies when reporting their educational experience. Start your reference check here.

- ✔ **Call current and former supervisors.** Getting information from employers is getting more difficult. Many businesspeople are rightfully concerned that they may be sued for libel or defamation of character if they say anything negative about current or former subordinates. Still, it doesn't hurt to try. You get a much better picture of your candidates if you speak directly to their current and former supervisors instead of to their firms' human resources department — especially if the supervisors you speak to have left their firms. The most you're likely to get from the human resources folks is a confirmation that the candidate worked at the firm during a specific period of time.

- ✔ **Check your network of associates.** If you belong to a professional association, union, or similar group of like-minded careerists, you have the opportunity to tap into the rest of the membership to get the word on your candidates. For example, if you're a certified public accountant (CPA) and want to find out about a few candidates for your open accounting position, you can check with the members of your professional accounting association to see whether anyone knows anything about them.

- ✔ **Do some surfing.** On the Web, that is. Plug your candidate's name into a search engine such as Google (www.google.com), perhaps along with the name of the company where the person last worked or the city where she lives. Or do a search for your candidate on Facebook (www.facebook.com) or LinkedIn (www.linkedin.com). You might be surprised by how much information you can uncover about a job candidate — good and bad — doing just a few simple Web searches.

Reviewing your notes

You did take interview notes, didn't you? Now's the time to drag them back out and look them over. Review the information package for each candidate — one by one — and compare your findings against your predetermined criteria. Take a look at the candidates' résumés, your notes, and the results of your reference checks. How do they stack up against the standards you set for the position? Do you see any clear winners at this point? Any clear losers? Organize your candidate packages into the following stacks:

✔ **Winners:** These candidates are clearly the best choices for the position. You have no hesitation in hiring any one of them.

✔ **Potential winners:** These candidates are questionable for some reason. Maybe their experience isn't as strong as that of other candidates, or perhaps you weren't impressed with their presentation skills. Neither clear winners nor clear losers, you hire these candidates only after further investigation or if you can't hire anyone from your pool of winners.

✔ **Losers:** These candidates are clearly unacceptable for the position. You simply don't consider hiring any of them.

Conducting a second (or third) round

When you're a busy manager, you have pressure to get things done as quickly as possible, and you're tempted to take shortcuts to achieve your goals. It seems that everything has to be done yesterday — or maybe the day before. When do you have the opportunity to really spend as much time as you want to complete a task or project? Time is precious when you have ten other projects crying for your attention. Time is even more valuable when you're hiring for a vacant position that's critical to your organization and needs to be filled right now.

Hiring is one area of business where you must avoid taking shortcuts. Remember, hire slowly and fire quickly (but within the rules). Finding the best candidates for your vacancies requires an investment of time and resources. Your company's future depends on it. Great candidates don't stay on the market long, though, so don't allow the process to drag on too long. Make sure the candidates know your required time frame, and stick to it!

Depending on your organization's policies or culture, or if you're undecided on the best candidate, you may decide to bring candidates in for several rounds of interviews. In this kind of system, lower-level supervisors, managers, or interview panels conduct initial screening interviews. Candidates who pass this round are invited back for another interview with a higher-level manager. Finally, the best two or three candidates interview with the organization's top manager.

But keep in mind that the timeline for an offer differs depending on the job you're interviewing for. Lower-level job hunters cannot afford to be unemployed (if they are) for long, and they often get and accept job offers quickly. A higher-level position — say, a general manager — gives you more time.

The ultimate decision on how many rounds and levels of interviews to conduct depends on the nature of the job itself, the size of your company, and your policies and procedures. If the job is simple or at a relatively low level in the company, a single phone interview may be sufficient to determine the best candidate. However, if the job is complex or at a relatively high level in the organization, you may need several rounds of testing and personal interviews to determine the best candidate.

Hiring the Best (and Leaving the Rest)

The first step in making a hiring decision is to rank your candidates within the groups of winners and potential winners that you established during the evaluation phase of the hiring process. You don't need to bother ranking the losers because you wouldn't hire them anyway — no matter what. The best candidate in your group of winners is first, the next best is second, and so on. If you've done your job thoroughly and well, the best candidates for the job are readily apparent at this point.

The next step is to get on the phone and offer your first choice the job. Don't waste any time — you never know whether your candidate has interviewed with other employers. It would be a shame to invest all this time in the hiring process only to find out that your top choice accepted a job with one of your competitors. If you can't come to terms with your first choice in a reasonable amount of time, go on to your second choice. Keep going through your pool of winners until you either make a hire or exhaust the list of candidates.

The following sections give you a few tips to keep in mind as you rank your candidates and make your final decision.

Being objective

In some cases, you may prefer certain candidates because of their personalities or personal charisma, regardless of their abilities or work experience. Sometimes the desire to like these candidates can obscure their shortcomings, while a better qualified, albeit less socially adept, candidate may fade in your estimation.

Be objective. Consider the job to be done, as well as the skills and qualifications that being successful requires. Do your candidates have these skills and qualifications? What would it take for your candidates to be considered fully qualified for the position?

Don't allow yourself to be unduly influenced by your candidates' looks, champagnelike personalities, high-priced hairstyles, or fashion-forward clothing ensembles. None of these characteristics can tell you how well your candidates will actually perform the job. The facts are present for you to see in your candidates' résumés, interview notes, and reference checks. If you stick to the facts, you can still go wrong, but the chances are diminished.

One more thing: Diversity in hiring is positive for any organization. Check your bias at the door!

Trusting your gut

Sometimes you're faced with a decision between two equally qualified candidates, or with a decision about a candidate who is marginal but shows promise. In such cases, you have weighed all the objective data and given the analytical side of your being free rein, but you still have no clear winner. What do you do in this kind of situation?

Listen to yourself. What do you feel in your gut? Not nausea, we hope. Although two candidates may seem equal in skills and abilities, do you have a feeling that one is better suited to the job? If so, go with it. As much as you may want your hiring decision to be as objective as possible, whenever you introduce the human element into the decision-making process, a certain amount of subjectivity is naturally present.

In reality, rarely are two candidates equally qualified, although often one or more people seem to have more to bring to the job than anticipated (for example, industry focus, fresh ideas, previous contacts, and so forth). This is again where your pre-work can be so valuable in keeping you focused. Can they both do the job? If so, the bonus traits can tip the scale.

Other options:

- Give them each a nonpaid assignment and see how they do.
- Try them each on a paid project.

When Bob once hired a bookkeeper for his business, his hiring team narrowed the applicants to two candidates, both of whom looked like they could do the job equally well. As a result, secondary information became more relevant. One of the candidates was a little less flexible in work schedule, lived farther from the office, and wanted $7 more an hour than the company was offering for the position. The second candidate didn't have any of those issues and, therefore, got the offer.

Keep in touch with other top candidates as additional needs arise or in case your first choice doesn't work out.

Revisiting the candidate pool

What do you do if, heaven forbid, you can't hire anyone from your group of winners? This unfortunate occurrence is a tough call, but no one said management is an easy task. Take a look at your stack of potential winners. What would it take to make your top potential winners into winners? If the answer is as simple as a training course or two, then give these candidates serious consideration — with the understanding that you can schedule the necessary training soon after hiring. Perhaps a candidate just needs a little more experience before moving into the ranks of the winners. You can make a judgment call on whether you feel that someone's current experience is sufficient until that person gains the experience you're looking for. If not, you may want to keep looking for the right candidate. After all, this person may be working with you for a long time — waiting for the best candidate only makes sense.

If you're forced to go to your group of almost-winners and no candidate really seems up to the task, don't hire someone simply to fill the position. If you do, you're probably making a big mistake. Hiring employees is far easier than unhiring them. The damage that an inappropriate hire can wreak — on coworkers, your customers, and your organization (not to mention the person you hired) — can take years and a considerable amount of money to undo. Not only that, but it can be a big pain in your neck! Other options are to redefine the job, reevaluate other current employees, or hire on a temporary basis to see whether a risky hire works out.

Top five hiring Web sites

Wondering where to find the best information on the Web about the topics addressed in this chapter? Here are our top five favorites:

✔ *The Wall Street Journal* Careers section: `online.wsj.com/public/page/news-career-jobs.html`

✔ *Entrepreneur* magazine: `www.entrepreneur.com/humanresources/hiring/index.html`

✔ BusinessTown.com: `www.businesstown.com/hiring/index.asp`

✔ CCH Business Owner's Toolkit: `www.toolkit.com/small_business_guide/sbg.aspx?nid=P05_0001`

✔ Federal hiring law Q&A (EEOC): `www.eeoc.gov/facts/qanda.html`

Chapter 6

Goal Setting Made Easy

*I*f you created a list of the most important duties of management, "setting goals" would likely be near the top of the list. In most companies, senior management sets the overall purpose — the vision — of the organization. Middle managers then have the job of developing goals and plans for achieving the vision senior management sets. Managers and employees work together to set goals and develop schedules for attaining them.

As a manager, you're probably immersed in goals — not only for yourself, but also for your employees, your department, and your organization. This flood of goals can cause stress and frustration as you try to balance the relative importance of each one.

Should I tackle my department's goal of improving turnaround time first, or should I get to work on my boss's goal of finishing the budget? Or maybe the company's goal of improving customer service is more important. Well, I think I'll just try to achieve my own personal goal of setting aside some time to eat lunch today.

As you discover in this chapter, sometimes having too many goals is as bad as not having any goals. This chapter helps you understand why setting strong, focused goals is essential to your success and that of your employees. We also guide you in communicating visions and goals and keeping both yourself and your employees on track to meet established goals.

Goals provide direction and purpose. Don't forget, if you can see it, you can achieve it. Goals help you see where you're going and how you can get there. And the *way* you set goals can impact how motivating they are to others.

Knowing Where You're Going

Believe it or not, Lewis Carroll's classic book *Alice in Wonderland* offers lessons that can enhance your business relationships. Consider the following passage, in which Alice asks the Cheshire Cat for advice on which direction to go.

> "Would you tell me, please, which way I ought to go from here?"
>
> "That depends a good deal on where you want to go," said the Cat.
>
> "I don't much care where — " said Alice.
>
> "Then it doesn't matter which way you go," said the Cat.
>
> " — so long as I get *somewhere,*" Alice added as an explanation.
>
> "Oh, you're sure to do that," said the Cat, "if you only walk long enough."

It takes no effort at all to get *somewhere.* Just do nothing, and you're there. (In fact, everywhere you go, there you are!) However, if you want to get somewhere meaningful and succeed as a manager, you first have to know where you want to go. And after you decide where you want to go, you need to make plans for how to get there. This practice is as true in business as in your everyday life.

For example, suppose that you have a vision of starting up a new sales office in Prague so that you can better service your Eastern European accounts. How do you go about achieving this vision? You have three choices:

- An unplanned, non-goal-oriented approach
- A planned, goal-oriented approach
- A hope and a prayer

Which choice do you think is most likely to get you to your goal? Go ahead, take a wild guess!

If you guessed the unplanned, non-goal-oriented approach to reaching your vision, shame on you! Please report to study hall. Your assignment is to write 500 times, "A goal is a dream with a deadline." Now, no talking to your classmates and no goofing off. We've got our eyes on you!

If you guessed the planned, goal-oriented approach, you've earned a big gold star and a place in the *Managing For Dummies* Hall of Fame. Congratulations!

Following are the main reasons to set goals whenever you want to accomplish something significant:

- ✓ **Goals provide direction.** For our preceding example (starting up a new sales office in Prague), you can probably find a million different ways to better serve your Eastern European business accounts. However, to get something done, you have to set a definite vision — a target to aim for and to guide the efforts of you and your organization. You can then translate this vision into goals that take you where you want to go. Without goals, you're doomed to waste countless hours going nowhere. With goals, you can focus your efforts and your team's efforts on only the activities that move you toward where you're going — in this case, opening a new sales office.

- ✓ **Goals tell you how far you've traveled.** Goals provide milestones to measure how effectively you're working toward accomplishing your vision. If you determine that you must accomplish several specific milestones to reach your final destination and you complete a few of them, you know exactly how many remain. You know right where you stand and how far you have yet to go.

- ✓ **Goals help make your overall vision attainable.** You can't reach your vision in one big step — you need many small steps to get there. If, again, your vision is to open a new sales office in Prague, you can't expect to proclaim your vision on Friday and walk into a fully staffed and functioning office on Monday. You must accomplish many goals — from shopping for office space, to hiring and relocating staff, to printing stationery and business cards — before you can attain your vision. Goals enable you to achieve your overall vision by dividing your efforts into smaller pieces that, when accomplished individually, add up to big results.

- ✓ **Goals clarify everyone's role.** When you discuss your vision with your employees, they may have some idea of where you want to go but no idea of how to go about getting there. As your well-intentioned employees head off to help you achieve your vision, some employees may duplicate the efforts of others, some employees may focus on the wrong strategies and ignore more important tasks, and some employees may simply do something else altogether (and hope that you don't notice the difference). Setting goals with your team clarifies what the tasks are, who handles which tasks, and what is expected from each employee and, ultimately, from the entire team.

- ✓ **Goals give people something to strive for.** People are typically more motivated when challenged to attain a goal that's beyond their normal level of performance — this is known as a *stretch goal*. Not only do goals give people a sense of purpose, but they also relieve the boredom that can come from performing a routine job day after day. Be sure to discuss the goal with them and seek feedback where appropriate to gain their commitment and buy-in.

For goals to be effective, they have to link directly to the manager's final vision. To stay ahead of the competition — or simply to maintain their current position in business — organizations create compelling visions, and then management and employees work together to set and achieve the goals to reach those visions. Look over these examples of compelling visions that drive the development of goals at several successful enterprises (which are perhaps even more important as they fight for competitive advantage in the face of depressed telecommunications and technology sectors):

✔ Samsung is a Korea-based manufacturer of electronics, chemicals, and heavy machinery, as well as a provider of architectural and construction services. Samsung's vision is to lead the digital convergence movement; this vision drives the organization's goals.

✔ Motorola, long known for its obsession with quality, has set a target of no more than two manufacturing defects per billion parts produced.

✔ A century ago, the chairman of AT&T created a vision for the organization comprising good, cheap, and fast worldwide telephone service. AT&T's vision today is "to be the most admired and valuable company in the world."

When it comes to goals, the best ones

✔ Are few in number but very specific and clear in purpose.

✔ Are stretch goals. They're attainable, but they aren't too easy or too hard.

✔ Involve people. When you involve others in a collaborative, team-based process, you get buy-in so it becomes their goal, not just yours.

Identifying SMART Goals

You can find all kinds of goals in all types of organizations. Some goals are short term and specific ("Starting next month, we will increase production by two units per employee per hour"); others are long term and vague ("Within the next five years, we will become a learning organization"). Employees easily understand some goals ("Line employees will have no more than 20 rejects per month"), but other goals can be difficult to measure and subject to much interpretation ("All employees are expected to show more respect to each other in the next fiscal year"). Still other goals can be accomplished relatively easily ("Reception staff will always answer the phone by the third ring"), whereas others are virtually impossible to attain ("All employees will master the five languages that our customers speak before the end of the fiscal year").

How do you know what kind of goals to set? The whole point of setting goals, after all, is to achieve them. It does you no good to go to the trouble of calling meetings, hacking through the needs of your organization, and burning up precious time only to end up with goals that aren't acted on or completed. Unfortunately, this scenario describes what far too many managers do with their time.

The best goals are *smart* goals — actually, *SMART* goals is the acronym to help you remember them. SMART refers to a handy checklist for the five characteristics of well-designed goals:

✔ **Specific:** Goals must be clear and unambiguous; broad and fuzzy thinking has no place in goal setting. When goals are specific, they tell employees exactly what's expected, when, and how much. Because the goals are specific, you can easily measure your employees' progress toward their completion.

✔ **Measurable:** What good is a goal that you can't measure? If your goals aren't measurable, you never know whether your employees are making progress toward their successful completion. Not only that, but your employees may have a tough time staying motivated to complete their goals when they have no milestones to indicate their progress.

✔ **Attainable:** Goals must be realistic and attainable by average employees. The best goals require employees to stretch a bit to achieve them, but they aren't extreme. That is, the goals are neither out of reach nor set too low. Goals that are set too high or too low become meaningless, and employees naturally come to ignore them.

✔ **Relevant:** Goals must be an important tool in the grand scheme of reaching your company's vision and mission. We've heard that 80 percent of workers' productivity comes from only 20 percent of their activities. You can guess where the other 80 percent of work activity ends up! This relationship comes from Italian economist Vilfredo Pareto's 80/20 rule. This rule, which states that 80 percent of the wealth of most countries is held by only 20 percent of the population, has been applied to many other fields since its discovery. Relevant goals address the 20 percent of workers' activities that has such a great impact on performance and brings your organization closer to its vision, thereby making it, and you, a success.

✔ **Time-bound:** Goals must have starting points, ending points, and fixed durations. Commitment to deadlines helps employees focus their efforts on completing the goal on or before the due date. Goals without deadlines or schedules for completion tend to be overtaken by the day-to-day crises that invariably arise in an organization.

SMART goals make for smart organizations. In our experience, many supervisors and managers neglect to work with their employees to set goals together. And for the ones that do, goals are often unclear, ambiguous, unrealistic, immeasurable, uninspiring, and unrelated to the organization's vision. By developing SMART goals with your employees, you can avoid these traps while ensuring the progress of your organization and your team.

Although the SMART system of goal setting provides guidelines to help you frame effective goals, you have additional considerations to keep in mind. The following considerations help you ensure that anyone in your organization can easily understand and act on the goals you and your employees agree on.

✔ **Ensure that goals are related to your employees' role in the organization.** Pursuing an organization's goals is far easier for employees when those goals are a regular part of their jobs and they can see how their contributions support the company. For example, suppose that you set a goal for employees who solder circuit boards to raise production by 2 percent per quarter. These employees spend almost every working moment pursuing this goal, because the goal is an integral part of their job. However, if you give the same employees a goal of "improving the diversity of the organization," what exactly does that have to do with your line employees' role? Nothing. The goal may sound lofty and may be important to your organization, but because your line employees don't make the hiring decisions, you're wasting both your time and theirs with that particular goal.

✔ **Whenever possible, use values to guide behavior.** What's the most important value in your organization? Honesty? Fairness? Respect? Whatever it is, ensure that leaders model this behavior and reward employees who live it.

✔ **Simple goals are better goals.** The easier your goals are to understand, the more likely the employees are to work to achieve them. Goals should be no longer than one sentence; make them concise, compelling, and easy to read and understand.

Goals that take more than a sentence to describe are actually multiple goals. When you find multiple-goal statements, break them into several individual, one-sentence goals. Goals that take a page or more to describe aren't really goals; they're books. File them away and try again.

Setting Goals: Less Is More

Coauthor Peter remembers the scene as if it were yesterday. His organization had determined that it needed to develop a long-range strategic plan. (Strategic planning was "in" at the time and seemed like a good thing to do.) The entire management team was marshaled for this effort; the team scheduled several all-day planning sessions, retained a high-priced consultant, and announced to the staff that something major was brewing at the top.

The management team threw itself wholeheartedly into the planning effort. The managers wanted to answer questions like the following:

✔ Why did the organization exist?

✔ Who were its customers?

✔ What were its values?

✔ What was its mission?

✔ What were its goals?

✔ How could the organization know when it achieved the goals?

Session after session, they had great idea after great idea. Before long, they had more than 12 poster-sized flip chart pages taped to the walls of the meeting room, each brimming with goals for the organization. "Improve customer service." "Provide quicker project turnaround." "Fix the heating and air conditioning system at corporate headquarters." And many more — in all, more than 200!

When the last planning meeting ended, the managers congratulated each other over their collective accomplishment and went back to their regular office routines. Before long, the goals were forgotten, the pages on which they were recorded neatly folded and stored away in someone's file cabinet. Meanwhile, business went on as usual, and the long-range planning effort went into long-term hibernation. Soon the organization's employees who knew that the management team had embarked on a momentous process of strategic planning finally tired of asking about it.

Don't let all your hard work be in vain. When you go through the exercise of setting goals, keep them to a manageable number that can realistically be followed up on. And when you finish one goal, move on to the next.

When it comes to goal setting, less is more.

The following guidelines can help you select the right goals — and the right number of goals — for your organization:

✔ **Pick two to three goals to focus on.** You can't do everything at once — at least, not well — and you can't expect your employees to, either. Attempt to complete only a few goals at any one time. Setting too many goals dilutes the efforts of you and your staff and can result in a complete breakdown in the process.

✔ **Pick the goals with the greatest relevance.** Certain goals bring you a lot closer to attaining your vision than do other goals. Because you have only so many hours in your workday, it clearly makes sense to concentrate your efforts on a few goals that have the biggest payoff rather than on a boatload of goals with relatively less impact to the business.

✔ **Focus on the goals that tie most closely to your organization's mission.** You may be tempted to take on goals that are challenging, interesting, and fun to accomplish but that are far removed from your organization's mission. Don't do it.

✔ **Regularly revisit the goals and update them as necessary.** Business is anything but static, and regularly assessing your goals is important in making sure that they're still relevant to the vision you want to achieve. Put in quarterly or midyear review schedules. If the goals remain important, great — carry on. If not, meet with your employees to revise the goals and the schedules for attaining them.

Avoid creating too many goals in your zeal to get as many things done as quickly as you can. Too many goals can overwhelm you — and they can overwhelm your employees, too. You're far better off setting a few significant goals and then concentrating your efforts on attaining them. Don't forget that management isn't measured by one huge success after another. Instead, it involves successfully meeting daily challenges and opportunities — gradually but inevitably improving the organization in the process.

Communicating Your Vision and Goals to Your Team

Having goals is great, but how do you get the word out to your employees? As you know, goals should align with the organization's vision. Establishing goals helps you ensure that employees focus on achieving the vision in the desired time frame and with the desired results. You have many possible ways to communicate goals to your employees, but some ways are better than others. In every case, you must communicate goals clearly, the receiver must understand the goals, and the relevant parties must follow through on achieving the goals.

The power of the annual goal at Marmot Mountain

When Steve Crisafulli was brought on as president of Marmot Mountain, Ltd., a California-based producer of super-high-quality outdoor clothing, he quickly discovered that Marmot was in big trouble. The company had no credit records, the computer inventory system was inadequate, and employees consistently were late in delivering financial statements to decision makers. Crisafulli planned to develop specific goals to lead the company to his vision of profitability. However, the job had to be done one step at a time.

The first problem Crisafulli focused on was the firm's recurring difficulties making deliveries to customers on time. In one particularly bad example, the entire winter clothing line — due to stores by Labor Day — wasn't delivered until January of the next year. As a result, business dropped precipitously. Soon Crisafulli made

timely delivery of Marmot products the firm's number one priority. Employees agreed to a goal of getting the next winter clothing line out no later than mid-September. To meet the goal, the management team implemented daily meetings, managers began to communicate with each other and with workers, quality control inspectors went out to check on key suppliers, and marketing budgets were increased.

To make a long story short, not only did Marmot achieve its goal, but the entire winter clothing line was shipped two weeks ahead of the mid-September deadline. Even today, the company retains the single-mindedness that delivered it from the brink of disaster years ago. At its annual strategic meeting, Marmot's management team decides on one goal for the following year.

Communicating your organization's vision is as important as communicating specific goals. You can communicate the vision in every way possible, as often as possible, throughout your organization and to significant others such as clients, customers, suppliers, and so forth. Be aware of possible obstacles, too: Often an organization's vision is pounded out in a series of grueling management meetings that leave the participants (you, the managers!) beaten and tired. By the time the managers reach their final goal of developing a company's vision, they're sick of it and ready to go on to the next challenge.

Many organizations drop the ball at this crucial point and are thereby slow to communicate the vision. Also, each succeeding layer of an organization tends to siphon off some of the vision's energy, so by the time it filters down to the front-line employees, the vision has become dull and lifeless.

When you communicate vision and goals, do it with energy and a sense of urgency and importance. You're talking about the future of your organization and your employees, not the score of last night's game! If your team doesn't think that you care about the vision, why should they? Simply put, they won't.

Companies usually announce their visions to employees — and the public — in ways that are designed to maximize the impact. Companies commonly communicate their vision in these ways:

- ✔ By conducting huge employee rallies where the vision is unveiled in inspirational presentations

- ✔ By branding their vision on anything possible — business cards, letter-head stationery, massive posters hung in the break rooms, newsletters, employee name tags, and more

- ✔ By proudly emblazoning their vision statements within corporate Web sites; on Facebook fan pages; and via electronic media campaigns, Twitter tweets, and other Internet-enabled methods of communication

- ✔ By mentioning the corporate vision in newspaper, radio, television, and other media interviews

- ✔ By encouraging managers to "talk up" the vision in staff meetings or other verbal interactions with employees and during recruiting

To avoid a cynical "fad" reaction from employees who may already be suspicious of management's motives when unveiling a new initiative, making consistent, casual and genuine reference to it is much more effective than hosting a huge, impersonal event. Again, in this case, less is often better.

Unlike visions, goals are much more personalized to the department or individual employees, and you must use more formal and direct methods to communicate them. The following guidelines can help:

- ✔ Write down your goals.

- ✔ Conduct one-on-one, face-to-face meetings with your employees to introduce, discuss, and assign goals.

    If physical distance prohibits this or you can't conduct a face-to-face meeting, conduct your meeting over the phone. The point is to make sure that your employees hear the goals, understand them and your expectations, and have the opportunity to ask for clarifications.

- ✔ Call your team together to introduce team-related goals.

    You can assign goals to teams instead of solely to individuals. If this is the case, get the team together and explain the role of the team and each individual in the successful completion of the goal. Make sure that all team members understand exactly what they are to do and whether a leader or co-leaders are ultimately responsible for the goals' completion. Get employee buy-in and try to make the goals resonate with each person. (We discuss the function of teams in more detail in Chapter 8.)

✔ Gain the commitment of your employees, whether individually or on teams, to work toward the successful accomplishment of their goals.

Ask your employees to prepare and present plans and milestone schedules explaining how they can accomplish the assigned goals in the agreed-upon timeline. After your employees begin working on their goals, regularly monitor their progress to ensure that they're on track, and collaborate with them to resolve any problems.

Juggling Priorities: Keeping Your Eye on the Ball

After you've decided what goals are important to you and your organization, you come to the difficult part. How do you, the manager, maintain the focus of your employees — and yourself, for that matter — on achieving the goals you've set?

The process of goal setting can generate excitement and engage employees in the inner workings of the business, whether the goals are set individually or by department or function. This excitement can quickly evaporate, though, when employees return to their desks. You, the manager, must take steps to ensure that the organization's focus remains centered on the agreed-upon goals, not on other matters (which are less important but momentarily more pressing). Of course, this task is much easier said than done.

Hallmark's many avenues of communication

The management of Hallmark Cards, Inc., the world's largest producer of greeting cards, firmly believes in the value of communicating the organization's vision, goals, and vital business information to its employees. According to former Hallmark president and CEO Irvine O. Hockaday, Jr., "The only sustainable edge for a corporation is the energy and cleverness of its people. To tap that, a chief executive must craft a vision, empower employees, encourage teamwork, and kindle the competitive fires."

To back up its commitment to getting the word out to employees, Hallmark developed an elaborate portfolio of formal employee publications. In addition to distributing a daily newsletter, Noon News, for all employees, Hallmark publishes Crown, a bimonthly magazine for employees, and a newsletter for managers titled Directions. However, Hallmark's commitment to communication doesn't end with newsletters and magazines — when Hockaday worked at Hallmark, he regularly invited workers from throughout the organization to join him for a meal to share information.

Staying focused on goals can be extremely difficult — particularly when you're a busy person and the goals compound your regular responsibilities. Think about situations that demand your attention during a typical day at work:

- ✔ How often do you sit down at your desk in the morning to prioritize your day, only to have your priorities completely changed five minutes later when you get a call from your boss?

- ✔ How many times has an employee unexpectedly come to you with a problem?

- ✔ Have you ever gotten caught in a so-called quick meeting that lasts for several hours?

In unlimited ways, you or your employees can get derailed and lose the focus you need to get your organization's goals accomplished. One of the biggest problems employees face is confusing activity with tangible results. Do you know anyone who works incredibly long hours — late into the night and on weekends — but never seems to get anything done? These employees always seem busy, but they're working on the wrong things. This is called the *activity trap,* and it's easy for you and your employees to fall into.

We previously mentioned the general rule that 80 percent of workers' productivity comes from 20 percent of their activity. The flip side of this rule is that only 20 percent of workers' productivity comes from 80 percent of their activity. This statistic illustrates the activity trap at work. What do you do in an average day? More important, what do you do with the 80 percent of your time that produces so few clear results? You can get out of the activity trap and take control of your schedules and priorities. However, you have to be tough, and you have to single-mindedly pursue your goals.

Achieving your goals is all up to you. No one, not even your boss (perhaps *especially* not your boss), can make it any easier for you to concentrate on achieving your goals. You have to take charge and find an approach that works for you. If you aren't controlling your own schedule, you're simply letting everyone else control your schedule for you.

Following are some tips to help you and your employees get out of the activity trap:

- ✔ **Complete your top-priority task first.** With all the distractions that compete for your attention, with the constant temptation to work on the easy stuff first and save the tough stuff for last, and with people dropping into your office just to chat or to unload their problems on you, concentrating on your top-priority task is always a challenge. However, if you don't do your top priority first, you're almost guaranteed to find yourself caught in the activity trap. That is, you'll find the same priorities on your list of tasks to do day after day, week after week, and month after month. If your top-priority task is too large, divide it into smaller chunks and focus on the most important piece first.

✔ **Get organized.** Getting organized and managing your time effectively are both incredibly important pursuits for anyone in business. If you're organized, you can spend less time trying to figure out what you should be doing and more time just doing it.

✔ **Just say no.** If someone tries to make his or her problems your problems, just say no! If you're a manager, you probably like nothing more than taking on new challenges and solving problems. However, the conflict arises when solving somebody else's problems interferes with your own work. You have to fight the temptation to lose control of your day. Always ask yourself, "How does this help me achieve my goals?"

Using Your Power for Good: Making Your Goals Reality

After you create a set of goals with your employees, how do you make sure they get done? How do you turn your priorities into your employees' priorities? The best goals in the world mean nothing if they aren't achieved. You can choose to leave this critical step to chance or you can choose to get involved.

You have the power to make your goals happen.

Power has gotten a bad rap lately. In reaction to the highly publicized leadership styles that signified greed and unethical behavior in American corporations, employees have increasingly demanded — and organizations are recognizing the need for — management that is principle centered and has a more compassionate, human face.

We believe that nothing is inherently wrong with power — everyone has many sources of power within. Not only do you have power, but you also exercise power to control or influence people and events around you on a daily basis (hopefully in a positive way). Generally, well-placed power is a positive thing. However, power can be a negative thing when abused or when someone acts in only self-interest. Manipulation, exploitation, and coercion have no place in the modern workplace.

You can use your positive power and influence to your advantage — and to the advantage of the people you lead — by tapping into it to help achieve your organization's goals. People and systems often fall into ruts or nonproductive patterns of behavior that are hard to break. Power properly applied can redirect people and systems and move them in the right direction — the direction that leads to the accomplishment of goals.

Everyone has five primary sources of power, as well as specific strengths and weaknesses related to these sources. Recognize your strengths and weaknesses and use them to your advantage. As you review the five sources of power that follow, consider your own personal strengths and weaknesses.

- ✔ **Personal power:** This is the power that comes from within your character. Your passion for greatness, the strength of your convictions, your ability to communicate and inspire, your personal charisma, and your leadership skills all add up to personal power.

- ✔ **Relationship power:** Everyone has relationships with people at work. These interactions contribute to the relationship power that you possess in your organization. Sources of relationship power include close friendships with top executives, partners, owners, people who owe you favors, and co-workers who provide you with information and insights that you wouldn't normally receive.

- ✔ **Knowledge power:** To see knowledge power in action, just watch what happens the next time your organization's computer network goes down. You'll see who really has the power in your organization — in this case, your computer network administrator. Knowledge power comes from the special expertise and knowledge gained during the course of your career. Knowledge power also comes from obtaining academic degrees (think MBA) or special training.

- ✔ **Task power:** Task power is the power that comes from the job or process you perform at work. As you've probably witnessed, people can facilitate or impede the efforts of their co-workers and others by using their task power. For example, when you submit a claim for payment to your insurance company and months pass with no action ("Gee, we don't seem to have your claim in our computer — are you sure you submitted one? Maybe you should send us another one just to be safe!"), you're on the receiving end of task power.

- ✔ **Position power:** This kind of power derives strictly from your rank or title in the organization and is a function of the authority that you wield to command human and financial resources. Whereas the position power of the receptionist in your organization is probably quite low, the position power of the chairman, president, or owner is at the top of the position power chart. The best leaders seldom rely on position power to get things done today.

Top five goal Web sites

Wondering where to find the best information on the Web about the topics in this chapter? Well, you've come to the right place! These sites are our top five favorites:

✔ For personal goal setting: `www.mind tools.com/page6.html`

✔ For business and personal goals: `www.mygoals.com`

✔ For business and personal goals for staying focused: `humanresources.about.com/od/performance management/a/goal_setting.htm`

✔ For goal setting with employees: `managementhelp.org/emp_perf/goal_set/goal_set.htm`

✔ For setting goals for management: `www.dummies.com/how-to/content/setting-smart-management-goals.html`

If you identify weakness in certain sources of power, you can strengthen them. For example, work on your weakness in relationship power by making a concerted effort to know your co-workers better and to cultivate relationships with higher-ranking managers or executives. Instead of passing on the invitations to get together with your co-workers after work, join them — have fun and strengthen your relationship power at the same time.

Be aware of the sources of your power and use your power in a positive way to help you and your employees accomplish the goals of your organization. For getting things done, a little power can go a long way.

Chapter 7

Developing Employees through Coaching and Mentoring

*O*ne recurring theme of today's new management reality is the new role of managers as people who support and encourage their employees instead of telling them what to do (or, worse, simply expecting them to perform). The best managers take time to develop their employees by staying actively involved in employee progress and development, helping to guide them along the way. The best managers also are *coaches* — that is, individuals who guide, discuss, and encourage others on their journey. With the help of coaches, employees can achieve outstanding results and organizations can perform better than ever.

Employee development doesn't just happen. Managers and employees must make a conscious, concerted effort. The best employee development is ongoing and requires that you support and encourage your employees' initiative. Recognize, however, that all development is self-development. You can really develop only yourself. You can't force your employees to develop; they have to want to develop themselves. You can, however, help set an environment that makes it more likely that they will want to learn, grow, and succeed. This chapter guides you through employee development, coaching, and mentoring, pointing to the large and small things you can do to help improve your employees' performance and position them for future success.

As the maxim goes . . .

> Tell me . . . I forget.
>
> Show me . . . I remember.
>
> Involve me . . . I learn.

Why Help Develop Your Employees?

Many good reasons exist for helping your employees develop and improve themselves. Perhaps the number one reason is that they'll perform more effectively in their current jobs. However, despite all the good reasons, development boils down to one important point: As a manager, you're the one person in the best position to provide your employees with the support they need to develop in your organization. You can provide them with not only the time and money required for training, but also unique on-the-job learning opportunities and assignments, mentoring, team participation, and more. Besides, you'll need *someone* capable of taking over your job when you get promoted, right? Employee development involves a lot more than just going to a training class or two. In fact, approximately 90 percent of development occurs on the job.

The terms *training* and *development* can have two distinctly different meanings. *Training* usually refers to teaching workers the short-term skills they need to know right now to do their jobs. *Development* usually refers to teaching employees the kinds of long-term skills they'll need in the future as they progress in their careers. For this reason, employee development is often known as *career development*.

Now, in case you're still not sure why developing your employees is a good idea, the following list provides just a few reasons. We're certain that many more exist, depending on your personal situation.

✔ **You may be taking your employees' knowledge for granted.** Have you ever wondered why your employees continue to mess up assignments that you know they can perform? Believe it or not, your employees may not know how to do those assignments. Have you ever actually seen your employee perform the assignments in question?

Suppose you give a pile of numbers to your assistant and tell him you want them organized and totaled within an hour. However, instead of presenting you with a nice, neat computer spreadsheet, your employee gives you a confusing mess. No, your assistant isn't necessarily incompetent; he may not know how to put together a spreadsheet on his computer. Find out! The solution may be as simple as walking through your within 60 days of purchase, (iii) textbooks returned with a receipt within 14 days of purchase, or (iv) original purchase was made through Barnes & Noble.com via PayPal. Opened music/DVDs/audio may not be returned, but can be exchanged only for the same title if defective.

After 14 days or without a sales receipt, returns or exchanges will not be permitted.

Magazines, newspapers, and used books are not returnable. Product not carried by Barnes & Noble or Barnes & Noble.com will not be accepted for return.

Policy on receipt may appear in two sections.

app... yee and then
hav...

✔ **Em...** mply put,
sm... elp your employ-
ee... ively — and
do... r organization
kn... employees don't
kr... them help with
w... chieved their
d... ation will reap
t'... veness, and you'll
s... manager.

✔ **!...** . Do you ever
... you going to go
... n't prepare your
... part of your job?
... what's going on at
... for a status update
... spend more time
... emselves.

... offices when they're
... their employees to
... , too. The future of

Return Policy

With a sales receipt, a full refund in the original form of payment will be issued from any Barnes & Noble store for returns of new and unread books (except textbooks) and unopened music/DVDs/audio made within (i) 14 days of purchase from a Barnes & Noble retail store (except for purchases made by check less than 7 days prior to the date of return) or (ii) 14 days of delivery date for Barnes & Noble.com purchases (except for purchases made via PayPal). A store credit for the purchase price will be issued for (i) purchases made by check less than 7 days prior to the date of return, (ii) when a gift receipt is presented within 60 days of purchase, (iii) textbooks returned with a receipt within 14 days of purchase, or (iv) original purchase was made through Barnes & Noble.com via PayPal. Opened music/DVDs/audio may not be returned, but can be exchanged only for the same title if defective.

After 14 days or without a sales receipt, returns or exchanges will not be permitted.

Magazines, newspapers, and used books are not returnable. Product not carried by Barnes & Noble or Barnes & Noble.com will not be accepted for return.

Policy on receipt may appear in two sections.

CUSTOMER COPY

...tion. When you allocate funds to ... Return Policy ...yees win by learning higher-level skills and new ways of viewing ... orld — and your organization wins because of increased employee motivation and improved work skills. When you spend money for employee development, you actually double the effect of your investment because of this dual effect. Most important, you prepare your employees to fill the roles your organization will need them to move into in the future.

✔ **Your employees are worth your time and money.** New employees cost a lot of money to recruit and train. You have to consider the investment not only in dollars, but also in time.

Back when coauthor Peter used to work in a real job, his secretary accepted a promotion to another department. The result was a parade of three or four temporary employees until Peter could recruit, interview, and hire a replacement. To say that this parade disrupted his organization is an understatement. Peter and his staff had to invest hours training the temp in the essentials of the job, only to have a new one suddenly appear in her place. Then it was time for another round of training, and thus it continued. The moral of the story is, when you have a trained employee, you must do everything to keep that person. Constantly training replacements can be disruptive and expensive.

When employees see that you have their best interests at heart, they're likely to want to work for you and learn from you. As a result, your organization will attract talented people. Invest in your employees now, or waste your time and money finding replacements later. The choice is yours.

✔ **The challenge stimulates your employees.** Face it, not every employee is fortunate enough to have the kind of exciting, jet-setting, make-it-happen job you have. Right? For this reason, some employees occasionally become bored, lackadaisical, and otherwise indisposed. Employees constantly need new challenges and new goals to maintain interest in their jobs. And if you don't challenge your employees, you're guaranteed to end up with either an unmotivated, low-achievement workforce or employees who jump at offers from employers who will challenge them. Which option do you prefer?

Getting Down to Employee Development

Employee development doesn't just happen all by itself. It takes the deliberate and ongoing efforts of employees with the support of their managers. If either employees or managers drop the ball, employees don't develop and the organization suffers the consequences of employees who aren't up to the challenges of the future. This outcome definitely isn't good. As a manager, you want your organization to be ready for the future the moment it arrives, not always trying to catch up to it.

The employees' role is to identify areas where development can help make them better and more productive workers and then to relay this information to their managers. After identifying further development opportunities, managers and employees can work together to schedule and implement them.

As a manager, your role is to be alert to the development needs of your employees and to keep an eye out for potential development opportunities. Managers in smaller organizations may have the assignment of determining where the organization will be in the next few years. Armed with that information, you're responsible for finding ways to ensure that employees are available to meet the needs of the future organization. Your job is then to provide the resources and support required to develop employees so that they're able to fill the organization's needs.

Taking a step-by-step approach

To develop your employees to meet the coming challenges within your organization, follow these steps:

1. **Meet with an employee about her career.**

   After you assess your employee, meet with her to discuss where you see her in the organization and also to find out where in the organization she wants to go. This effort has to be a joint one. Having elaborate plans for an employee to rise up the company ladder in sales management doesn't do you any good if she hates the idea of leaving sales to become a manager of other salespeople.

2. **Discuss your employee's strengths and weaknesses.**

   Assuming that, in the preceding step, you discover that you're on the same wavelength as your employee, the next step is to have a frank discussion regarding her strengths and weaknesses. Your main goal here is to identify areas the employee can leverage — that is, strengths she can develop to continue her upward progress in the organization and to meet the future challenges your business faces. Focus most of your development efforts and dollars on these opportunities.

   Most important, you need to spend more time developing your strengths than improving your weaknesses. You can excel in an area that comes easy to you, resulting in more value for you and your organization than if you forced yourself to be merely adequate at tasks others excel in.

3. **Assess where your employee is now.**

   The next step in the employee-development process is to determine the current state of your employee's skills and talents. Does Jane show potential for supervising other warehouse employees? Which employees have experience in doing customer demos? Is the pool of software quality assurance technicians adequate enough to accommodate a significant upturn in business? If not, can you develop internal candidates, or will you have to hire new employees from outside the organization? Assessing your employees provides you with an overall road map to guide your development efforts.

4. **Create career development plans.**

   A career development plan is an agreement between you and your employee that spells out exactly what formal support (tuition, time off, travel expenses, and so on) she'll receive to develop her skills and when she'll receive it. Career development plans include milestones.

5. **Follow through on your agreement, and make sure your employee follows through on hers.**

   Don't break the development plan agreement! Provide the support that you agreed to provide. Make sure that your employee upholds her end of the bargain, too. Check on her progress regularly. If she misses a schedule because of other priorities, reassign her work as necessary to ensure that she has time to focus on her career development plans.

So when is the best time to sit down with your employees to discuss career planning and development? The sooner the better! Unfortunately, many organizations closely tie career discussions to annual employee performance appraisals. On the plus side, doing so ensures that a discussion about career development happens at least once a year; on the minus side, development discussions become more of an afterthought than the central focus of the meeting. Because of that limitation, along with the current rapid changes in competitive markets and technology, once a year just isn't enough to keep up.

Conducting a career development discussion twice a year with each of your employees is definitely not too frequent, and quarterly is even better. Include a brief assessment in each discussion of the employee's development needs. Ask your employee what she can do to fulfill them. If those needs require additional support, determine what form of support the employee needs and when to schedule the support. Career development plans are best adjusted and resources best redirected as necessary.

Creating career development plans

The career development plan is the heart and soul of your efforts to develop your employees. Unfortunately, many managers don't take the time to create development plans with their employees. Instead, they're trusting that, when the need arises, they can find training to accommodate that need. This kind of reactive thinking ensures that you're always playing catch-up to the challenges your organization will face in the years to come.

Why wait for the future to arrive before you prepare to deal with it? Are you really so busy that you can't spend a little of your precious time planting the seeds that your organization will harvest years from now? No! Although you do have to take care of the seemingly endless crises that arise in the here and now, you also have to prepare yourself and your employees to meet the challenges of the future. To do otherwise is an incredibly shortsighted and ineffective way to run your organization.

All career development plans must contain at least the following key elements:

- ✔ **Specific learning goals:** When you meet with an employee to discuss development plans, you identify specific *learning goals*. And don't forget, every employee in your organization can benefit from having learning goals. Don't leave anyone out!

  For example, say that your employee's career path will start at the position of junior buyer and work up to manager of purchasing. The key learning goals for this employee may be to learn material requirements planning (MRP), computer spreadsheet analysis techniques, and supervision.

- ✔ **Resources required to achieve the designated learning goals:** After you identify your employee's learning objectives, you have to decide how he will reach them. Development resources include a wide variety of opportunities that support the development of your employees. Assignment to teams, job shadowing, *stretch assignments* (assignments that aren't too easy or too hard and that involve some learning and discomfort), formal training, and more may be required. Formal training may be conducted by outsiders, by internal trainers, or perhaps in a self-guided series of learning modules. If the training requires funding or other resources, identify those resources and make efforts to obtain them.

- ✔ **Employee responsibilities and resources:** Career development is the joint responsibility of an employee and his manager. A business can and does pay for training and development opportunities, but so can employees (as any employee who has paid out of her own pocket to get a college degree can attest). A good career development plan should include what the employee is doing on her own time.

- ✔ **Required date of completion for each learning goal:** Plans are no good without a way to schedule the milestones of goal accomplishment and progress. Each learning goal must have a corresponding date of completion. Don't select dates that are so close that they're difficult or unduly burdensome to achieve, or so far into the future that they lose their immediacy and effect. The best schedules for learning goals allow employees the flexibility to get their daily tasks done while keeping ahead of the changes in the business environment that necessitate the employees' development in the first place.

- ✔ **Standards for measuring the accomplishment of learning goals:** For every goal, you must have a way to measure its completion. Normally, the manager assesses whether the employees actually use the new skills they've been taught. Whatever the individual case, make sure that the standards you use to measure the completion of a learning goal are clear and attainable and that both you and your employees are in full agreement with them.

The career development plan of a junior buyer may look like Figure 7-1.

Career Development Plan
Sarah Smith

Skill goal:

- Become proficient in material requirements planning (MRP).

Learning goal:

- Learn the basics of employee supervision.

Plan:

Figure 7-1:
Sample
junior buyer
career
develop-
ment plan.

- Shadow supervisor in daily work for half days, starting immediately.
- Attend quarterly supervisor's update seminar on the first Wednesday of January, April, July, and October. (No cost: in-house.)
- Complete class "Basics of MRP" no later than the first quarter of fiscal year XX. ($550 plus travel costs.)
- Successfully complete class "Intermediate MRP" no later than the second quarter of fiscal year XX. ($750 plus travel costs.)
- Continue self-funded accounting certificate program at local community college.

As you can see, this career development plan contains each of the four necessary elements that we describe. A career development plan doesn't have to be complicated to be effective. In fact, when it comes to employee development plans, simpler is definitely better. The exact format you decide on isn't so important — the most important point is that you do career development plans.

Balancing development and downsizing

Most companies aren't immune when the economy turns south. Maybe your organization has felt the sharp knife of layoffs, downsizing, or reductions in force. If so, you may ask, "Isn't employee development too difficult to perform when everything is changing so fast around me? My employees may not even have careers next year, much less the need to plan for developing them."

Actually, nothing is further from the truth. Although businesses are going through rapid change, employee development is more important than ever. As departments are combined, dissolved, or reorganized, employees have to be ready to take on roles they may never have performed. In some cases, employees may have to compete internally for positions or sell themselves to other departments to ensure that they retain their employment with the firm. In this time of great uncertainty, many employees may feel that they've lost control of their careers and even their lives.

Career planning and development gives employees in organizations undergoing rapid change the tools they need to regain control of their careers. The following list tells what some of the largest American companies have done to help their employees get through massive corporate downsizings and reorganizations:

✔ As a result of dramatic organizational changes, General Electric provided targeted career training for its crucial engineering employees. The firm also scheduled informal follow-up meetings with graduates of this engineering career training.

✔ At AT&T, management offered special three-day career development seminars to its employees nationwide in response to dramatic staff reductions.

✔ IBM overhauled the career plans of thousands of employees who transitioned from staff positions to sales positions as a result of a massive corporate reorganization.

Despite the obvious negative effects of downsizing on employee morale and trust, these times of change provide managers with a unique opportunity to shape the future of their organizations. For many managers, this moment is the first time they have such an opportunity to help remake the organization.

Ten easy ways to develop employees

Although you can develop employees in many different ways, some are definitely better than others. Here are ten of the best — and easiest:

1. Give employees opportunities to learn and grow.

2. Be a mentor to an employee.

3. Let an employee fill in for you in staff meetings.

4. Assign an employee to a team.

5. Allow employees to pursue and develop any idea they have.

6. Provide employees with a choice of assignments.

7. Send an employee to a seminar on a new topic.

8. Bring an employee with you when you call on customers.

9. Introduce an employee to top managers in your organization and arrange to have her perform special assignments for them.

10. Allow an employee to shadow you during your workday.

Employee development is more important than ever as employees are called upon to take on new and often more responsible roles in your organization. Your employees need your support now; make sure you're there to provide it. This help just may be one of the most valuable gifts you can give your employees.

Coaching Employees to Career Growth and Success

Coaching plays a critical part in the learning process for employees who are developing their skills, knowledge, and self-confidence. Your employees don't learn effectively when you simply tell them what to do. In fact, they usually don't learn at all.

With the right guidance, anyone can be a good coach. In this section, we consider what effective coaches do and how they do it so that you can coach your employees toward successful results.

Serving as both manager and coach

Even if you have a pretty good sense of what it means to be a manager, do you really know what it means to be a coach? A coach is a colleague, counselor, and cheerleader, all rolled into one. Based on that definition, are you a coach? How about your boss? Or your boss's boss? Why or why not?

We bet you're familiar with the role of coaches in other nonbusiness activities. A drama coach, for example, is almost always an accomplished actor or actress. The drama coach's job is to conduct auditions for parts, assign roles, schedule rehearsals, train and direct cast members throughout rehearsals, and support and encourage the actors and actresses during the final stage production. These roles aren't all that different from the roles managers perform in a business, are they?

Coaching a team of individuals isn't easy, and certain characteristics make some coaches better than others. Fortunately, as with most other business skills, you can discover, practice, and improve the traits of good coaches. You can always find room for improvement, and good coaches are the first to admit it. Following are key characteristics and tasks for coaches:

✔ **Coaches set goals.** Whether an organization's vision is to become the leading provider of wireless telephones in the world, to increase revenues by 20 percent a year, or simply to get the break room walls painted this year, coaches work with their employees to set goals and deadlines for completion. They then go away and allow their employees to determine how to accomplish the goals.

✔ **Coaches support and encourage.** Employees — even the best and most experienced — can easily become discouraged from time to time. When employees are learning new tasks, when a long-term account is lost, or when business is down, coaches are there, ready to step in and help the team members through the worst of it. "That's okay, Kim. You've learned from your mistake, and I know that you'll get it right next time!"

✔ **Coaches emphasize team success over individual success.** The team's overall performance is the most important concern, not the stellar abilities of a particular team member. Coaches know that no one person can carry an entire team to success; winning takes the combined efforts of all team members. The development of teamwork skills is a vital step in an employee's progress in an organization.

✔ **Coaches can quickly assess the talents and shortfalls of team members.** The most successful coaches can quickly determine their team members' strengths and weaknesses and, as a result, tailor their approach to each. For example, if one team member has strong analytical skills but poor presentation skills, a coach can concentrate on providing support for the employee's development of better presentation skills. "You know, Mark, I want to spend some time with you to work on making your viewgraph presentations more effective."

✔ **Coaches inspire their team members.** Through their support and guidance, coaches are skilled at inspiring their team members to the highest levels of human performance. Teams of inspired individuals are willing to do whatever it takes to achieve their organization's goals.

✔ **Coaches create environments that allow individuals to succeed.** Great coaches ensure that their workplaces are structured to let team members take risks and stretch their limits without fear of retribution if they fail.

Coaches are available to advise their employees or just to listen to their problems, as needed. "Carol, do you have a minute to discuss a personal problem?"

✔ **Coaches provide feedback.** Communication and feedback between coach and employee is a critical element of the coaching process. Employees must know where they stand in the organization — what they're doing right and what they're doing wrong. Equally important, employees must let their coaches know when they need help or assistance. And both parties need this dialogue in a timely manner, on an ongoing basis — not just once a year in a performance review.

Firing someone doesn't constitute effective feedback. Unless an employee has engaged in some sort of intolerable offense (such as physical violence, theft, or intoxication on the job — see Chapter 19 for more details), a manager needs to give the employee plenty of verbal and written feedback before even considering termination. Giving your employee several warnings offers her an opportunity to correct deficiencies that she may not be able to see.

Identifying a coach's tools

Coaching is not a one-dimensional activity. Because every person is different, the best coaches tailor their approach to their team members' specific, individualized needs. If one team member is independent and needs only occasional guidance, recognize where she stands and provide that level of support. This support may consist of an occasional, informal progress check while making the rounds of the office. On the other hand, if another team member is insecure and needs more guidance, the coach must recognize this employee's position and assist as needed. In this case, support may consist of frequent, formal meetings with the employee to assess progress and provide advice and direction as needed.

Although you have your own coaching style, the best coaches employ certain techniques to elicit the greatest performance from their team members:

- ✔ **Make time for team members.** Managing is primarily a people job. Part of being a good manager and coach is being available to your employees when they need your help. If you're not available, your employees may seek out other avenues to meet their needs — or simply stop trying to work with you. Always keep your door open to your employees and remember that they are your first priority. Manage by walking around. Regularly get out of your office and visit your employees at their workstations. "Do I have a minute, Elaine? Of course, I always have time for you and the other members of my staff."

- ✔ **Provide context and vision.** Instead of simply telling employees what to do, effective coaches explain the why. Coaches provide their employees with context and a big-picture perspective. Instead of spouting long lists of do's and don'ts, they explain how a system or procedure works and then define their employees' parts in the scheme of things. "Chris, you have a very important part in the financial health and vitality of our company. By ensuring that our customers pay their invoices within 30 days after we ship their products, we're able to keep our cash flow on the plus side, and we can pay our obligations such as rent, electricity, and your paycheck on time."

- ✔ **Transfer knowledge and perspective.** A great benefit of having a good coach is the opportunity to learn from someone who has more experience than you do. In response to the unique needs of each team member, coaches transfer their personal knowledge and perspective. "We faced this exact situation about five years ago, Dwight. I'm going to tell you what we did then, and I want you to tell me whether you think it still makes sense today."

✔ **Be a sounding board.** Coaches talk through new ideas and approaches to solving problems with their employees. Coaches and employees can consider the implications of different approaches to solving a problem and role-play customer or client reactions before trying them out for real. By using active listening skills, coaches can often help their employees work through issues and come up with the best solutions themselves. "Okay, David, you've told me that you don't think your customer will buy off on a 20 percent price increase. What options do you have to present the price increase, and are some more palatable than others?"

✔ **Obtain needed resources.** Sometimes coaches can help their employees make the jump from marginal to outstanding performance simply by providing the resources those employees need. These resources can take many forms: money, time, staff, equipment, or other tangible assets. "So, Gene, you're confident that we can improve our cash flow if we throw a couple more clerks into collections? Okay, we'll give it a try."

✔ **Offer a helping hand.** For an employee who is learning a new job and is still responsible for performing her current job, the total workload can be overwhelming. Coaches can help workers through this transitional phase by reassigning current duties to other employees, authorizing overtime, or taking other measures to relieve the pressure. "John, while you're learning how to troubleshoot that new network server, I'm going to assign your maintenance workload to Rachel. We can get back together at the end of the week to see how you're doing."

Teaching through show-and-tell coaching

Besides the obvious coaching roles of supporting and encouraging employees in their quest to achieve an organization's goals, managers as coaches also teach their employees how to achieve an organization's goals. Drawing from your experience, you lead your workers step by step through work processes or procedures. After they discover how to perform a task, you delegate full authority and responsibility for its performance to them.

For the transfer of specific skills, you can find no better way of teaching, and no better way of learning, than the *show-and-tell* method. Developed by a post–World War II American industrial society desperate to quickly train new workers in manufacturing processes, show-and-tell is beautiful in its simplicity and effectiveness.

Show-and-tell coaching has three steps:

1. **You do, you say. Sit down with your employees and explain the proce-dure in general terms while you perform the task.**

2. **They do, you say. Now have the employees do the same procedure as you explain each step in the procedure.**

3. **They do, they say. Finally, as you observe, have your employees per-form the task again as they explain to you what they're doing.**

As you go through these steps, have employees create a "cheat sheet" of the new steps to refer to until they become habit.

Making turning points big successes

Despite popular impressions to the contrary, 90 percent of management isn't the big event — the blinding flash of brilliance that creates markets where none previously existed, the magnificent negotiation that results in unheard-of levels of union-management cooperation, or the masterful stroke that cata-pults the firm into the big leagues. No, 90 percent of a manager's job consists of the daily chipping away at problems and the shaping of talents.

When the coach needs a coach

Sometimes even coaches need to be coached. Scott McNealy, chairman of Sun Microsystems, has used a combination of drive, passion, and tough financial controls to shepherd his com-pany from $39 million in sales in 1984, when he took over, to $11.4 billion in 2009. Calling the stand-alone personal computer a "hairball on the desktop," McNealy has pushed the concept of network computing for years — long before the Internet became the "in" place to be. Sun is the leading maker of UNIX-based servers used to power corporate computer networks and Web sites, and an increasing number of companies has adopted Sun's Internet-ready networks for internal use, among them Gap, Federal Express, and AT&T Universal Card Services.

However, despite his success, McNealy hired a "CEO coach" to help him become even more effective. The coach, Chuck Raben of Delta Consulting Group, Inc., asked McNealy's man-agers to report areas where they thought their boss could improve. Raben compiled the sur-veys and summarized the responses. According to Sun's management team, McNealy needs to become a better listener. So McNealy now carries with him a reminder to respond to the points his managers raise in meetings.

The best coaches are constantly on the lookout for *turning points* — the daily opportunities to succeed that are available to all employees.

The big successes — the victories against competitors, the dramatic surges in revenues or profits, the astounding new products — are typically the result of building a foundation of countless small successes along the way. Making a voice-mail system more responsive to your customers' needs, sending an employee to a seminar on time management, writing a great sales agreement, conducting a meaningful performance appraisal with an employee, meeting a prospective client for lunch — all are turning points in the average business day. Although each event may not be particularly spectacular on its own, when aggregated over time, they can add up to big things.

This is the job of a coach. Instead of using dynamite to transform the organization in one fell swoop (and taking the chance of destroying their organizations, their employees, or themselves in the process), coaches are like the ancient stonemasons who built the great pyramids of Egypt. The movement and placement of each individual stone may not have seemed like a big deal when considered as a separate activity. However, each was an important step in achieving the ultimate result — the construction of awe-inspiring structures that have withstood thousands of years of war, weather, and tourists.

Incorporating coaching into your day-to-day interactions

Coaches focus daily on spending time with employees to help them succeed — to assess their progress and to find out what they can do to help the employees capitalize on the turning points that present themselves every day. Coaches complement and supplement the abilities and experience of their employees by bringing their own abilities and experience to the table. They reward positive performance and help their employees learn important lessons from making mistakes — lessons that, in turn, help the employees improve their future performance.

For example, suppose that you have a young and inexperienced, but bright and energetic, sales trainee on your staff. Your employee has done a great job of contacting customers and making sales calls, but she hasn't yet closed her first deal. When you talk to her about this, she confesses that she's nervous about her own personal turning point: She's worried that she may become confused in front of the customer and blow the deal at the last minute. She needs your coaching.

Top five coaching Web sites

Wondering where to find the best information on the Web about the topics addressed in this chapter? Here are our top five favorites:

✔ The Coaching and Mentoring Network: `www.coachingnetwork.org.uk/`

✔ International Coach Federation: `www.coachfederation.org/`

✔ The Coaching Connection: `thecoachingconnection.wordpress.com`

✔ *Fast Company* magazine: `www.fastcompany.com/magazine/05/coach2.html`

✔ About.com: `www.humanresources.about.com/cs/coachingmentoring/`

The following guidelines can help you, the coach, handle any employee's concerns:

✔ **Meet with your employee.** Make an appointment with your employee as soon as possible for a relaxed discussion of the concerns. Find a quiet place free of distractions, and put your phone on hold or forward it to voice mail.

✔ **Listen!** One of the most motivating things one person can do for another is to listen. Avoid instant solutions or lectures. Before you say a word, ask your employee to bring you up-to-date with the situation, her concerns, and any possible approaches or solutions she's considered. Let her do the talking while you do the listening.

✔ **Reinforce the positive.** Begin by pointing out what your employee did right in the particular situation. Let your employee know when she's on the right track. Give her positive feedback on her performance.

✔ **Highlight areas for improvement.** Point out what your employee needs to do to improve and tell her what you can do to help. Agree on the assistance you can provide, whether your employee needs further training, an increased budget, more time, or something else. Be enthusiastic about your confidence in the employee's ability to do a great job.

✔ **Follow through.** After you determine what you can do to support your employee, do it! Notice when she improves. Periodically check up on the progress your employee is making and offer your support as necessary.

Above all, be patient. You can't accomplish coaching on your terms alone. At the outset, understand that everyone is different. Some employees catch on sooner than others and some employees need more time to develop. Differences in ability don't make certain employees any better or worse than their co-workers — they just make them different. Just as you need time to build relationships and trust in business, your employees need time to develop skills and experience.

Finding a Mentor, Being a Mentor

When you're an inexperienced employee working your way up an organization's hierarchy, having someone with more experience to help guide you along the way is invaluable. Someone who's already seen what it takes to get to the top can advise you about what you should and shouldn't do as you work your way up. This someone is called a *mentor*.

Isn't a manager supposed to be a mentor? No. A mentor is most typically an individual high up in the organization who isn't your boss. A manager's job is clearly to coach and help guide employees. Although managers certainly can act as mentors for their own employees, mentors most often act as confidential advisers and sounding boards to their chosen employees and, therefore, aren't typically in the employee's direct chain of command.

The day that a mentor finds you and takes you under his wing is a day for you to celebrate. Why? Not everyone is lucky enough to find a mentor. And don't forget that someday you'll be in the position to be a mentor to someone else. When that day comes, don't be so caught up in your busy business life to neglect to reach out and help someone else find his way up the organization.

Mentors provide definite benefits to the employees they mentor, and they further benefit the organization by providing needed guidance to employees who may not otherwise get it. The following reasons are why mentors are a real benefit, both to your employees and to your organization:

- ✔ **Mentors explain how the organization really works.** Mentors are a great way to find out what's really going on in an organization. You've probably noticed that a big difference exists between what's formally announced to employees and what really goes on in the organization — particularly within the ranks of upper management. Your mentor quite likely has intimate knowledge of details behind the formal pronouncements and can convey that knowledge to you (at least, the knowledge that isn't confidential) without your having to find it out the hard way.

- ✔ **Mentors teach by example.** By watching how your mentor gets tasks done in the organization, you can discover a lot. Your mentor has likely already seen it all and can help you discover the most effective and efficient ways to get things done. Why reinvent the wheel or get beaten up by the powers-that-be when you don't have to?

✔ **Mentors provide growth experiences.** A mentor can help guide you to activities above and beyond your formal career development plans that are helpful to your growth as an employee. For example, though your official development plan doesn't identify a specific activity, your mentor may strongly suggest that you join a group such as Toastmasters, to improve your public-speaking skills. Your mentor makes this suggestion because he knows that public speaking skills are important to your future career growth.

✔ **Mentors provide career guidance and discussion.** Your mentor has probably seen more than a few employees and careers come and go over the years. He knows which career paths in your organization are dead ends and which offer the most rapid advancement. This knowledge can be incredibly important to your future as you make career choices within an organization. The advice your mentor gives you can be invaluable.

The mentoring process often happens when a more experienced employee takes a professional interest in a new or inexperienced employee. Employees can also initiate the mentoring process by engaging the interest of potential mentors while seeking advice or working on projects together. However, recognizing the potential benefits for the development of their employees, many organizations — including Merrill Lynch, Federal Express, and the Internal Revenue Service — have formalized the mentoring process and made it available to a wider range of employees than the old informal process ever could. If a formal mentoring program isn't already in place in your organization, why don't you recommend starting one?

Top five mentoring Web sites

Wondering where to find the best information on the Web about the topics addressed in this chapter? Here are our top five favorites:

✔ Service Corps of Retired Executives: www.score.org

✔ Business Gateway Scotland: www.businessmentoringscotland.org

✔ SBA Find a Mentor: www.sba.gov/smallbusinessplanner/start/findamentor/index.html

✔ GreenBiz.com Mentoring Handbook: www.greenbiz.com/research/tool/2002/02/15/mentoring-handbook

✔ SBA Office of Women's Business Ownership: www.sba.gov/womeninbusiness/wnet.html

Chapter 8

It's a Team Thing

A revolution is taking place in business today. That revolution is deciding what work to do, how to accomplish it, what goals an organization strives for, and who's responsible for achieving them. That revolution is also touching everyone in an organization, from the very top to the very bottom. What is this revolution? It's called *teams*.

A team is two or more people working together to achieve a common goal. Why use teams? Teams offer an easy way to tap the knowledge and resources of all employees — not just supervisors and managers — to solve the organization's problems. A well-structured team draws together employees from all different functions and levels of the organization to find the best way to approach an issue. Smart companies have discovered (and not-so-smart companies are just now starting to figure out) that, to remain competitive, they can no longer rely solely on management to guide work processes and organizational goals. Companies need to involve employees who are closer to the problems and the organization's customers — the front-line workers.

This chapter discusses the changes in today's global business environment that set the stage for the movement toward teams. We look at the major kinds of teams and how they work, examine the impact of new computer-based technology on teams, and offer insights into conducting the best team meetings ever.

Identifying Advantages of Empowered Teams

When employees gain more authority and autonomy from top management, they tend to be more responsive to the customers' needs and to resolve problems at the lowest possible level in the organization. The transfer of power, responsibility, and authority from higher-level to lower-level employees is called *empowerment*.

By empowering workers, managers place the responsibility for decision making with the employees who are in the best position to make the decision. In the past, many managers felt that *they* were in the best position to make decisions that affected a company's products or customers. In reality, this is often not the case.

Freeing up manager time and boosting morale

Effective managers know the value of empowering their workers. Not only are customers better served when front-line workers have the responsibility and authority to address their needs, but managers are free to pursue other important tasks that only they can do. These tasks include coaching, "big-picture" communicating, long-range planning, walking the walk, and talking the talk. The result is a more efficient, more effective organization.

The following tales demonstrate the clear benefit of empowered teams:

✔ The personal insurance division of the Fireman's Fund Insurance Company in Novato, California, divided its employees into work units organized around its customers. The company cut several levels of management and, whenever possible, assigned individuals cradle-to-grave project responsibility instead of fragmented work tasks. With these changes, employees felt they had a real stake in making customers happy. Efficiency increased by 35–40 percent, systems investments declined by $5 million a year, and endorsement turnaround decreased from 21 days to 48 hours.

✔ Helicopter parts manufacturer Lord Aerospace Products (a division of the Lord Corporation in Dayton, Ohio) energized the company's employees by putting together a small team of workers to take the initiative to solve technical problems. Productivity increased 30 percent and absenteeism dropped 75 percent.

Empowerment is also a great morale booster in an organization. Managers who empower their workers show that they trust them to make decisions that are important to the company's success. Employees return the favor by becoming more loyal and more engaged in their work. For more information on creating an engaged workforce, see Chapter 4.

Spotlighting quality

Today's businesses have discovered a lot from the improvement movement. Taking a cue from successful Japanese businesses — noted for their high-quality automobiles and innovative consumer electronic products — U.S. businesses embarked on a quest for quality in the 1980s. U.S. managers quickly discovered that the cornerstone of many Japanese programs was the empowerment of workers to make decisions regarding their work processes.

For example, many U.S. businesses have instituted *quality circles,* groups of employees who meet regularly to suggest ways to improve the organization, borrowing the Japanese technique of participative decision making. A quality circle's suggestions carry great weight with management.

As an example of employee empowerment, Motorola management considers employee teams to be a crucial part of its strategy for quality improvement. Self-directed teams at its Arlington Heights, Illinois, mobile telephone equipment manufacturing plant not only decide on their own training programs and schedule their own work, but they're also involved in hiring and firing co-workers.

Operating in a smaller and nimbler way

Teams not only have the potential to make better decisions, but they can also make faster decisions. Because team members are closest to the problems and to one another, they can skip unnecessary communication channels, resulting in minimal lag time. Some teams are given the authority to make decisions and take action without seeking further approval from others in the organization.

Large organizations often have a hard time competing in the marketplace against smaller, more nimble competitors. Smaller units within a large organization — such as teams — also are better able to compete. The rate and scope of change in the global business environment has led to increased competitive pressures on organizations in nearly every business sector.

Because customers can get products and services faster, they demand to have them at top speed (those darn customers!). Because they can buy products more cheaply as a result of technology improvements or global competition, they expect lower prices as well (double-darn them!). And customers' expectation of quality in relation to price has dramatically increased over the years — especially because consumers can obtain more advanced electronics and computer technology for progressively lower prices. In short, customer values are changing so that customers now want products and services "any time, any place." They also want to pay less than they did last year.

Staying innovative and adaptable

Teams can also bring about increased innovation. According to former Harvard economist Robert Reich in the *Harvard Business Review,* "As individual skills are integrated into a group, the collective capacity to innovate becomes something greater than the sum of its parts."

Teams are also more adaptive to the external environment as it quickly or constantly changes. Thus, a team's size and flexibility give it a distinct advantage over the more traditional organizational structure of competing organizations. At Xerox and Hewlett-Packard, for example, design, engineering, and manufacturing functions are now closely intertwined in the development of new products, dramatically shortening the time from concept to production.

Teams used to be considered useful only for projects of short duration. However, many companies no longer follow this thinking. Indeed, the team concept has proven itself to be a workable long-term solution to the needs of many organizations. A team's members may change, but the team itself can remain in place for years or even decades.

Setting Up and Supporting Your Teams

The first point you need to consider when setting up a team is what kind of team to create. And the job doesn't stop there. Regardless of type, all teams need managerial support to operate successfully in the real business environment. This section introduces you to the three main types of teams and guides you through what you can (and should) do to support your teams.

Deciding on the type of team

Three major kinds of teams exist: *formal, informal,* and *self-managed.* Each type of team offers advantages and disadvantages, depending on the specific situation, timing, and the organization's needs.

Formal teams

A *formal team* is chartered by an organization's management and tasked to achieve specific goals. These goals can range from developing a new product line, to determining the system for processing customer invoices, to planning a company picnic. Types of formal teams include the following:

✔ **Task forces:** These teams are assembled on a temporary basis to address specific problems or issues. For example, a task force may be assembled to determine why the number of rejects for a machined part has risen from 1 in 10,000 to 1 in 1,000. A task force usually has a deadline for solving the issue and reporting its findings to management.

✔ **Committees:** These long-term or permanent teams are created to perform an ongoing, specific organizational task. For example, some companies have committees that select employees to receive awards for their performance or that make recommendations to management for safety improvements. Although committee membership may change from year to year, the committees continue their work, regardless of who belongs to them.

✔ **Command teams:** These teams consist of a manager or supervisor and all the employees who report directly to that person. Such teams are hierarchical by nature and represent the traditional way tasks are communicated from managers to workers. Examples of command teams include company sales teams, management teams, and executive teams.

Formal teams are important to most organizations because much of the communication within an establishment traditionally occurs within the team. News, goals, and information pass from employee to employee via formal teams. The teams provide the structure for assigning tasks and soliciting feedback from team members on accomplishments, performance data, and so on.

Informal teams

Informal teams are casual associations of employees that spontaneously develop within an organization's formal structure. Such teams include groups of employees who eat lunch together every day or simply like to hang out together, both during and after work. The membership of informal teams is in a constant state of flux as members come and go, and friendships and other associations between employees change over time.

Although informal teams have no specific tasks or goals assigned by management, they're important to organizations for the following reasons:

✔ Informal teams provide a way for employees to get information outside of formal, management-sanctioned communications channels.

> ✔ Informal teams provide a (relatively) safe outlet for employees to let off steam about issues that concern them and to find solutions to problems by discussing them with employees from other parts of the organization — unimpeded by the walls of the formal organization.

For example, a group of women employees at the Verizon Communications Northeast Bureau created *mentoring circles*. The purpose of these informal teams — developed outside the formal organization — was to fill the void created by a lack of female top-level managers to serve as mentors for other women in the organization. Organized in groups of 8–12 employees, the circles provided the kind of career networking, support, and encouragement that mentors normally provide to their charges.

Ad hoc groups are informal teams of employees assembled on an impromptu basis to solve a problem, often (though not always) by regular employees. For example, you may form an ad hoc team when you select employees from your human resources and accounting departments to solve a problem with the system for tracking and recording pay changes in the company's payroll system. You don't invite participants from shipping to join this informal team, because they probably can't provide meaningful input to the problem.

Self-managed teams

Self-managed teams combine the attributes of both formal and informal teams. Generally chartered by management, self-managed teams often quickly take on lives of their own as members accept responsibility for the day-to-day workings of the team. Self-managed teams usually consist of employees whose job is to find solutions to common worker problems. Self-managed teams are also known as *high-performance teams, cross-functional teams,* and *superteams.*

To save time and gain benefits, an organization's self-managing teams must be

> ✔ Made up of people from different parts of the organization.
>
> ✔ Small, because large groups create communication problems.
>
> ✔ Self-managing and empowered to act, because referring decisions back up the line wastes time and often leads to poorer decisions.
>
> ✔ Multifunctional, because that's the best — if not the only — way to keep the actual product and its essential delivery system clearly visible and foremost in everyone's mind.

Consider this example of a self-managing team at the Tennessee Valley Authority (TVA). A TVA civil engineering unit had the monthly responsibility of checking the operation of 100 warning sirens at a local nuclear power plant. When a second plant opened nearby, this team was given responsibility for checking 105 additional sirens, double the normal workload. On their own initiative, the team put together a work schedule that ensured the work was completed on time, while streamlining reporting requirements. The initiative was a great success: Deadlines were met and the TVA saved the money it would've had to spend hiring more people to inspect the sirens.

Increasingly, when management is willing to turn over the reins of absolute authority to workers, self-managing teams are rising to the challenge and making major contributions to the success of their firms. Indeed, the future success of many businesses lies in the successful implementation of self-managed teams.

Helping teams work in the real world

Empowerment is beautiful when it flourishes in an organization. However, real empowerment is still rare. Many plastic substitutes are out there masquerading as empowerment. Although many managers talk a good story about how they empower their employees, few actually do it. When they're real and not pale imitations, empowered teams typically

- ✔ Make the most of the decisions that influence team success.
- ✔ Choose their leaders.
- ✔ Add or remove team members.
- ✔ Set their goals and commitments.
- ✔ Define and perform much of their training.
- ✔ Receive rewards as a team.

Unfortunately, employee empowerment may largely be only an illusion. A survey of team members showed that plenty of room for change and improvement in the workings of teams still exists. Survey respondents clearly felt that the areas of intragroup trust, group effectiveness, agenda setting/ meeting content, and role and idea conformity can use some improvement.

Conducted by management expert Dr. Bob Culver, a recent study of managers, team leaders, and team members at nine different companies discovered that real-world teams are more participative than empowered. Basically, top management is still making the real decisions. Those pesky backsliders! Using Culver's study results as a basis, you can apply the following specific recommendations to counter the ineffectiveness of many teams:

- ✔ **Make your teams empowered, not merely participative:** Instead of just inviting employees to participate in teams, grant team members the authority and power to make independent decisions. Follow these guidelines:

    - Allow your teams to make long-range and strategic decisions, not just procedural ones.

- Permit the team to choose the team leaders.

- Allow the team to determine its goals and commitments.

- Make sure the team knows you're an advocate for it.

- Make sure all team members have influence by involving them in the decision-making process.

✔ **Remove the source of conflicts:** Despite their attempts to empower employees, managers are often unwilling to live with the results. Be willing to start up a team and then accept the outcome by doing the following:

- Recognize and work out personality conflicts.

- Provide adequate resources to the team (and to individual members).

- Fight turf protection and middle-management resistance.

- Work to unify manager and team member views.

- Minimize the stress of downsizing and process improvement tasks.

✔ **Change other significant factors that influence team effectiveness:** Each of these factors indicates that an organization has not yet brought true empowerment to its employees. You have the power to change this situation by doing the following:

- Allow the team to discipline poorly performing members.

- Make peer pressure less important in attaining high team performance.

- Recognize the contributions of the team and individuals.

- Train as many team members as you train managers or team leaders.

Although you can find clear examples of companies in which management has truly empowered its teams (they're out there somewhere), team empowerment doesn't just happen. Supervisors and managers must make concerted and ongoing efforts to ensure that authority and autonomy pass from management to teams. You can, too!

Taking advantage of new technology in team operations

According to a *Fortune* magazine article, three dominant forces are shaping 21st-century organizations:

✔ A high-involvement workplace with self-managed teams and other devices for empowering employees

✔ A new emphasis on managing business processes instead of functional departments

✔ The evolution of information technology, to the point that knowledge, accountability, and results can be distributed rapidly anywhere in the organization

The integrating ingredient of these three dominant forces is information. Information technology and the way information is handled are increasingly becoming the keys to an organization's success.

In a team environment, *process management information* moves precisely to where the team needs it, unfiltered by a hierarchy. Raw numbers go straight to the people who need them in their jobs, because front-line workers such as salespeople and machinists have been trained in how to use that information. By letting information flow wherever the team needs it, a horizontal self-managed company isn't only possible, it's also inevitable. Information technology–enabled team support systems include e-mail, computer conferencing, and videoconferencing that coordinate both geographically and across time zones more easily than ever. The development and use of computer software to support teams also is growing. An example is the expanding body of software called *groupware.* Groupware consists of computer programs specifically designed to support collaborative work groups and processes.

As organizations make better use of information technology, they don't need middle managers as often to make decisions. The result? Companies can dramatically reduce the number of management levels and the number of managers. Jobs, careers, and knowledge shift constantly. Typical management career paths are eliminated, and workers advance by learning more skills to be of greater value to the organization.

The managers who remain need to take on new skills and attitudes to become more of a coach, supporter, and facilitator to the front-line employees. Supervisors and managers no longer have the luxury of spending time trying to control the organization — instead, they must change it. Their job is to seek out new customers at the same time they respond to the latest needs of their established customers. Managers still have considerable authority, but instead of commanding workers, their job is to inspire them.

Meetings: Putting Teams to Work

So what is a discussion about meetings doing in a chapter on teams? Well, meetings are the primary forum in which team members conduct business and communicate with one another. And with the proliferation of teams in business today, it pays to master the basic skills of meeting management.

Teams are a better idea at GE

Jack Welch, former chairman of General Electric (GE), determined that if the company was going to succeed, it had to move away from the old model of autocratic meetings and direction from top management. Welch's solution was to initiate a town hall concept of meetings throughout the entire organization. These meetings, called *workout* meetings, brought workers and managers together in open forums where workers were allowed to ask any question they wanted and managers were required to respond.

The company's core business strategies were shaped in regular meetings of senior executives, each of whom represented one of GE's individual business units. In these high-energy meetings, attendees were encouraged to explore every possible avenue and alternative and remain open to new ideas. GE's recent ventures in Mexico, India, and China are a direct result of these meetings.

At GE's Bayamón, Puerto Rico, lightning arrester plant, employees have been organized into teams that are responsible for specific plant functions — shipping, assembly, and so forth. However, instead of tapping only employees from shipping to be on the shipping team, for example, teams consist of employees from all parts of the plant. This process enables representatives from all affected departments to discuss how suggested changes or improvements may affect their part of the operation. Hourly workers run the meetings on their own, and *advisers* — GE's term for salaried employees — participate in meetings only at the team's request.

Results of the Bayamón experiment produced clear and convincing evidence that General Electric's approach is quite successful. A year after start-up, the plant's employees measured 20 percent higher in productivity than their closest counterparts in the mainland United States. And if that weren't enough, management projected a further 20 percent increase in the following year.

As organizations continue to flatten their hierarchies and empower front-line workers with more responsibility and authority, teams are the visible and often inevitable result. This transition is good news to the burgeoning industry of consulting and seminars in business team building.

Avoiding common problems with meetings

Most meetings are a big waste of time. Meeting experts have determined that approximately 53 percent of all the time spent in meetings — and this means the time that *you* spend in meetings — is unproductive, worthless, and of little consequence. And when you realize that most businesspeople spend at least 25 percent of their working hours in meetings, with upper management spending more than double that time in meetings, you can begin to appreciate the importance of learning and applying effective meeting skills. With today's business imperative to get more done with less, making every meeting count is more important than ever.

So what's wrong with meetings, anyway? Why do so many meetings go so wrong, and why can't you ever seem to do anything about it? Consider a few reasons:

- **Too many meetings take place.** The problem isn't just the number of meetings. The problem is that many meetings are unnecessary, unproductive, and a waste of time.

- **Attendees are unprepared.** Some meetings happen prematurely, before a real reason to meet arises. Other times, neither the individuals leading the meeting nor the participants are prepared. In this case, the participants stumble around blindly for a long period of time trying to figure out why the meeting was called in the first place.

- **Certain individuals dominate the proceedings.** You generally find one or two of these people in every crowd — you know, the people who think they know it all and make sure their opinion is heard loudly and often during the course of a meeting. These folks may be good for occasional comic relief, if nothing else, but they often intimidate the other participants and stifle their contributions.

- **Meetings last too long.** Yes, yes, yes. Make sure a meeting doesn't last longer than it needs to — no less, no more. Most managers let meetings expand to fill the time allotted to them and hold the participants hostage even after the business at hand is completed.

- **The meeting has no focus.** Meeting leadership isn't a passive occupation. Many pressures work against keeping meetings on track and on topic, and managers often fail to step up to the challenge. The result is the proliferation of personal agendas, digressions, diversions, off-topic tangents, and worse.

Following the eight keys to great meetings

Meetings that produce results don't just happen by accident. Fortunately, your dysfunctional meeting blues have a cure. Here's the good news again: The cure is readily available, inexpensive, and easy to swallow.

- **Be prepared.** You need only a little time to prepare for a meeting, and the payoff is increased meeting effectiveness. Instead of wasting time trying to figure out why you're meeting, your preparation gets results as soon as the meeting starts.

✔ **Have an agenda.** An agenda is your road map, your meeting plan. With it, you and the other participants recognize the meeting goals and know what you're going to discuss. And if you distribute the agenda and other documents to participants before the meeting, you multiply its effectiveness because the participants can prepare for the meeting in advance. This preparation saves time and improves the quality of dialogue and decision making.

✔ **Start on time and end on time (or sooner).** Maybe you've gone to a meeting on time, but the meeting leader, muttering about an important phone call or visitor, arrives 15 minutes late. Even worse is when the meeting leader ignores the scheduled ending time and lets the meeting go on and on. Respect your participants by starting and ending your meetings on time. You don't want them to spend the entire meeting looking at their watches and worrying about how late you're going to keep them!

✔ **Have fewer — but better — meetings.** Call a meeting only when a meeting is absolutely necessary. When you do call a meeting, make the meeting a good one. Do you really have to meet to discuss a change in your travel reimbursement policy? Wouldn't an e-mail message to all company travelers do just as well? Or how about the problem you've been having with the financial reports? Instead of calling a meeting, maybe a phone call can do the trick. Whenever you're tempted to call a meeting, make sure you have a good reason for doing so.

✔ **Think inclusion, not exclusion.** Be selective about whom you invite to your meetings — select only as many participants as needed to get the job done. But don't exclude people who may have the best insight into your issues simply because of their ranks in the organization or their lifestyles, appearance, or beliefs.

You never know who in your organization is going to provide the best ideas, and you only hurt your chances of getting those great ideas by excluding people for non-performance-related reasons.

✔ **Maintain the focus.** Ruthlessly keep your meetings on topic at all times. Although doing everything but talking about the topic at hand can be a lot of fun, you called the meeting for a specific reason. Stick to the topic. If you finish the meeting early, then by all means end it.

✔ **Capture action items.** Make sure you have a system for capturing, summarizing, and assigning action items to individual team members. Flip charts — those big pads of paper you hang from an easel in front of the group — are great for this purpose. Have you ever come out of a meeting wondering why the meeting took place? Was it a meeting with no purpose, no direction, and no assignments or follow-up actions? Make sure that your meetings have purpose and that you assign action items to the appropriate people.

✔ **Get feedback.** Feedback can be a great way to measure the effectiveness of your meetings. Not only can you find out what you did right, but you can find out what you did wrong and get ideas on how to make your future meetings more effective. After the meeting, ask participants to give you their honest and open feedback — verbally or in writing — and then use it. You can never see yourself as others do unless they show you.

Leveraging Internet meeting tools

The Internet has forever changed the way we do business, and it touches us in ways we never imagined possible. One of these ways is through the proliferation of Web-enabled meeting tools. Using them in your own business can save you both time and money. Why fly across the country — or halfway around the world — when you can fire up your Web browser and conduct the meeting using your computer and a Web cam for free?

As technology improves and the widespread availability of fast Internet connections increases, businesses are moving their meetings onto the Web. Be aware of these meeting tools:

✔ **Internet voice and video call software:** If your meeting involves a small group, an Internet voice and video calling software program like Skype (available at www.skype.com) may be all you need. Using voice over IP (VoIP) technology, Skype enables you to make free video calls to anyone who also has the Skype software installed on a computer. This includes someone down the street or on the other side of the globe.

✔ **Meeting software:** A number of Web-enabled meeting software programs are available. These are particularly handy for larger meetings or for meetings with participants who work in more than two locations. Most of these programs enable you to load PowerPoint presentations and documents that meeting participants can view. GoToMeeting (available at www.gotomeeting.com) is one of the most popular online meeting providers. Although you'll pay a monthly fee for the service, you can try before you buy, with a 30-day free trial period. Other popular programs include WebEx (www.webex.com) and MegaMeeting (www.megameeting.com). If you have a Blackberry, iPhone, or other smartphone, some of these programs will also run on your mobile unit.

Chapter 9

Managing Virtual Employees

. . . .

In This Chapter

▶ Managing a new flavor of employee

▶ Leveraging the Internet to manage virtual employees

▶ Monitoring far-away employees

▶ Leading different shifts

. . . .

The past decade has seen a major shift in the attitudes of companies — and the attitudes of the men and women who run them — toward a more worker-friendly workplace. Today's managers are much more flexible and willing to work with the unique needs of their employees than ever. Why? Because savvy managers realize that they can get more from employees with a little consideration (and employees increasingly expect this). So whether employees need to drop off their kids at school in the morning, work only on certain days of the week, or take an extended leave of absence to care for an ill relative, managers are more likely to do whatever they can to accommodate workers' needs.

This shift in attitudes (as well as changes in the nature of work, the improvement of technology, and reduced levels of management in many organizations) has led to its eventual conclusion — virtual employees who spend most of their work hours away from established company offices and worksites, employees managed from a distance, employees who work a variety of shifts or have differing starting and ending times, and employees who telecommute to the office from the comfort of their homes.

Of course, these changes haven't been easy for the managers who are required to implement them. For managers who are used to having employees nearby and ready to instantly respond to the needs of customers and clients, managing off-site employees can be a bit disconcerting. But that doesn't have to be the case. Virtual employees can be just as good as the ones in the office with you. In fact, they can be more loyal, more effective, and more highly motivated . . . as long as you know how to manage them effectively.

In this chapter, we consider this new kind of work arrangement and how best to work with virtual employees. We explore strategies for effectively managing far-away employees and employees who work differing shifts, and we take a look at the future of telecommuting.

Making Room for a New Kind of Employee

A new kind of employee is out there — the *virtual* employee. Exactly what do we mean by *virtual employee*? A virtual employee is simply someone who regularly works somewhere outside of the regular bricks-and-mortar offices that house a company's business operations. Virtual employees join employees who have accepted (and often clamored for) a variety of alternative working arrangements, including alternate work schedules and flexible work schedules.

According to a U.S. Labor Department report, approximately one in ten employees today has an alternative work arrangement. These alternative work arrangements can range from something as simple as starting and ending the workday outside the standard (or core) business hours, all the way to working full-time from home.

But don't these kinds of arrangements cost a company more or result in less productive employees? At this time, the evidence says no. IBM found that it saves an average of 40 to 60 percent of its real estate expenses each year by eliminating offices for all employees except those who truly need them. The company recorded productivity gains of 15 to 40 percent after instituting a virtual workplace. Hewlett-Packard doubled revenues per salesperson after it created virtual workplace arrangements for its people. And Andersen Consulting discovered that its consultants spent 25 percent more time with clients when their regular physical offices were eliminated.

Managing people who aren't physically located near you can be particularly challenging, and you must approach it differently than managing employees who work in the same physical location. Perhaps your employees are located at a different facility or even in a different state (called *remote* employees), or maybe they're telecommuting from their homes, a local library, or even a coffee shop. But regardless of the reason for the separation, these new distance-working relationships make it harder for managers to identify and acknowledge desired behavior and performance. You must be more systematic and intentional in determining whether employees are fully performing their duties to the same standard as employees housed in a regular office.

Preparing to get virtual

Is your company ready for virtual employees? Are you ready for virtual employees? The following quick-and-easy checklist can help you determine whether your organization is ready and taking steps to make it so:

❏ Your company has established work standards to measure employee performance.

❏ Prospective virtual employees have the equipment they need to properly perform their work off-site.

❏ The work can be performed off-site.

❏ The work can be completed without ongoing interaction with other employees.

❏ Prospective virtual employees have demonstrated that they can work effectively without day-to-day supervision.

❏ Supervisors can manage and monitor employees by their results rather than by direct observation.

❏ Any state or local requirements for virtual workers (including overtime pay requirements) have been discussed with your legal and human resources departments.

❏ The company policy on flexible work arrangements is clear and has been well communicated.

❏ A standard agreement is in place to be used to document the terms of each customized work arrangement.

❏ Employee worksites have been examined to ensure that they're adequately equipped.

If you have several check marks, your organization is ready, willing, and able to initiate alternative work arrangements with your employees. If you have several empty boxes, you have your work cut out for you before you can reasonably expect virtual employees to be a viable option in your organization.

To make your organization more ready for virtual employees, take another look at the checklist. By addressing each box that doesn't have a check mark, you bring your company closer to making virtual employees a reality. For example, if your company doesn't have the equipment virtual employees need to do their work off-site — say, laptop computers, wireless modems, and Blackberry phones — then you can budget for and buy them. Or if you don't have a clear company policy on flexible work arrangements, you can create one. As you address each of the unchecked boxes, you're one step closer to your goal.

Understanding changes to the office culture

One of the key concerns for managers when an increasing number of employees become virtual employees is this: What happens to the company's culture (and employee performance) as more workers work outside the office? After all, a company's culture is mostly defined by the day-to-day interactions of employees within a company's four walls. Employees who work outside these interactions probably have no grounding in an organization's culture and have little attachment to other employees or to the organization's values and goals. The result? Employees who are potentially less productive than regular employees, with lowered teamwork and loyalty.

The good news is that you can take a number of steps to help your virtual workers plug into your company's culture, become team players, and gain a stake in the organization's goals in the process.

Consider the following ideas:

- ✔ **Schedule regular meetings that everyone attends — in person or by telephone conference call or Internet videoconferencing system.** Discuss current company events and set aside time for the group to tackle and solve at least one pressing organizational issue — or more, if time permits.

- ✔ **Create communication vehicles that everyone can be a part of.** Bob once worked with a limousine company that gave all its drivers a monthly cassette tape. The tape updated the company's employees — most of whom were out on the road doing their jobs — on current company happenings, policies, questions and answers, and more, to listen to in their cars. With the technology of today, you could do the same by sending employees digital recordings or podcasts to listen to when and where convenient.

- ✔ **Hire a facilitator and schedule periodic team-building sessions with all your employees — virtual and nonvirtual — to build working relationships and trust among employees.**

- ✔ **Initiate regular, inexpensive group events that draw out your virtual employees to mingle and get to know regular employees — and each other.** Going out to lunch on the company's tab, volunteering to help a local charity, having a potluck at a local park — the possibilities are endless.

As a manager, you need to consider the reality that virtual employees face issues and challenges that conventional in-house employees don't:

✔ Virtual employees may find that they're not fairly compensated by their employers for the home resources (office space, computers, electricity, furniture, and so forth) that they contribute to the job. Many employers feel that employees should contribute these items for nothing — as a *quid pro quo* for being allowed to work outside the office.

✔ Virtual employees may feel that their personal privacy is being violated if management efforts are too intrusive. Remember that your employee is (we assume) not available 24/7. Respect his or her work hours and use work phone numbers and e-mail addresses — not home contact information — when you want to communicate.

✔ Regular employees may become jealous of virtual employees' "special privileges."

✔ Family duties may intrude on work duties much more often for employees who work at home than for employees who work in traditional offices.

These issues don't mean that you should just forget about offering your employees alternative working arrangements. It just means that you need to be aware of them and work to ensure that they don't cause problems for your virtual — or regular — employees.

Weighing the pros and cons of telecommuting

With the proliferation of personal computers — both at work and at home — and the availability of fast and inexpensive broadband Internet hookups and communications software, telecommuting is becoming a common arrangement with many benefits. According to studies, employee productivity can increase by 30 percent, less time is lost as people sit in cars or mass transit to and from work, workers are more satisfied with their jobs, and society (and our lungs) benefits from fewer cars on the road every rush hour.

When her fiancé accepted a job in New Mexico, Amy Arnott, an analyst at Chicago-based Morningstar, Inc., was faced with a tough decision. Should she quit her job and move to New Mexico with her husband-to-be, or should she try maintaining a long-distance romance? Fortunately for Arnott, she didn't have to make the choice. Morningstar allowed Arnott to telecommute each day from Los Alamos to Chicago — a journey of more than 1,000 miles each way. Arnott used her computer and modem to tap into the Morningstar mutual fund database. By using the database, along with off-the-shelf word processing, spreadsheet, and e-mail software, Arnott performed her job just as well as if she were at her old office in Chicago.

Although the idea of virtual employees seems to be catching on in the world of business, you, as a manager, need to consider some pros and cons when your thoughts turn to the idea of telecommuting.

Following are some advantages to telecommuting:

- ✔ Depending on the job, employees can set their own schedules.
- ✔ Employees can spend more time with customers.
- ✔ Distracting office politics are often reduced.
- ✔ Employees can conduct more work because everything is there where they need it. (And when they get bored on a Saturday afternoon, they just may do an hour or two of work.)
- ✔ You may be able to save money by downsizing your facilities.
- ✔ Costs of electricity, water, and other overhead are reduced.
- ✔ Employee morale is enhanced because they have the opportunity to experience the freedom of working from their own homes or other locations of their choice.

And following are some of the disadvantages to telecommuting:

- ✔ Monitoring employee performance is more difficult.
- ✔ Scheduling meetings can be problematic.
- ✔ You may have to pay to set up your employees with the equipment they need to telecommute.
- ✔ Employees can lose their feelings of being connected to the organization.
- ✔ You must be more organized in making assignments.

For many employees, the prospect of being able to work out of their own home is much more appealing than merging onto the freeway each morning. For example, Scott Bye still gets out of bed at about the same time he did when he worked at a large corporate publisher, but now his commute is a few steps down the hall instead of an hour and 15 minutes of bumper-to-bumper, smog-filled, Los Angeles stop-and-go traffic. By 9:30 a.m. (15 minutes before his old starting time), Bye has already made several calls to his East Coast clients, sent a fax or two to publishing contacts overseas, and created a sales presentation on his computer.

However, telecommuting isn't just a plus for your current employees. It can be a powerful recruiting tool when you're on the hunt for new people to supplement your workforce. As the Baby Boom generation retires and moves on to greener pastures, the younger generations (Generation X and Generation Y) will have fewer people to replace them. Long story short, as the economy rebounds in coming years, a shortage of good workers is going to arise. Anything you can do to attract and retain good employees in the future will become not just a nicety, but a necessity.

Managing from a Distance

With the changing nature of work today, managers have to adapt to new circumstances for managing employees. How can managers keep up with an employee's performance when that employee may not even have physical contact with the manager for weeks or months at a time? It's hard enough for many managers to keep up with the employees who are in the office, much less a group of employees who are now working outside it.

Increasing your interaction

Today's managers have to work harder to manage distant employees. If you value strong working relationships and clear communication (and you should), you need to reach out to your virtual employees to be sure adequate communication is taking place. Some of the answers to managing virtual employees effectively lie in a return to the following basics of human interaction:

- **Make time for people.** Nothing beats face time when it comes to building trusting relationships. Managing is a people job — if you're a manager, you need to take time for people. It's a part of the job. And you need to do so not only when taking time is convenient, but also whenever employees are available and need to meet.

- **Increase communication as you increase distance.** The greater the distance from one's manager, the greater the effort both parties have to make to keep in touch. And although some employees want to be as autonomous as possible and want to minimize their day-to-day contact with you, other employees quickly feel neglected or ignored if you don't make a routine effort to communicate with them. Increase communication by sending regular updates and scheduling meetings and visits more frequently. Also encourage your employees to contact you (communication is a two-way street, after all), and go out of your way to provide the same types of communication meetings with each work shift or to arrange meetings that overlap work shifts or duplicate awards for each facility.

✔ **Use technology.** Don't let technology use you. Use technology as a more effective way to communicate with your employees, not just to distribute data. Promote the exchange of information and encourage questions. Have problem discussion boards or host chat rooms with managers or executives, or create an electronic bulletin board to capture the exchange of individual employee and team progress, problems, and solutions. You can set these up on your company intranet or within a password-protected area of your company's Web site.

Providing long-distance recognition

Every employee needs to be recognized by a manager for a job well done. Just because an employee is out of sight doesn't mean that person should be out of mind. Consider some steps you can take to make sure your virtual employees feel just as appreciated as your regular employees:

✔ Ask virtual team members to keep the leader and other team members apprised of their accomplishments, because they can't be as readily seen.

✔ Keep a recognition log of remote team members so that they don't fall into the cracks — a particularly important consideration for mixed teams (with both traditional and virtual team members).

✔ Make sure that virtual team members are appropriately included in recognition programs by passing around recognition item catalogs and by ensuring that remote employees are kept fully in the loop.

✔ Provide some "treat" for virtual team members who can't join in face-to-face socials and celebrations.

✔ Utilize recognition activities and items that are appropriate for a mobile workforce, such as thank-you cards and gift certificates.

✔ Tap into the recognition capabilities of e-mail, such as virtual flowers or greeting cards.

✔ Involve executives in recognition activities by way of conference calls, videoconferencing, or periodic in-person awards programs.

✔ Make a point of employing a variety of team recognition items (such as coffee mugs, T-shirts, jackets, and so forth) when rewarding members of virtual teams. Such items help remind them of their team membership.

Using the Internet

It's hard to believe that just a couple decades ago, only a small handful of academic researchers and government employees used the Internet. Today the Internet touches most all of us, either at work or at home. You can do so many things on the Internet — the possibilities are endless. However, we're most interested in using the Internet to manage your virtual employees.

Managing employees is a challenge when you've got them right there in front of you. However, when your employees are across town — or on the other side of the globe, nine time zones away — this challenge is multiplied many times. The good news is that, just as the Internet has brought the world closer together in many different ways, the Internet can help bring your far-flung employee team closer together while making your job of managing easier. These tools can do just that.

- ✔ **Teleconferencing and videoconferencing:** The widespread proliferation of broadband Internet connections has finally provided most business-people with the bandwidth they need to make real-time phone telecon-ferencing and videoconferencing work on their computers. You can find a number of Internet-enabled teleconferencing Web sites, including www. freeconferencecall.com and www.accuconference.com. Some of these sites provide service for free, but others require you to pay. All offer a variety of different features, including instant conference calls, scheduled calls, recording, conversation transcription, and more. If you want to conduct videoconferences, many of the teleconferencing com-panies' sites can also do that. However, Skype (www.skype.com) allows you to set up videoconferences for free.

- ✔ **Virtual meetings:** If you've got a group larger than just a few people and you want to integrate your computer into the proceedings (to display documents, spreadsheets, graphics, and so forth), consider checking out some of the providers of virtual meetings services. Some of the most popular are Microsoft Office Live Meeting (included along with the Microsoft Office software product) and www.gotomeeting.com. Prices for these services vary, but most offer a free trial period, so be sure to try before you buy.

- ✔ **Project collaboration sites:** One of the most difficult challenges in manag-ing virtual employees arises when you're working together on a project. Usually team members need to swap a lot of documents and files, plus occasional get-togethers are necessary to ensure that everyone is working from the same page. Project collaboration Web sites such as Basecamp (www.basecamp.com) and Easy Projects (www.easyprojects.net) make the job much easier and more effective. Most offer a variety of online project-collaboration tools such as project milestone charts, proj-ect updates and check-ins, shared task lists, virtual brainstorm sessions, and much more. Again, prices and exact services vary, so be sure the system meets your needs before you make a long-term commitment.

Of course, you can still use your telephone as well as e-mail or text messages to conduct the majority of your interactions with your virtual employees. And don't forget to schedule an occasional in-person team meeting where everyone has an opportunity to spend some time together and put faces behind the voices. However, when you need to manage a project or pull together a meeting with more than an employee or two, these Internet-based tools give you a distinct advantage.

Managing Different Shifts

The challenge of managing today's employees is made harder by the fact that the nature of work is changing so dramatically and so quickly. Employers have increasingly supplemented traditional work schedules with more flexible scheduling options. Managing employees who work differing shifts is a special challenge for today's managers.

Following are some strategies to consider when making the most of working with shift employees:

✔ **Take time to orient shift employees.** All employees need to get their bearings, and shift employees can often be at a disadvantage because they're working outside a company's normal hours. Be sure to let them know what they can expect about the job and the organization, including work policies you expect them to abide by. And create opportunities for them to personally meet all other individuals they need to know or work with.

✔ **Give them the resources to be productive.** Giving them the resources can range from the right equipment to do the job, to access to others when they have a question. Other resources include the right instruction and training, especially about company products and services, work processes, internal procedures, and administrative requirements.

✔ **Make an ongoing effort to communicate.** The importance of communication is almost a cliché, but we say it anyway: You can't underestimate its value. Many employees prefer to silently suffer through poor directions instead of running the risk that they'll seem slow to grasp an assignment — and possibly be labeled as difficult to work with. Constantly check with shift employees to see if they have questions or need help. Make every personal interaction count to find out how the employees are doing and how you can better help them.

Some managers schedule meetings at shift change to get two shifts at once or host a dinner with later shifts for a question-and-answer session around key initiatives. Have key staff contacts from your human resources, finance, and legal departments come in occasionally to answer questions as well.

✔ **Appreciate employees for the jobs they do.** Even if an employee is at work only outside the standard work schedule, his need to be recognized for hard work and accomplishments is still as great as any other employee's, although his circumstances make it more inconvenient to thank him. Fortunately, a little appreciation can go a long way. Take the time to find out what may motivate extra performance and then deliver such rewards when you receive the desired performance.

✔ **Treat shift employees the way you want them to act.** If you want shift employees to have a long-term perspective, treat them with a long-term perspective. Make them feel a part of the team. Treating shift employees with courtesy and professionalism can help establish your reputation as a desirable employer to work for and thus attract additional talent when you need it.

Managing employees who work different shifts is an achievable task if done with the right effort at the right time. Make the time and the effort, and you'll reap the benefits.

Top five virtual management Web sites

Wondering where to find the best information on the Web about the topics addressed in this chapter? Here are our top five favorites:

✔ @Brint: `www.brint.com/EmergOrg.htm`

✔ StartWright: `www.startwright.com/virtual.htm`

✔ The Economist: `graphics.eiu.com/upload/eb/NEC_Managing_virtual_teams_WEB.pdf`

✔ Center for Coordination Science: `ccs.mit.edu`

✔ CoWorking: `coworking.com`

Chapter 10

Monitoring Performance and Execution

*1*n Chapter 6, we discuss the whys and wherefores of setting goals. Setting goals — for individuals, for teams, and for the overall organization — is extremely important. Goals help provide the internal motivation that makes things happen. However, ensuring that the organization is making progress toward the successful completion of goals (in the manner and time frames agreed to) is equally important. You can't have one without the other. The organization's performance depends on each individual who works within it. Achieving goals is what this chapter is all about.

Measuring and monitoring the performance of individuals in your organization is like walking a tightrope: You don't want to overmeasure or overmonitor your employees. Doing so only leads to needless bureaucracy, lack of trust, and demotivation, all of which can negatively affect your employees' ability to perform their tasks. Nor do you want to undermeasure or undermonitor your employees. This lack of watchfulness can lead to nasty surprises when a task is completed late, over budget, or not at all. For managers, this means a real balancing act as they try to ensure that goals are completed yet seek to avoid the kind of micromanagement that most employees dislike.

Keep in mind that, as a manager, your primary goal in measuring and monitoring your employees' performance is not to punish them for making a mistake or missing a milestone. Instead, your primary goal is to help your employees stay on schedule and discover whether they need additional assistance or resources to do so. Whatever the reason, few employees like to admit that they need help getting an assignment done. Because of this built-in reluctance, you must systematically check on the progress of your employees, regularly give them feedback on how they're doing, and provide support to them as necessary. And if they just can't get the job done, you need to identify this situation quickly and replace the employee with someone who can get the job done.

If you don't *monitor* desired performance, you won't *achieve* desired performance. Don't leave achieving your goals to chance; develop systems to monitor progress and ensure that your goals are achieved.

Turning Goals into Action

The term *execution* is a popular one in business today. Execution in business simply means the act of successfully carrying out a task — it's all about turning goals into action.

The first step in checking your employees' progress in executing their goals is to determine the key indicators of a goal's success. If you follow the advice in Chapter 6, you set goals with your employees that are few in number and *SMART* (specific, measurable, attainable, relevant, and time bound).

When you quantify a goal in precise numerical terms, your employees have no confusion over how their performance is measured and when their job performance is adequate (or less than adequate). If you measure performance in terms of the quantity of sprockets produced per hour, your workers know exactly what you mean. If the goal is to produce 100 sprockets per hour with a reject rate of 1 or less, your employees clearly understand that producing only 75 sprockets per hour with 10 rejects is unacceptable performance. Nothing is left to the imagination, and the goal isn't subject to individual interpretation or to the whims of individual supervisors or managers.

How you measure and monitor the progress of your employees toward completion of their goals depends on the nature of the goals. For example, you can measure some goals in terms of time, others in terms of units of production, and others in terms of delivery of a particular work product (such as a report or a sales proposal).

The following are examples of different goals and the ways you can measure them:

✔ **Goal:** Plan and implement a company newsletter before the end of the second quarter of the current year.

Measurement: The specific date (for example, June 30) the newsletter is mailed (time).

✔ **Goal:** Increase the number of mountain bike frames produced by each employee from 20 to 25 per day.

Measurement: The exact number of mountain bike frames produced by the employee each day (quantity).

✔ **Goal:** Increase profit on the project by 20 percent in fiscal year 2012.

Measurement: The total percentage increase in profit from January 1 through December 31, 2012 (percentage increase).

Although noting when your employees attain their goals is obviously important, recognizing your employees' incremental progress toward attaining their goals is just as important. For example:

✔ The goal for your drivers is to maintain an accident-free record. This goal is ongoing, with no deadline. To encourage them in their efforts, you prominently post a huge banner in the middle of the garage that reads "153 Accident-Free Days." You increase the number for each day of accident-free driving.

✔ The goal of your fiscal clerks is to increase the average number of transactions from 150 per day to 175 per day. To track their progress, you publicly post a summary of each employee's daily production counts at the end of each week. As production increases, you praise the progress of your employees toward the final goal.

✔ The goal set for your reception staff is to improve the percentage of "excellent" responses on customer feedback cards by 10 percent. You tabulate the monthly counts for each receptionist and announce the results at department staff meetings. The department manager buys lunch for the receptionist with the highest total each month.

The secret to performance measuring and monitoring is the power of positive feedback. When you give positive feedback (increased number of units produced, percentage increase in sales, and so on), you encourage the behavior you want. However, when you give negative feedback (number of errors, number of workdays lost, and so on), you aren't encouraging the behavior you want; you're only discouraging the behavior that you don't want. Consider the following examples:

✔ Instead of measuring the number of defective cartridges, measure the number of correctly assembled cartridges.

✔ Instead of measuring the number of days late, measure the number of days on time.

✔ Instead of measuring the quantity of backlogged transactions, measure the quantity of completed transactions.

You may wonder whether the feedback you give to employees regarding their performance should be public or private. Do you put the information out there for everyone to see, or do you get a better response by making the information confidential? From our experience as managers, we find that you're much more likely to get the results you want when you put group performance measures (total revenues, average days sick, and so on) out in the open for everyone to see but keep individual performance measures (sales performance by employee, on-time rankings by employee, and so on) private. The intent is to get a team to work together to improve its performance — tracking and publicizing group measures and then rewarding improvement can lead to dramatic advances in the performance you seek. You *don't* want to embarrass your employees or subject them to ridicule by other employees when their individual performance isn't up to par. Instead, counsel them privately and coach them (and provide additional training and support, as necessary) to improve performance.

Developing a System for Immediate Performance Feedback

You can measure an infinite number of behaviors or performance characteristics. What you measure and the values you measure against are up to you and your employees. In any case, keep certain points in mind when you design a system for measuring and monitoring your employees' performance. Build your system on the *MARS* system, an acronym for *milestones, actions, relationships,* and *schedules.* We describe each element of the MARS system in the following sections.

Applying each characteristic — milestones, actions, relationships, and schedules — results in goals that you can measure and monitor. If you can't measure and monitor your goals, chances are, your employees will never achieve them and you won't know the difference. And wouldn't that be a shame?

Setting your checkpoints: The milestones

Every goal needs a starting point, an ending point, and points in between to measure progress along the continuum. *Milestones* are the checkpoints, events, and markers that tell you and your employees how far along you are on the road to reaching the goals you've set together.

For example, suppose that you establish a goal of finalizing corporate budgets in three months. The third milestone along the way to your ultimate goal is that draft department budgets be submitted to division managers no later than June 1. If you check with the division managers on June 1 and they haven't submitted the draft budgets, you quickly and unambiguously know that the project is behind schedule. However, if all the budgets are in on May 15, you know that the project is ahead of schedule and that you may reach the final goal of completing the corporate budgets sooner than you originally estimated.

Reaching your checkpoints: The actions

Actions are the individual activities that your employees perform to get from one milestone to the next. To reach the third milestone in your budgeting project, your employees must undertake and complete several actions after they reach the second milestone in the project. Each action gets your employees a little closer to reaching the third milestone in the project (completion of draft corporate budgets by June 1, for example) and is therefore a critical element in your employees' performance.

In this example, these actions may include the following:

1. **Review prior-year expenditure reports and determine the relationship, if any, to current activities.**

2. **Review current year-to-date expenditure reports and project final year-end numbers.**

3. **Meet with department staff to determine their training, travel, and capital equipment requirements for the new fiscal year.**

4. **Review possible new hires, terminations, and pay raises to determine the impact on payroll cost.**

5. **Create a computerized draft budget spreadsheet using numbers developed in the preceding actions.**

6. **Print the draft budget and manually double-check the results. Correct entries and reprint, if necessary.**

7. **Submit the draft budget to the division manager.**

 When developing a plan for completing a project, note each action in writing. By taking notes, you make focusing easier for your employees because they know exactly what they must do to reach a milestone, how far they have gone, and how much farther they have to go.

Sequencing your activity: The relationships

Relationships are how milestones and actions interact with one another. Relationships shape the proper sequencing of activities that lead you and your employees to the successful, effective accomplishment of your goals. Although sequence doesn't always matter, it usually can be more effective to perform certain actions before others and to attain certain milestones before others.

For example, in the list of actions needed to achieve the third project milestone (refer to the previous section), trying to perform the fifth action before the first, second, third, or fourth isn't going to work. If you haven't figured out the right numbers to put into your spreadsheet before you fill in the blanks, your results will be meaningless.

However, keep in mind that you may have more than one way to reach a milestone, and give your employees the latitude to find their own ways to reach their goals. Doing so empowers your employees to take responsibility for their work and to learn from their mistakes and successes. The results are successful performance and happy, productive employees.

Establishing your time frame: The schedules

How do you determine how far apart your milestones must be and how long project completion will take? You can plan better by estimating the *schedule* of each individual action in your project plan. How long does it take to review current year-to-date expenditure reports and project final year-end numbers? A day? A week? How long does it take you to meet with all your staff members to assess their needs?

Using your experience and training to develop schedules that are realistic and useful is important. For example, you may know that if everything goes perfectly, meeting with all your employees will take exactly four days. However, you also know that if you run into problems, the process can take as long as six days. Therefore, for planning purposes, you decide that five days is an appropriate schedule to apply to this particular action. This schedule allows for some variability in performance while ensuring that you meet the milestone on time.

Measuring instead of counting

According to management guru Peter Drucker, most businesspeople spend too much time counting and too little time actually measuring the performance of their organizations. What does Drucker mean by this? He's talking about the tendency of managers to be shortsighted in their application of management controls such as budgets. For example, most budgets are meant to ensure that company funds are spent only where authorized. They're control mechanisms that prevent spending from going out of control unnoticed by counting the number of dollars spent for a particular activity. However, Drucker suggests that, instead of using budgets only to count, managers can use them to measure quantities that are even more important to the future of the business (such as the number of satisfied customers). Managers can relate proposed expenditures to future results, for example, and provide follow-up information to show whether the desired results were achieved.

Drucker likens this counting issue to a doctor using an X-ray machine to diagnose an ill patient. Although some ailments — broken bones, pneumonia, and such — show up on an X-ray, other, more life-threatening illnesses such as leukemia, hypertension, and AIDS don't. Similarly, most managers use accounting systems to X-ray the organization's financial performance. However, accounting systems don't measure a catastrophic loss of market share or a failure of the firm to innovate until it's already too late and the "patient" has been damaged — perhaps permanently.

Putting Performance Measuring and Monitoring into Practice

Theory is nice, but practice is better. How does measuring and monitoring employee performance really happen? Following are a couple real-life cases; each takes a different path to achieve the same end: successful employee performance.

Case 1: Revamping processes for world-class performance

Several years ago, before coauthor Bob started his own company, he took over his previous employer's product customization department. At the time, the department was in shambles — project management was haphazard, at best, with no clear system of organization, and customers had to wait weeks or even months to receive their customized products, which often came to them with countless errors. Clearly, a change was needed, and Bob was given the task of straightening the mess out.

After reviewing the department's operations and collecting data from internal and external customers, Bob developed a checklist of tasks to bring the organization up to a world-class level of performance. At the heart of Bob's plan was a complete revamping of the department's system of measuring and monitoring performance.

Step 1: Setting goals with employees

The first two steps Bob took after drafting a checklist of what he wanted to accomplish were to talk to the employees in his new department and to interview users. And did they talk! By the time he'd finished collecting everyone's feedback, Bob had filled seven pages with negative comments about the department, work processes, finished products, and more. An example of the kind of problems Bob's employees talked about was vividly illustrated on his first day in the office, when a company salesperson called in some urgently needed changes to one of the projects completed the day before, only to find out that the software version of that product was lost.

All performance starts with clear goals. After Bob figured out exactly what was interfering with his employees' ability to do a good job, he discussed department needs and changes with his employees. Bob and the department agreed on a set of mutually acceptable goals and a game plan. Together Bob and the employees set the stage for the next step in achieving world-class performance.

Step 2: Changing the performance-monitoring system

When he reviewed the department's systems for measuring and monitoring employee performance, Bob quickly noticed that the measurements were all negative. All the talk was about problems: late projects, the number of mistakes, backlogged orders, and so on. The department wasn't tracking any positive performance measures.

Bob wanted to start some positive tracking to establish a baseline for performance and to build positive momentum. He installed a new system that focused on only one performance measure: a positive one — the number of on-time projects. From only a few on-time projects when Bob took over, the department racked up an amazing 2,700 on-time projects (in a row!) by the end of two years. Not only did this tremendous increase in performance make Bob happy, but the difference in the morale of his employees was like night and day. Instead of dreading the requests for customized products — and never having management appreciate their efforts or consider them "good enough" — Bob's department looked forward to the challenge of exceeding the high standards of performance they'd set for themselves.

Step 3: Revising the plan

As project performance improved, Bob pushed for other improvements: 24-hour project quotes, project indexing, software storage, streamlining of royalty and invoicing systems, and more. At the same time the improvements were planned and implemented, Bob walked a tightrope between addressing the long-term needs of system improvements and getting the short-term work done.

Before long, top management noticed what was going on in Bob's department. As the department's performance continued to improve, its work went from being a liability to the firm (that many salespeople refused to use) to being a major competitive advantage in the marketplace. By this time, the department completed 80 percent of its projects within two weeks after receipt, and the customization function became a leading competitive advantage for the company.

Case 2: Helping employees give 100 percent

You may not always measure the results you want for your organization in terms of the number of widgets produced or the percentage increase in an employee's contributions to profitability. Sometimes you simply want your employees to show up on time and to at least seem to be engaged in their work during the hours they spend on the job each day. If your employees' morale is poor, their productivity is likely to be poor, too.

A survey of employees at Cascades Diamond, Inc., that's cited in Bob's book *1001 Ways to Reward Employees* showed that 79 percent of employees felt they weren't being rewarded for a job well done, 65 percent felt that management treated them disrespectfully, and 56 percent were pessimistic about their work. Fortunately, company managers recognized that they had a problem. What follows is what they did to fix it.

Step 1: Create a program based on the behaviors you want

The first step the management of Cascades Diamond took was to create a brand new club in the company. The company developed the 100 Club to reinforce the behaviors that management wanted to promote throughout the organization: attendance, punctuality, and safety.

The plan was to award points to employees based on certain measurable criteria related to these behaviors. Any employee who attained a total of 100 points received an award — in this case, a nylon jacket with the company logo and the words "The 100 Club" imprinted on it.

Step 2: Assign points to the desired behaviors

The next step was to assign points to each desired behavior. Depending on whether employees exhibit the desired behavior, they can either receive points or have them taken away. For example, employees receive 25 points for a year of perfect attendance. However, for each full or partial day of absence, they have points deducted from their totals. Employees who go an entire year without formal disciplinary actions receive 20 points, and employees who work for a year without injuries resulting in lost time receive 15 points. Employees can also earn points for making cost-saving or safety suggestions, or participating in community service projects such as Red Cross blood drives or the United Way.

In assigning points to each behavior, management made sure the number of points was proportionate to the behavior's importance to the organization. Furthermore, management ensured that, although the numeric goals weren't too easy to attain — that is, employees had to stretch themselves to reach them — they weren't impossible to reach and, thereby, weren't demotivating.

Step 3: Measure and reward employee performance

Measurement and reward of the desired employee behavior constitute the heart of Cascades Diamond's program. Supervisors and managers closely track the performance of their employees and assign points for each of the factors. When employees reach the coveted 100-point level, they're inducted into the 100 Club, and the jacket — and all the pride that goes along with it — is theirs.

You may think this program is trivial — who really cares about getting a jacket with a company logo and three words, "The 100 Club," printed on it? Your employees, that's who! A local bank teller tells a story about a Cascades Diamond employee who once visited the bank to proudly model her new 100 Club jacket to bank customers and employees. According to the woman, "My employer gave this to me for doing a good job. It's the first time in the 18 years I've been there that they've recognized the things I do every day."

Even more telling, in the first year of the program, Cascades Diamond saved $5.2 million, increased productivity by nearly 15 percent, and reduced quality-related mistakes by 40 percent. In addition, 79 percent of employees said their work quality concerned them more now than before the program started, 73 percent reported that the company showed concern for them as people, and an amazing 86 percent of employees said the company and management considered them to be either "important" or "very important." Not bad results for a $40 baby blue jacket!

Measuring Progress with Bar Charts, Flowcharts, and Other Yardsticks

In some cases, measuring your employees' progress toward achieving a goal doesn't take much. For example, if the goal is to increase the number of widgets produced from 100 per hour to 125 per hour, a simple count can tell you whether your employees have achieved that goal. However, if the goal is to fabricate a prototype electric-powered vehicle in six months, the job of measuring and monitoring individual performance gets much more complicated and confusing.

Although you may decide to write out all the different milestones and actions (as we did in the corporate budgeting example earlier in this chapter), reading and understanding a graphical representation of the project is often much easier for complex projects. *Gantts*, *PERTs*, and other yardsticks perform this vital service for businesspeople around the world 24 hours a day, 7 days a week.

Bar charts

Bar charts, also known as *Gantt charts* (named for industrial engineer Henry L. Gantt), are probably one of the simplest and most common means of illustrating and monitoring project progress. With a quick glance, a manager can easily see exactly where the project is at any given date and can compare actual progress against planned progress.

The three key elements of bar charts are the following:

- ✔ **Timeline:** The timeline provides a scale with which you measure progress. You can express the timeline in any units you want: days, weeks, months, or whatever is most useful for managing the project. In most bar charts, the timeline appears along the horizontal axis (the *x-axis*, for you math majors).

- ✔ **Actions:** Actions are the individual activities that your employees perform to get from one milestone to the next. In a bar chart, each action is listed — usually in chronological order — vertically along the left side of the chart (that's the *y-axis*, math experts!).

- ✔ **Bars:** Now, what would a bar chart be without bars? Bars are the open blocks that you draw on your bar chart to indicate the length of time a particular action is estimated to take. Short bars mean short periods of time; long bars mean long periods of time. What's neat about bars is that, as an action is completed, you can fill in the bar, providing a quick visual reference of complete and incomplete actions.

We use our earlier example again to show the use of a bar chart. Figure 10-1 shows a typical bar chart; in this case, the chart illustrates the actions that lead up to the third milestone in the corporate budgeting example.

As Figure 10-1 shows, the timeline is along the top of the bar chart, just as we said it would be. In this example, the timeline stretches from April 15 to June 1, with each increment of 5 representing one week. The six actions necessary to reach the third milestone are listed vertically along the left side of the bar chart. Finally, you see those neat little bars that are really the heart and soul of the bar chart. Leave the bars unfilled until an action is completed; you may color them in then, if you like.

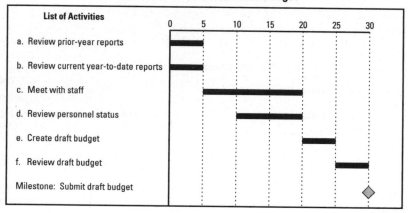

Third Milestone: Submit Draft Budget

Figure 10-1:
A bar chart illustrating actions leading up to the third milestone.

If all actions are completed according to the bar chart, the third milestone will be reached on June 1. If some actions take longer to complete than estimated, you may not reach the milestone on time and someone may end up in hot water. Conversely, if some actions take less time than estimated, the milestone can be reached early (sounds like a bonus is in order!).

The advantages of the Gantt chart are its simplicity, ease of preparation and use, and low cost. Although Gantt charts work fine for a simple project such as preparing a budget, they're generally unsuitable for large, complex projects such as building a space shuttle or doing your taxes.

Flowcharts

When the going gets tough, the tough get going — and they reach for their flowcharts. Although bar charts are useful for simple projects, they don't illustrate the sequential flow of actions in a project (and, therefore, aren't as useful for complex projects). On the other hand, *flowcharts* do a good job of illustrating this sequential flow. Although flowcharts look completely different than bar charts, they also have three key elements:

- ✔ **Actions:** In the case of flowcharts, arrows indicate actions. Arrows lead from one event to the next on a flowchart until the project is completed. The length of the arrows doesn't necessarily indicate the duration of an action. The arrows' primary purpose in a flow chart is to illustrate the sequential relationship of actions to one another.

- ✔ **Events:** Events, represented in flowcharts by numbered circles, signify the completion of a particular action.

- ✔ **Time:** Time estimates are inserted alongside each action (arrow) in the flowchart. By adding the number of time units along a particular path, you can estimate the total time for the completion of an action.

Figure 10-2 shows a flowchart of the corporate budgeting example illustrated in Figure 10-1. As you can see, the flowchart shows exactly how each action relates to the others. By following the longest path in terms of time, you can determine the *critical path* of the project. This kind of analysis is called the *critical path method (CPM)* and assumes that the time to complete individual actions can be estimated with a high degree of certainty. The CPM highlights the actions that determine the soonest that a project can be completed — in this case, 30 days.

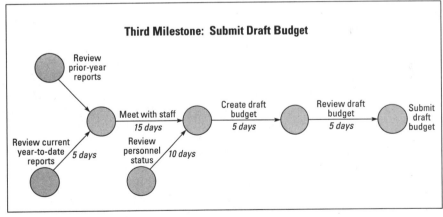

Figure 10-2: A flowchart for the corporate budgeting example.

PERT, short for *program evaluation and review technique,* is a variation of CPM used when the time to complete individual actions can't be estimated with a high degree of certainty. Using some interesting statistical techniques (okay, maybe not so interesting), PERT averages a range of possible times to arrive at an estimate for each action.

Software/Web tools

Fortunately for those of you who missed out on calculus in high school, the wonderful world of computers and software has now touched project monitoring and measurement. What you used to do with hours of drawing, erasing, redrawing, and so on, you can now accomplish with only a few well-placed keystrokes.

Microsoft Office Project, one of the foremost project-planning software packages on the market today, enables you to create and revise project schedules quickly and easily. Setting up a project with Microsoft Office Project is as easy as 1, 2, 3:

1. **Enter the actions to be completed.**

2. **Enter the sequence of the actions and their dependencies on other actions.**

3. **Enter the resources (people and money) required to complete the action.**

As a project progresses, you can input data such as actual start and completion dates, actual expenditures, and more to get a realistic picture of where the project is at any time. You can print these results in the form of tables, charts, or graphs — whatever your preference — and then save them for future reference.

The good news is that a variety of project management software options are available to you. Some popular options include Tenrox Project Management Software, Project Kickstart, Mindview, and Genius Project for Domino. Check the features and specifications before you buy, to ensure that they best meet your needs.

Aside from software-in-a-box solutions like Microsoft Office Project, an increasing number of online project management options exist. These solutions make it easy for you to collaborate with colleagues anywhere, anytime. Some popular Web-based project management sites include the following:

- Tenrox Online Project Management (www.tenrox.com)
- @Task (www.attask.com)
- Clarizen (www.clarizen.com)
- Basecamp (www.basecamphq.com)
- Easy Projects .NET (www.easyprojects.net)

A humorous look at a project's six phases

Some management techniques are so popular that they're copied and passed from employee to employee and from company to company in an informal system of communication that outperforms the formal communication system of many organizations. These tongue-in-cheek lists, diagrams, and cartoons help many employees find humor in their own workplaces and brighten their days. Of course, in some organizations, these items might ring a little too true. The following compilation of six phases of a project list has been floating around for many,

many years — our copy looks like it's at least fifth generation:

1. Enthusiasm
2. Disillusionment
3. Panic
4. Search for the guilty
5. Punishment of the innocent
6. Praise and honors for the nonparticipants

Most providers of these Web-based solutions offer free trial periods, so you can try before you buy. This gives you the opportunity to see whether a particular solution will work for you and your organization before you make a long-term commitment.

Assessing Execution and Moving Forward

You've set up your goals, you've set performance measures, and you've obtained pages of data for each of your employees. Now you determine whether the expected results were achieved, as follows.

- ✔ **Compare results to expectations:** What is the expected goal? Suppose that the goal is to complete the budget by June 1. When was the budget completed? It was completed on May 17 — well ahead of the deadline. Super! The mission was accomplished with time to spare.

- ✔ **Record the results:** Make note of the results — perhaps put them in the files that you maintain for each employee or print them and post them in the work area.

- ✔ **Praise, coach, or counsel your employees:** If the job was done right, on time, and within budget, congratulate your employees for a job well done and reward them appropriately: a written note of appreciation, a day off with pay, a formal awards presentation — whatever you decide.

However, if the expected results weren't achieved, find out why and determine what you can do to ensure that the expected results are achieved the next time. If the employees need only additional support or encouragement, coach them for a better performance. You can listen to your employees, refer them to other employees, or provide your own personal examples. If the poor results stem from a more serious shortcoming, counsel or discipline your employees. (For more on this subject, turn to Chapter 18.)

Top five project management Web sites

Wondering where to find the best information on the Web about the topics addressed in this chapter? Here are our top five favorites:

✔ The PM Forum: www.pmforum.org

✔ The Balanced Scorecard Institute: www.balancedscorecard.org

✔ American Productivity and Quality Center: www.apqc.org

✔ Gantt Chart and Timeline Center: www.smartdraw.com/resources/centers/gantt

✔ Performance Measurement Association: www.performanceportal.org

Part III
Tools and Techniques for Managing

The 5th Wave   By Rich Tennant

STRENGTHS/WEAKNESSES

✓ NEVER CONVICTED
✓ INVESTIGATION STALLED
✓ AUDITS INCONCLUSIVE

"Okay, let's hear some weaknesses."

In this part . . .

Management is all about getting things done through others. In this part, we address some of the most common and effective tools and techniques for managing, including delegating work to others, communicating, conducting performance evaluations, budgeting and accounting, using technology the right way, and adopting corporate social responsibility.

Chapter 11

Delegating to Get Things Done

. . . .

In This Chapter

▶ Managing through delegation

▶ Debunking the myths about delegation

▶ Putting delegation to work

▶ Choosing which tasks to delegate

▶ Checking up on your employees

. . . .

*T*he power of effective management comes not from your efforts alone (sorry to burst your bubble), but from the sum of all the efforts of each person within your work group. If you're responsible for only a few employees, with extraordinary effort, you perhaps can do the work of your entire group if you so desire (and if you want to be a complete stranger to your friends and family).

However, when you're responsible for a larger organization, you simply can't be an effective manager by trying to do all of your group's work. In the best case, the group may view you as a *micromanager* who gets too involved in the petty details of running an organization, spending more time on other people's work than your own. In the worst case, your employees may take less responsibility for their work because you're always there to do it (or check it) for them. They will be less engaged in their work, and morale will plummet. Why should they bother trying to do their best job if you don't trust them enough to do it?

Managers assign responsibility for completing tasks through *delegation*. But as we explain in this chapter, simply assigning tasks and then walking away isn't enough. To delegate effectively, managers must also give employees authority and ensure that they have the resources necessary to complete tasks effectively. Finally, managers who delegate like experts can monitor the progress of their employees toward meeting their assigned goals.

Delegating: The Manager's Best Tool

Now that you're a manager, you're required to develop skills in many different areas. You need good technical, analytical, and organizational skills, but most important, you also must have good people skills. Of all the people skills, the one skill that can make the greatest difference in your effectiveness is the ability to delegate well. Delegating is a manager's number one management tool, and the inability to delegate well is the leading cause of management failure.

Why do managers have such a hard time delegating? A variety of possible reasons exist:

- ✔ You're too busy and just don't have enough time.
- ✔ You don't trust your employees to complete their assignments correctly or on time.
- ✔ You're afraid to let go.
- ✔ You're concerned that you'll no longer be the center of attention.
- ✔ You have no one to delegate to (lack of resources).
- ✔ You don't know how to delegate effectively.

Perhaps you're still not convinced that managers need to delegate at all. If you're a member of this particular group of reluctant managers, consider these reasons why you must let go of your preconceptions and inhibitions and start delegating today:

- ✔ **Your success as a manager depends on it.** Managers who can successfully manage team members — each of whom has specific responsibilities for a different aspect of the team's performance — prove that they're ready for bigger and better challenges. Nice perks often accompany these challenges, including bigger and better titles, fatter paychecks, and other niceties of business life, such as offices with windows and larger budgets to play with.

- ✔ **You can't do it all.** No matter how great a manager you are, shouldering the entire burden of achieving your organization's goals isn't in your best interest unless you want to work yourself into an early grave. Besides, wouldn't it be nice to see what life is like outside the four walls of your office?

- ✔ **You have to concentrate on the jobs that you can do and your staff can't.** They pay you the big bucks to be a manager — not a software programmer, truck driver, accounting clerk, or customer service representative. Do your job, and let your employees do theirs.

✔ **Delegation gets workers in the organization more involved.** When you give employees the responsibility and authority to carry out tasks — whether individually or in teams — they respond by becoming more involved in the day-to-day operations of the organization. Instead of acting like drones with no responsibility or authority, they become vital to the success of the work unit and the entire organization. And if your employees succeed, you succeed!

✔ **Delegation gives you the chance to develop your employees.** If you make all the decisions and come up with all the ideas, your employees never learn how to take initiative and see tasks through to successful completion. And if they don't learn, guess who's going to get stuck doing everything forever? (Hint: Take a look in the mirror.) In addition, doing everything yourself robs your employees of a golden opportunity to develop their work skills. Today's employees increasingly report learning and development opportunities as one of the top motivators. See Chapter 7 for more about developing your employees.

As a manager, you're ultimately responsible for all your department's responsibilities. However, most managers find that personally executing all the tasks necessary for your department to fulfill its responsibilities and for you to achieve your organizational goals is neither practical nor desirable.

Suppose, for example, that you're the manager of the accounting department for a health care consulting firm. When the firm had only a few employees and sales of $100,000 a year, it was no problem for you to personally bill all your customers, cut checks to vendors, run payroll, and take care of the company's taxes every April. However, now that employment has grown to 150 employees and sales are at $50 million a year, you can't even pretend to do it all — you don't have enough hours in the day. You now have specialized employees who take care of accounts payable, accounts receivable, and payroll, and you have farmed out the completion of income tax work to a CPA.

Each employee that you've assigned to a specific work function has specialized knowledge and skills in a certain area of expertise. If you've made the right hiring decisions (see Chapter 5), each employee is a talented and specialized pro in a specific field. Sure, you could personally generate payroll if you had to, but you've hired someone to do that job for you. (By the way, your payroll clerk is probably a lot better and quicker at it than you are.)

On the other hand, you're uniquely qualified to perform numerous responsibilities in your organization. These responsibilities may include developing and monitoring your operations budget, conducting performance appraisals, and helping to plan the overall direction of your company's acquisitions. In the section "Sorting Out What to Delegate and What to Do Yourself," later in this chapter, we tell you which tasks to delegate to your employees and which ones to retain.

Debunking Myths about Delegation

Admit it, you may have many different rationalizations for why you can't delegate work to your employees. Unfortunately, these reasons have become part of the general folklore of being a manager. And they're guaranteed to get in the way of your ability to be an effective manager.

You can't trust your employees to be responsible

If you can't trust your employees, who can you trust? Assume that you're responsible for hiring at least a portion of your staff. Now, forgetting for a moment the ones you didn't personally hire, you likely went through quite an involved process to recruit your employees. Remember the mountain of résumés you had to sift through and then divide into winners, potential winners, and losers? After hours of sorting and then hours of interviews, you selected the best candidates — the ones with the best skills, qualifications, and experience for the job.

You selected your employees because you thought they were the most talented people available and deserved your trust. Now your job is to give them that trust without strings attached.

You usually reap what you sow. Your staff members are ready, willing, and able to be responsible employees; you just have to give them a chance. Sure, not every employee is going to be able to handle every task you assign. If that's the case, find out why. Does someone need more training? More time? More practice? Maybe you need to find a task that's better suited to an employee's experience or disposition. Or perhaps you simply hired the wrong person for the job. If that's the case, face up to the fact and fire or reassign the employee before you lose even more time and money. To get responsible employees, you have to give responsibility.

You'll lose control of a task and its outcome

If you delegate correctly, you don't lose control of the task or its outcome. You simply lose control of the way the outcome is achieved. Picture a map of the world. How many different ways can a person get from San Francisco to Paris? One? One million? Some ways are quicker than others. Some are more scenic, and others require a substantial resource commitment. Do the differences in these ways make any of them inherently wrong? No.

In business, getting a task done doesn't mean following only one path. Even for tasks that are spelled out in highly defined steps, you can always leave room for new ways to make a process better. Your job is to describe to your employees the outcomes that you want and then let them decide how to accomplish the tasks. Of course, you need to be available to coach and counsel them so that they can learn from your past experience, if they want, but you need to let go of controlling the *how* and instead focus on the *what* and the *when*.

You're the only one with all the answers

You're joking, right? If you think that you alone have all the answers, have we got a thing or two to tell you! As talented as you may be, unless you're the company's only employee, you can't possibly have the only answer to every question in your organization.

On the other hand, a certain group of people deals with an amazing array of situations every day. The group talks to your customers, your suppliers, and each other — day in and day out. Many members of this group have been working for the company far longer than you, and many of them will be there long after you're gone. Who are these people? They are your employees.

Your employees have a wealth of experience and knowledge about your business contacts and the intimate, day-to-day workings of the organization. They are often closer to the customers and problems of the company than you are. To ignore their suggestions and advice is not only disrespectful, but also shortsighted and foolish. Don't ignore this resource. You're already paying for it, so use it.

You can do the work faster by yourself

You may think that you're completing tasks faster when you do them than when you assign them to others, but this belief is merely an illusion. Yes, discussing a task and assigning it to one of your employees may require more of your time when you first delegate that task, but if you delegate well, you'll spend significantly less time the next time you delegate that same task.

What else happens when you do it yourself instead of delegating it? When you do the task yourself, you're forever doomed to doing the task — again and again and again. When you teach someone else to do the task and then assign that person the responsibility for completing it, you may never have to do it again. Your employee may even come to do it faster than you can. Who knows? That employee may actually improve the way that you've always done it, perhaps reducing costs or increasing customer satisfaction.

Delegation dilutes your authority

Delegation does the exact opposite of what this myth says — it actually extends your authority. You're only one person, and you can do only so much by yourself. Now imagine all 10, 20, or 100 members of your team working toward your common goals. You still set the goals and the timetables for reaching them, but each employee chooses his own way of getting there.

Do you have less authority because you delegate a task and transfer authority to an employee to carry out the task? Clearly, the answer is no. What do you lose in this transaction? Nothing. Your authority is extended, not diminished. The more authority you give to employees, the more authority your entire work unit has and the better able your employees are to do the jobs you hired them to do.

As you grant others authority, you gain an efficient and effective workforce — employees who are truly empowered, feel excited by their jobs, and work as team players. You also gain the ability to concentrate on the issues that deserve your undivided attention.

You relinquish the credit for doing a good job

Letting go of this belief is one of the biggest difficulties in the transition from being a doer to being a manager of doers. When you're a doer, you're rewarded for writing a great report, developing an incredible market analysis, or programming an amazing piece of computer code. When you're a manager, the focus of your job shifts to your performance in reaching an overall organizational or project goal through the efforts of others. You may have been the best darn marketing assistant in the world, but that talent doesn't matter anymore. Now you're expected to develop and lead a team of the best darn marketing analysts in the world. The skills required are quite different, and your success is a result of the indirect efforts of others and your behind-the-scenes support.

Wise managers know that when their employees shine, they shine, too. The more you delegate, the more opportunities you give your employees to shine. Give your workers the opportunity to do important work — and do it well. And when they do well, make sure you tell everyone about it. If you give your employees credit for their successes publicly and often, they'll more likely want to do a good job for you on future assignments. Don't forget, when you're a manager, you're primarily measured on your team's performance, not what you're personally able to accomplish. Chapter 3 covers everything you ever wanted to know about employee motivation and rewards.

Delegation decreases your flexibility

When you do everything yourself, you have complete control over the progress and completion of tasks, right? Wrong! How can you, when you're balancing multiple priorities at the same time and dealing with the inevitable crisis (or two or three) of the day? Being flexible is pretty tough when you're doing everything yourself. Concentrating on more than one task at a time is impossible. While you're concentrating on that one task, you put all your other tasks on hold. Flexibility? Not!

The more people you delegate to, the more flexible you can be. As your employees take care of the day-to-day tasks necessary to keep your business running, you're free to deal with those surprise problems and opportunities that always seem to pop up at the last minute.

Taking the Six Steps to Delegate

Delegation can be scary, at least at first. But as with anything else, the more you do it, the less scary it gets. When you delegate, you're putting your trust in another individual. If that individual fails, you're ultimately responsible — regardless of whom you give the task to. A line like this isn't likely to go very far with your boss: "Yeah, I know that we were supposed to get that proposal to the customer today, but that employee of mine, Joe, dropped the ball." When you delegate tasks, you don't automatically abdicate your responsibility for their successful completion.

As a part of this process, you need to understand your employees' strengths and weaknesses. For example, you probably aren't going to delegate a huge task to someone who has been on the job for only a few days. As with any other task that you perform as a manager, you have to work at delegating — and keep working at it. Ultimately, delegation benefits both workers and managers when you do it correctly. Follow these six steps in effectively delegating:

1. **Communicate the task.**

   Describe exactly what you want done, when you want it done, and what end results you expect. Ask for any questions your employee might have.

2. **Furnish context for the task.**

   Explain why the task needs to be done, its importance in the overall scheme of things, and possible complications that may arise during its performance.

3. **Determine standards.**

   Agree on the standards you plan to use to measure the success of a task's completion. Make these standards realistic and attainable.

4. **Grant authority.**

   You must grant employees the authority to complete the task without constant roadblocks or standoffs with other employees.

5. **Provide support.**

   Determine the resources necessary for your employee to complete the task, and then provide them. Successfully completing a task may require money, training, or the ability to check with you about progress or obstacles as they arise.

6. **Get commitment.**

   Make sure your employee has accepted the assignment. Confirm your expectations and your employee's understanding of and commitment to completing the task.

Sorting Out What to Delegate and What to Do Yourself

In theory, you can delegate anything you're responsible for to your employees. Of course, if you delegate all your duties, why is your company bothering to pay you? The point is, some things you, the manager, are better able to do, and some things your employees are better able to do. As a result, some tasks you make an effort to delegate to your employees and other tasks you retain for yourself.

When you delegate, begin with simple tasks that don't substantially impact the firm if they aren't completed on time or within budget. As your employees gain confidence and experience, delegate higher-level tasks. Carefully assess the level of your employees' expertise, and assign tasks that meet or slightly exceed that level. Set schedules for completion and then monitor your employees' performance against them. This is a good opportunity to see if an employee isn't being challenged or is bored. When you get the hang of it, you'll find that you have nothing to be afraid of when you delegate.

Pointing out appropriate tasks for delegation

Certain tasks naturally lend themselves to being delegated. Take every opportunity to delegate the following kinds of work to your employees.

Detail work

As a manager, you have no greater time-waster than getting caught up in details — you know, tasks such as double-checking pages, spending days troubleshooting a block of computer code, or personally auditing your employees' timesheets. An old saying holds that 20 percent of the results come from 80 percent of the work, which illustrates why the company selected you to be a manager. You can no doubt run circles around almost anyone on those detailed technical tasks that you used to do all the time.

But now that you're a manager, you're being paid to orchestrate the workings of an entire team of workers toward a common goal — not just to perform an individual task. Leave the detail to your employees, but hold them accountable for the results. Concentrate your efforts on tasks that have the greatest payoff and that allow you to most effectively leverage the work of all your employees.

Information gathering

Browsing the Web for information about your competitors, spending hours poring over issues of *Fortune* magazine, and moving into your local library's reference stacks for weeks on end isn't an effective use of your time. Still, most managers get sucked into the trap. Not only is reading newspapers, reports, books, magazines, and the like fun, but it also give managers an easy way to postpone the more difficult tasks of management. You're being paid to look at the big picture, to gather a variety of inputs and make sense of them. You can work so much more efficiently when someone else gathers needed information, freeing you to take the time you need to analyze the inputs and devise solutions to your problems.

Repetitive assignments

What a great way to get routine tasks done: Assign them to your employees. Many of the jobs in your organization arise again and again; drafting your weekly production report, reviewing your biweekly report of expenditures versus budget, and approving your monthly phone bill are just a few examples. Your time is much too important to waste on routine tasks that you mastered years ago.

If you find yourself involved in repetitive assignments, first take a close look at their particulars. How often do the assignments recur? Can you anticipate the assignments in sufficient time to allow an employee to successfully complete them? What do you have to do to train your employees in completing the tasks? When you figure all this out, develop a schedule and make assignments to your employees.

Surrogate roles

Do you feel that you have to be everywhere all the time? Well, you certainly can't be everywhere all the time — and you shouldn't even *try*. Every day, your employees have numerous opportunities to fill in for you. Presentations, conference calls, client visits, and meetings are just a few examples. In some cases, such as in budget presentations to top management, you may be required to attend. However, in many other cases, whether you attend personally or send someone to take your place really doesn't matter.

The next time someone calls a meeting and requests your attendance, send one of your employees to attend in your place. This simple act benefits you in several different ways. Not only do you have an extra hour or two in your schedule, but also your employee can present you with only the important outcomes of the meeting. In any case, your employee has the opportunity to take on some new responsibilities, and you have the opportunity to spend the time you need on your most important tasks. Your employee may even discover something new in the process.

Future duties

As a manager, you must always be on the lookout for opportunities to train your staff in their future job responsibilities. For example, one of your key duties may be to develop your department's annual budget. By allowing one or more of your employees to assist you — perhaps in gathering basic market or research data, or analyzing trends in previous-year budgets — you can give your employees a taste of what goes into putting together a budget.

Don't fall into the trap of believing that the only way to train your employees is to sign them up for an expensive class taught by someone with a slick color brochure who knows nothing about *your* business. Opportunities to train your employees abound within your own business. An estimated 90 percent of all development occurs on the job. Not only is this training free, but also by assigning your employees to progressively more important tasks, you build their self-confidence and help pave their way to progress in the organization.

Knowing what tasks should stay with you

Some tasks are part and parcel of the job of being a manager. By delegating the following work, you fail to perform your basic management duties.

Long-term vision and goals

As a manager, you're in a unique position. Your position at the top provides you with a unique perspective on the organization's needs — the higher up you are in an organization, the broader your perspective. As we discuss in Chapter 1, one of the key functions of management is vision. Although employees at any level of a company can give you input and make suggestions that help shape your perspectives, developing an organization's long-term vision and goals is up to you. Employees can't collectively decide the direction in which the organization should move. An organization is much more effective when everyone moves together in the same direction.

Positive performance feedback

Rewarding and recognizing employees when they do good work is an important job for every manager. If this task is delegated to lower-level employees, however, the workers who receive it won't value the recognition as much as if it came from their manager. The impact of the recognition is therefore significantly lessened.

Performance appraisals, discipline, and counseling

In the modern workplace, a strong relationship between manager and employee is often hard to come by. Most managers are probably lucky to get off a quick "Good morning" or "Good night" between the hustle and bustle of a typical workday. Given everyone's hectic schedules, you may have times when you don't talk to one or more of your employees for days at a time.

However, sometimes you absolutely have to set time aside for your employees. When you discipline and counsel your employees, you're giving them the kind of input that only you can provide. You set the goals for your employees, and you set the standards by which you measure their progress. Inevitably, you decide whether your employees have reached the marks you've set or whether they've fallen short. You can't delegate away this task effectively — everyone loses as a result.

Politically sensitive situations

Some situations are just too politically sensitive to assign to your employees. Say, for example, that you're in charge of auditing the travel expenses for your organization. The results of your review show that a member of the corporation's executive team has made several personal trips on company funds. Do you assign a worker the responsibility of reporting this explosive situation? No! As a manager, you're in the best position to present this information, to defend it, and to absorb any repercussions.

Not only do such situations demand your utmost attention and expertise, but placing your employee in the middle of the line of fire in this potentially explosive situation is also unfair. Being a manager may be tough sometimes, but you're paid to make the difficult decisions and to take the political heat that your work generates.

When delegation goes wrong

Sometimes delegation goes wrong — way wrong. How can you identify the danger signs before it's too late, and what can you do to save the day? You can monitor the performance of your workers in several ways:

✔ **Personal follow-up:** Supplement your formal tracking system with an informal system of visiting your workers and checking their progress on a regular basis.

✔ **Sampling:** Take periodic samples of your employees' work and make sure that the work meets the standards you agreed to.

✔ **Progress reports:** Regular progress reporting from employees to you can give you advance notice of problems and successes.

✔ **A formalized tracking system:** Use a formal system to track assignments and due dates. The system can be manual (perhaps a big chart pinned to your wall) or computerized.

If you discover that your employees are in trouble, you have several options for getting everything back on track:

✔ **Increasing your monitoring:** Spend more time monitoring employees who are in trouble, keeping closer track of their performance.

✔ **Counseling:** Discuss the problems with your employees and agree on a plan to correct them.

✔ **Rescinding authority:** If problems continue despite your efforts to resolve them through counseling, you can rescind your employees' authority to complete the tasks independently. (They still work on the task, but under your close guidance and authority.)

✔ **Reassigning activities:** As the ultimate solution when delegation goes wrong, if your employees can't do their assigned tasks, give the tasks to workers who are better able to perform them successfully.

Personal assignments

Occasionally, your boss may assign a specific task to you with the intention that you personally perform it. Your boss may have good reasons for doing so: You may have a unique perspective that no one else in your organization has, or you may have a unique skill required to complete the assignment quickly and accurately. Whatever the situation, if a task is assigned to you with the expectation that you, and only you, carry it out, then you can't delegate it to your staff. You may decide to involve your staff in gathering input, but you must retain the ultimate responsibility for the final execution of the task.

Confidential or sensitive circumstances

As a manager, you're likely privy to information that your staff isn't, such as wage and salary figures, proprietary data, and personnel assessments. Releasing this information to the wrong individuals can be damaging to an organization. For example, salary information should remain confidential.

Similarly, if your competitors get their hands on some secret process that your company has spent countless hours and money to develop, the impact on your organization and employees can be devastating. Unless your staff has a compelling need to know, retain assignments involving these types of information.

Checking Up Instead of Checking Out

Assume that you've already worked through the initial hurdles of delegation: You assigned a task to your employee, and you're eagerly waiting to see how she performs. You defined the scope of the task and gave your employee the adequate training and resources to get it done. You also told her what results you expect and exactly when you expect to see them. What do you do next?

Here's one option: An hour or two after you make the assignment, you check on its progress. In a couple more hours, you check again. As the deadline rapidly approaches, you increase the frequency of your checking until, finally, your employee spends more time answering your questions about the progress she has made than she spends actually completing the task. Every time you press her for details about her progress, she gets a little more distracted from her task and a little more frustrated with your seeming lack of confidence in her abilities. When the appointed hour arrives, she submits the result on time, but the report is inaccurate and incomplete. The employee is also stewing because of your micromanagement.

Here's another option: After you make the assignment to your employee, you do nothing. Yes, you heard right. You do nothing. Instead of checking on your employee's progress and offering your support, you assign the task and move on to other concerns. When the appointed hour arrives, you're surprised to discover that the task is not completed. When you ask your employee why she didn't meet the goal that you had mutually agreed upon, she tells you that she had trouble obtaining some information and, instead of bothering you with this problem, she decided to try to construct it for herself. Unfortunately, this diversion required an additional two days of research before she found the correct set of numbers.

Clearly, neither of these two extremes is a productive way to monitor the delegation process. In between lies the answer to how to approach this delicate but essential task. Depending on the situation, this may mean daily or weekly progress updates from your employee.

Each employee is unique. One style of monitoring may work with one employee but not with another. New and inexperienced employees naturally require more attention and hand-holding than employees who are seasoned at their jobs. Veteran employees don't need the kind of day-to-day attention that less experienced employees need. In fact, they may resent your attempts to closely manage the way in which they carry out their duties.

Effective monitoring of delegation requires the following:

- ✔ **Tailor your approach to the employee.** If your employee performs his or her job with minimal supervision on your part, then establish a system of monitoring with only a few, critical checkpoints along the way. If your employee needs more attention, create a system (formal, in writing, or informal) that incorporates several checkpoints along the way to goal completion.

- ✔ **Diligently use a written or computer-based system for tracking the tasks that you assign to your employees.** Use a daily planner, a calendar, or project-management software to keep track of the what, who, and when of task assignments. Making a commitment to get organized is important.

- ✔ **Keep the lines of communication open.** Make sure your employees understand that you want them to let you know if they can't surmount a problem. Of course, this means making time for your employees when they come by to ask you for help. Find out whether they need more training or better resources. Finding out too early — when you can still do something about it — is better than finding out too late.

- ✔ **Follow through on the agreements that you make with your employees.** If a report is late, hold your employees accountable. Despite the temptation to let these failures slip ("Gee, he's had a rough time at home lately"), ignoring them does both you and your employees a disservice. Make sure your employees understand that the importance of taking personal responsibility for their work and that the ability of your group to achieve its goals depends on their meeting commitments. Be compassionate if your employee has indeed gone through a tough personal challenge (a parent died, a spouse was diagnosed with cancer, and so on) — you may need to assign someone else to cover his or her duties for a short period of time. However, if an employee consistently misses goals and shows no hope of improvement, perhaps that person is in the wrong job.

- ✔ **Reward performance that meets or exceeds your expectations, and counsel performance that falls below your expectations.** If you don't let your employees know when they fail to meet your expectations, they may continue to fail to meet your expectations. Do your employees, your organization, and yourself a big favor and call attention to both the good and the bad that your employees do. Remember the old advice (which happens to be accurate advice) to praise in public and criticize privately. You can find many more details about counseling employees in Chapters 7 and 13.

Top five delegation Web sites

Wondering where to find the best information on the Web about the topics addressed in this chapter? Here are our top five favorites:

✔ The Project Management Hut: `www.pmhut.com/12-rules-of-delegation`

✔ Mind Tools: `www.mindtools.com/pages/article/newLDR_98.htm`

✔ ITtoolkit.com: `www.ittoolkit.com/articles/projects/ease_delegation.htm`

✔ Businessballs.com: `www.businessballs.com/delegation.htm`

✔ Time-Management-Guide.com: `www.time-management-guide.com/delegation-skill.html`

Chapter 12

Communicating Your Message

· ·

In This Chapter

▶ Valuing informal communication over formal communication

▶ Discovering new ways to communicate

▶ Listening to others

▶ Communicating your thoughts in writing

▶ Making effective presentations

▶ Identifying the real side of communication

· ·

Getting your message across to your employees, peers, boss, clients, vendors, and customers is very important in the business world. Conveying that message means you have to be a good communicator — and it's extremely difficult to be an effective manager if you don't communicate well.

The twist is that you have more ways to communicate today than at any other point in the long history of business, and many more avenues are on the way. Just a couple decades ago, managers had only a few different communications skills to master; telephones, letters, face-to-face conversations, and the occasional speech or presentation were about it. Now, however, you have all kinds of exciting and new ways to tell your counterpart on the other side of the world to take a hike. You have e-mail — both on local networks within companies and on the Internet — voice mail, voice pagers, conference calls, teleconferencing, faxes, mobile phones, satellite uplinks, satellite downlinks, and on and on. Certain airlines even offer in-flight Wi-Fi, so you can access the Internet and send and receive e-mail messages from 40,000 feet above Earth.

This chapter is about communicating with others and, in particular, mastering the way in which you do it so that you can become a more effective manager.

Understanding Communication: The Cornerstone of Business

Effective communication is all-important for the growth, survival, and long-term success of today's organizations. The size of the organization doesn't matter — communication must be the cornerstone of every organization.

In business, communication takes place in a variety of formats. Table 12-1 shows the order in which the bulk of business communication occurs, contrasted with the focus of the formal communication training most Americans get in school.

Table 12-1	The Format of Business Communications and Formal Education	
Communication Format	*Frequency of Use*	*Training Provided*
Listening	Most frequent	Little formal training offered
Speaking/Presentation	Next-most frequent	Optional class
Writing	Next-most frequent	4 years English courses
Reading	Least frequent	4 years English courses

As you can see, *informal* communication is more important than *formal* communication in business. Many managers fail because they don't understand this critical point. The occasional speeches you make, the beautifully hand-crafted memos you write, and the articles you read in *The Wall Street Journal* don't have any effect on how you really communicate with your employees. You make a bigger difference when you talk to your employees one-on-one, face-to-face, day in and day out. Listening to them and really hearing what they have to say is vital.

During the past couple decades, business communication has undergone a fundamental change in style. Previously, most business communication — whether verbal or in writing — was formal and constrained. This style matched the older business view that considered workers to be significantly less important to the success of an organization than managers. In this now-obsolete view of business, the formal hierarchy — with bosses ruling strictly over workers — meant everything. If a line worker had an idea to improve customers' lives and save the company money, to boot, that worker had a right way and a wrong way to communicate the idea.

The right way was to write a formal memorandum to the boss. If the boss liked the idea, he passed it up to the next level, and so on until it found its way to the top of the organization. If the big boss liked the idea, the memo — probably rewritten several times by each manager along the way — got the stamp of approval and was passed back down the line for implementation. The process was slow and bureaucratic, but the procedure was "proper."

The wrong way was to skip any of the steps in the formal hierarchy or to make the change without the explicit approval of the powers-that-be. Woe to the employees who strayed outside the approved lines of communication. They were renegades bucking the status quo, and they often found themselves on the way out the door.

Today the "wrong way" of business communication is now the right way. Modern business communication is, above all, informal and nonhierarchical. Fast and furious, up, down, and across the organization. Quick and dirty. Of course, formal communication still has its place — in contracts, licensing agreements, and stern letters to wayward suppliers, for example.

Getting the Message by Being an Active Listener

You're a busy person. You probably have 10 million things on your mind at any given time, but when you don't give the person on the other side of your desk your full attention, you shortchange both you and the other person. Not only do you miss out on getting the message, but your inattention sends its own special message: "I don't really care what you have to say." Is that the message you really want to convey? When you listen actively, you increase the likelihood that you'll understand what the other person is saying — and depending upon what you're talking about, understanding can be quite important.

Don't leave listening to chance. Communication is a two-way street, and you have to do your part. Be an active listener. When someone has something to say to you, make a decision to either participate in the communication or let the other person know that you're busy and have to get back to him later. "Sorry, Tony, I've got to get these numbers together before lunch. Can we get together later this afternoon?" If you decide to communicate, clear your mind of all distractions. Forget for a moment the proposal that has to go out in a few hours, the spreadsheets awaiting your approval, and that growling in the pit of your stomach. Give the other person your full attention.

Of course, making an effort to give someone your full attention is easier said than done. How can you focus on the other person and not be distracted by all the people and tasks vying for your attention? You have a tough job, but someone has to do it. And that someone is you! The following tips may help:

- **Express your interest.** One of the best listening techniques is to be interested in what your counterpart has to say. For example, give your counterpart your full attention and ask questions that clarify what he has to say, such as, "That's really interesting. What brought you to that particular conclusion?" There's no bigger turn-off to communication than for you to yawn, look around the room aimlessly, or otherwise show that you're not interested in what your co-worker is saying. The more interest you show your counterpart, the more interesting that person becomes.

- **Maintain your focus.** People speak at the rate of approximately 150 words per minute. However, people think at approximately 500 words per minute. This gap leaves a lot of room for your mind to wander. Make a point of keeping your mind focused on listening to what the other person has to say. If your mind starts to wander, rein it back in right away. Ask a question or make a comment to get reengaged with the other person.

- **Ask questions.** If something is unclear or doesn't make sense to you, ask questions to clarify the subject. Not only does this practice keep communication efficient and accurate, but it also demonstrates to the speaker that you're interested in what he has to say. *Reflective listening* — summarizing what the speaker has said and repeating it back to him — is a particularly effective way of ensuring accuracy in communication and demonstrating your interest. For example, you can say, "So you mean that it's your belief that we can sell our excess capacity to other firms?"

- **Seek the key points.** What exactly is your counterpart trying to tell you? Anyone can easily get lost in the forest of details of a conversation and, as a result, miss seeing the trees. As you listen, make a point to place what your speaker has to say into two different categories: information that's key to the discussion and information that isn't really relevant. If you need to ask questions to help you decide which is which, don't be shy — ask away! "What does that have to do with meeting our goals?"

- **Avoid interruptions.** Although asking clarifying questions and employing reflective listening techniques is okay, constantly interrupting the speaker or allowing others to do so is not okay. When you're having a conversation with an employee, make him the most important focus in your life at that moment. If someone telephones you, don't answer it — that's what voice mail is for, after all. If someone knocks on your door and asks whether she can interrupt, say no, but offer to talk to her after you finish your current conversation. Of course, if your building is on fire, *then* you may feel free to interrupt the speaker.

✔ **Listen with more than your ears.** Communication involves a lot more than the obvious verbal component. According to communications experts, up to 90 percent of the communication in a typical conversation is nonverbal. Facial expressions, posture, position of arms and legs, and much more add up to the nonverbal component of communication. Therefore, you must use all your senses when you listen — not just your ears.

✔ **Take notes.** Remembering all the details of an important conversation hours, days, or weeks after it took place can be quite difficult. Be sure to take notes when necessary. Jotting down notes can be a terrific aid to listening and remembering what other people said. Plus, when you review your notes later, you can take the time to organize what was said and make better sense of it.

Practicing the preceding listening habits helps you understand the message and lets your co-workers know that you consider them important enough to give them your full attention. You do consider them to be an important part of your organization, don't you? Listen early and often.

Harnessing the Power of the Written Word

At first glance, you may think that all these new ways of communicating have made the written word less important. Nothing is farther from the truth. Indeed, instead of making the written word less important, these new ways of communicating have actually increased the variety of written media at your beck and call, and increased the speed at which the written word travels. Writing well in business is more important than ever — you need to write concisely and with impact.

Regardless of whether you're writing a one-paragraph e-mail message or a 100-page report for your boss, all business writing shares common characteristics. Review the following list of writing tips and don't forget to practice these tips every opportunity you get. The more you write, the better you get at it. So write, write, and then write some more.

✔ **Get to the point.** Before you set pen to paper (or fingertip to keyboard), think about exactly what you want to achieve. What information are you trying to convey, and what do you want the reader to do as a result? Who is your audience, and how can you best reach it?

✔ **Get organized.** Organize your thoughts before you start to write. Jotting down a few notes or creating a brief outline of your major points may be beneficial. Bounce your ideas off co-workers and business associates, or find other ways to refine them and get the all-important reality check.

✔ **Write the same way you speak.** Written communication and spoken communication have a lot more in common than many people think; the best writing most closely resembles normal, everyday speech. Writing that is too formal or stilted is less accessible and harder to understand than conversational writing. Although this doesn't mean that you should start using slang like *gonna* and *ain't* in your reports and memos, it does mean you should loosen up!

✔ **Make it brief and concise.** Write every word with a purpose. Make your point, support it, and then move on to the next point. Don't —repeat, don't — fill your memos, letters, and other correspondence with needless fluff simply to give them more weight or to make them seem more impressive. The only person you'll impress is *you.* If you can make your point in three sentences, don't write three paragraphs or three pages to accomplish the same goal.

✔ **Keep it simple.** Simplicity is a virtue. Avoid the tendency to use a word that most people would need to look up in a dictionary to understand when a simpler one works. Don't use cryptic acronyms and jargon that mean nothing outside of a small circle of industry insiders; replace them with more common terminology whenever possible.

✔ **Write and then rewrite.** Few writers can get their thoughts into writing perfectly on the first try. The best approach is to write your first draft without worrying too much about whether you've completed it perfectly. Next, read through your draft and edit it for content, flow, grammar, and readability. Keep polishing your work until it shines. However, keep in mind that there is such a thing as too much editing. Balance the desire for perfection with the very real need to get things done. Too much editing and too much time spent reviewing and revising causes inefficiency.

✔ **Convey a positive attitude.** No one likes to read negative memos, letters, reports, or other business writing. Instead of making the intended points with intended targets, negative writing often only reflects poorly on its author, and the message gets lost in the noise. Be active, committed, and positive in your writing. Even when you convey bad news, your writing can indicate that a silver lining follows even the worst storm.

If you're interested in developing better writing skills, you can find plenty of books to help. However, coauthor Peter stills swears by the timeworn 1971-vintage printing of *The Elements of Style,* by William Strunk, Jr., and E. B. White, which he bought in seventh grade. The book's advice is timeless, the writing direct and compelling. Consider Rule 13:

Omit needless words. Vigorous writing is concise. A sentence should contain no unnecessary words, a paragraph no unnecessary sentences, for the same reason that a drawing should have no unnecessary lines and a machine no unnecessary parts. This requires not that the writer make all his sentences short, or that he avoid all detail and treat his subjects only in outline, but that every word tell.

Making Presentations

Although many people dread the idea of standing up in front of a group of people — especially a large group of people they don't know — and making a speech, the ability to give oral presentations, speeches, and the like is a key skill for managers. Whether you already know the value of being able to give effective presentations or you're a new manager with relatively little experience presenting to others, this section guides you through the process of putting together and giving an effective presentation to employees.

Preparing to present

When you see great speakers or presenters in action, you may think that because of their extraordinary skill, making a presentation takes little preparation. This is kind of like saying that because an Olympic gymnast makes her floor routine look so perfect and so easy, she never has to practice it. What you don't see are the years of almost daily preparation that lead to her 90 seconds of glory.

Preparation is the key to giving a great presentation. The following tips can help you in preparing your presentation:

- ✔ **Determine what you want to accomplish.** Briefly outline the goals of your presentation. What exactly do you want to accomplish? Are you trying to convince decision makers that they should give you a bigger budget or extend your deadline to design a product that actually works? Are you seeking to educate your audience or to train employees in a new procedure? Are you presenting awards to employees in a formal ceremony? Each kind of presentation requires a different approach; tailor your approach accordingly.

- ✔ **Develop the heart of your presentation.** Build an outline of the major points that you want to communicate to your audience. Under each point, note any subpoints that are important to support your presentation. Don't try to accomplish too much; limit your major points to no more than a few. Sketch out any visual aids (if any) that you need to reinforce and communicate the ideas you're presenting verbally.

✔ **Write the introduction and conclusion.** When you finish the heart of your presentation, you can decide on your introduction and conclusion. Make the introduction accomplish three goals:

- Tell your audience members what they're going to gain from your presentation.

- Tell your audience members why the presentation is important to them.

- Get your audience's attention.

The conclusion is just as important, as is the final punctuation — the period — of your presentation. Write your conclusion to accomplish three objectives:

- Briefly summarize your key points.

- Refer your listeners back to the introduction.

- Inspire your audience.

✔ **Prepare your notes.** Preparing notes to use as an aid in your presentation is always a good idea. Not only are notes a confidence builder that can help you find your way when you get lost, but they also ensure that you cover all the topics that you planned to cover. Write brief but specific notes. The idea is for notes to trigger your thoughts on each key point and subpoint, not to be a word-for-word script.

✔ **Practice makes perfect.** After you sketch out your presentation, practice it. Depending on your personal situation, you may be comfortable simply running through your notes a few times the night before the big event. Alternately, you may want to rehearse your presentation in front of a co-worker or even a video camera so that you can review it at your leisure. Don't forget, the more presentations you make, the better you get at giving them.

Make the most of the time you have before your presentation. Preparation and practice pay off in a big way when it comes time to get up in front of your audience and start your performance.

Making an impact with pictures

Studies show that approximately 85 percent of all information the human brain receives is garnered visually. Think about that statistic the next time you make a presentation. Your spoken remarks may convey a lot of valuable information, but your audience is likely to remember more of the information when you present it to them visually.

Consider the following example. Peter was called to make a presentation to his company's executive team. His task was to present the most recent financial performance of the company's Western Group. Faced with piles of financial data stacked high to the ceiling, Peter realized that he had to find a way to present the essence of his message without getting himself and his audience lost in the details.

Figure 12-1 illustrates what some of the financial data looked like in a spreadsheet format. As a little extra incentive, Peter had seen what happened to managers who tried to present and explain lots of numbers: They tripped over their tongues and then lost their way. Not a pretty sight!

Western Group Financials

	Past Year	Current Year
Direct Labor	$19,887,000	$21,896,000
Fringe Benefits	$7,504,000	$8,259,000
Overhead Applied	$9,945,000	$10,938,000
Cost of Money	$13,000	$14,000
Travel	$2,801,000	$1,952,000
Other Direct Cost	$278,000	$356,000
G&A Applied	$4,973,000	$5,475,000
Total	$45,401,000	$48,890,000

Figure 12-1: Financial data in spreadsheet format.

So instead of developing an extensive spoken presentation, Peter had his controller develop a simple bar graph that summarized the piles of financial information visually. The graph compared current-year performance against past-year performance, and it contained only the information essential to decision makers. Figure 12-2 shows the vastly improved bar graph version of the same financial information that appears in Figure 12-1.

When Peter made his presentation, he kept his remarks brief, concentrating instead on walking his audience through the bar graphs. Sure, Peter could have given a highly detailed presentation of the numbers, but the results would have been more talk and less communication, a lot of wasted time, and a very numb group of executives! Instead, by using a simple visual presentation, Peter helped his audience grasp his message quickly and easily, and they concentrated on the message instead of the medium.

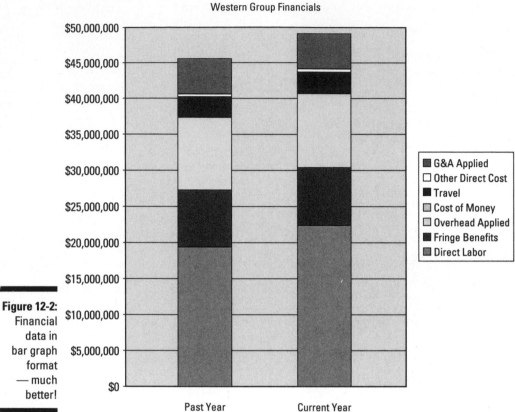

Figure 12-2:
Financial
data in
bar graph
format
— much
better!

The Nelson/Economy axiom of visual learning is

> If you don't see it, you can't believe it (and you sure won't remember it!).

Whenever possible, add visual elements to your presentation. The following are just a few of your options:

- ✔ Charts
- ✔ Displays
- ✔ Graphs
- ✔ Maps
- ✔ Photographs
- ✔ Product samples

✔ Prototypes

✔ Role plays

Presentation tools, visual aids, and other props serve several purposes. First, they convey your information much more quickly than do your spoken words. Second, people retain visual information longer than other kinds of information. Finally, presentation tools, visual aids, and other such props give your audience a welcome break from your oral presentation.

Consider using the following presentation tools and props whenever possible:

✔ **PowerPoint:** For presentations in front of large groups, computer projections — most often coupling a laptop computer with a high-power liquid crystal display (LCD) projector and the Microsoft PowerPoint software program — are the choice of the pros (just ask coauthor Bob!). Not only are presentations crystal clear, but you can easily fit one or more complete presentations into your laptop computer and carry it with you anywhere. One danger with computer presentations, however, is that if your computer goes on the fritz or your destination has no suitable projector to hook your computer to, your presentation is going to be notably absent. On more than a few occasions, Bob has flown many thousands of miles to make a PowerPoint presentation from his laptop computer and at the last minute discovered that his client hadn't arranged for an LCD projector in advance. Unfortunately, when this happened, Bob had no way to fix the problem, and he had to make his presentation without his visual aids.

✔ **Flip charts/whiteboards:** If you're presenting to a smaller group — say, up to about 30 people — flip charts and whiteboards are a handy way to present visual information. Flip charts are those big pads of paper that you can hang from an easel at the front of the room. You can set up your whole presentation on the flip charts before your presentation and, as with transparencies, scribble notes on them for emphasis as you speak. Throw in a dash of fun (oh, boy!) by using different colors of markers throughout.

✔ **Handouts:** Giving your audience handouts of the information you plan to cover — either before or after your presentation, depending on your personal preference — can be an effective way to ensure that they get your message.

Don't fall victim to the practice of providing handouts and then reading directly from them, word for word. Nothing is more boring to an audience than following a presenter's handouts as he or she reads through pages and pages of text. *Just say no!*

When using visual aids, keep the following advice in mind to ensure a happy audience:

✔ **Don't try to jam too much information into each of your aids.** Keep the type large, limit the words and numbers used, and add color for emphasis only when appropriate.

✔ **Have everything ready well in advance of your presentation.** Don't start your presentation by spending five minutes fumbling to set up your projector or paging through a disorganized stack of transparencies. This flustering doesn't impress your audience — and it doesn't bolster your self-confidence, either. Get everything set up well before you take the stage. Also make sure that your electronics, sound, lights, and other tools are working before you find out otherwise at a key point in your presentation. If someone else is going to run your audio-video presentation while you're speaking, touch base with her beforehand and make sure she's got everything she needs. You might even consider doing a couple of dry runs to ensure everything goes off without a hitch. *Remember:* You have only one chance to make a first impression!

✔ **Don't forget that you're the center of attention — not your visual aids.** Use visual aids to support your presentation — don't use your presentation to support your visual aids.

Delivering your presentation

The waiting is over and your audience is gathered, raptly waiting to hear the pearls of wisdom that you're going to fling all about the room. At this point, all your hours of preparation pay off. Follow these steps as you begin your presentation:

✔ **Relax!** What do you have to be nervous about? You're thoroughly prepared for your presentation. Your notes are in order, your visual aids are positioned and ready to go, and your audience is sincerely interested in what you have to say. As you wait for the presentation to start, breathe deeply and stay alert.

✔ **Greet your audience members.** One of the pluses of arriving early is that you can welcome the individual audience members as they arrive. Not only does this practice establish an initial level of rapport and interest, but getting a chance to talk to your audience members before you launch into your presentation helps you feel more at ease in front of the group.

✔ **Listen closely to your introduction.** Make sure that the facts are accurate, and listen for comments that you can incorporate into your initial remarks. For example, if the individual who introduces you mentions that you're both a brilliant manager and an avid skier, you can work a humorous anecdote about skiing into the beginning of your presentation.

✔ **Wait for your audience's attention.** As a presenter, you must capture the full attention of your audience. One particularly effective technique is to stand in front of your audience and say nothing until everyone's attention is focused on you.

✔ **Make your presentation:** Start at the beginning, finish when you're done, and have fun with everything in between! This presentation really is your opportunity to shine — make the most of it!

Scrutinizing Communication: What's Real and What's Not

One of the best ways to determine how well you fit into an organization is to see how well you communicate. But deciphering the *real* meaning of communication in an organization takes some practice. How do you determine the real meaning of words in your organization? You can best get to the underlying meanings by observing behavior, reading between the lines, and, when necessary, knowing how to obtain sensitive information.

Believing actions, not words

One way to decipher the real meaning of communication is to pay close attention to the corresponding behavior of the communicator. The values and priorities (that is, the ethics) of others tend to come through more clearly in what they do than in what they say.

For example, if your manager repeatedly says he's trying to get approval for a raise for you, look at what actions he has taken toward that end. Did he make a call to his boss or hold a meeting? Did he submit the necessary paperwork or establish a deadline to accomplish this goal? If the answers to these questions are no, or if he's continually waiting to hear, the action is probably going nowhere fast. To counter this situation, try to get higher up on your boss's list of priorities by suggesting actions that he can take to get you your raise. You may find that you need to do some or all of the footwork yourself. Alternatively, your manager's actions may indicate that your boss is not a power player in the organization. If so, make a point to attract the attention of the power players in your organization who can help you get the raise you deserve.

Reading between the lines

In business, don't take the written word at face value. Probe to find out the real reasons behind what is written. For example, here's a typical notice in a company newsletter announcing the reorganization of several departments:

> With the departure of J. R. McNeil, the Marketing Support and Customer Service department will now be a part of the Sales and Administration division under Elizabeth Olsen, acting vice president. The unit will eventually be moved under the direct supervision of the sales director, Tom Hutton.

Such an announcement in the company newsletter may seem to be straightforward on the surface, but if you read between the lines, you may be able to conclude some interesting information:

> J. R. McNeil, who never did seem to get along with the director of sales, finally did something bad enough to justify getting fired. Tom Hutton apparently made a successful bid with the board of directors to add the area to his empire, probably because his sales were up 30 percent from last year. Elizabeth Olsen will be assigned the acting vice president for an interim period to do some of Tom's dirty work by clearing out some of the deadwood. Tom will thus start with a clean slate, 20 percent lower expenses, and an almost guaranteed increase in profits for his first year in the job. This all fits very nicely with Tom's personal strategy for advancement. *(P.S.: A congratulatory call to Tom may be in order.)*

Announcements like these have been reworked dozens of times by so many people that they appear to be logical and valid when you initially read them. By reading between the lines, however, you can often determine what's really going on. Of course, you have to be careful not to jump to the wrong conclusions. J. R. may have simply gone on to better opportunities and the company has taken advantage of that event to reorganize. Be sure to validate your conclusions with others in the company to get the real story.

Probing for information

In general, you can get ongoing information about your organization by being a trusted listener to as many people as possible. Show sincere interest in the affairs of others, and they'll talk about themselves openly. After they begin talking, you can shift the topic to work, work problems, and eventually more sensitive topics. Ask encouraging questions and volunteer information as necessary to keep the exchange equitable. Managers should also research their company, attend all company update meetings, and read the company's Web site (press releases, annual report, and so forth) to validate information they're hearing.

Even after you've developed such trusted relationships, you need to know how to probe to uncover the facts about rumors, decisions, and hidden agendas. Start by adhering to the following guidelines:

- Check the information through two sources.
- Promise anonymity whenever possible.
- Generally know the answers to the questions you ask.
- Be casual and nonthreatening in your approach.
- Assume that the initial answer is superficial.
- Ask the same question different ways.
- Be receptive to whatever information you're given.

One more thing to consider: Every organization has its share of politics, but spending too much time worrying about it is certainly counterproductive, and it can't be good for your well-being. While you can't avoid politics on the job, you should avoid being drawn into this situation. Getting caught up in office politics decreases efficiency and may create a negative perception of you with others in the organization.

Top five communication Web sites

Wondering where to find the best information on the Web about the topics addressed in this chapter? Here are our top five favorites:

- Business Communication Headline News: `www.businesscommunication blog.com/blog`

- Presentations.com: `www.presenta tions.com`

- Business Exchange: `bx.business week.com/business-communica tions`

- Business Communications Resources: `www.writerswrite.com/busi nesscommunications/links.htm`

- AltaVista translation services: `babel fish.altavista.com`

Chapter 13

The Fine Art of Performance Evaluations

● ●

In This Chapter

▶ Considering the importance of performance evaluations

▶ Developing performance evaluations

▶ Avoiding evaluation mistakes

▶ Making evaluations better

● ●

*T*imely and accurate performance evaluations are an important tool for every business manager or supervisor. So why do most managers and supervisors dread doing them, and why do so many employees dread receiving them? According to studies on the topic, an estimated 40 percent of all workers never receive performance evaluations. At all. Ever. And for the 60 percent of the workers who do receive performance evaluations, most evaluations are poorly done. Very few employees actually receive regular, formal performance evaluations that are thoughtful, complete, and beneficial to the employee.

Ask any human resources manager whether formal performance evaluations are really necessary. The answer you get will likely be a resounding "Yes!" However, if you look a little below the surface, the reality may echo something quite different. Although most managers consider performance evaluations a necessary tool in developing their employees, reinforcing good performance, and correcting poor performance, these evaluations are often too little, too late. They miss the mark as tools for developing employees and for requesting their employees' input on how they're doing and what they need. If performance evaluations are done poorly, managers are better off not doing them at all — especially if the alternative is more frequent coaching.

In this chapter, we consider the benefits of performance evaluations and explore the right and wrong ways to do them.

Evaluating Performance: Why Bother?

You can find many good reasons for conducting regular formal performance evaluations with your employees. Formal performance evaluations are just one part of an organization's system of delegation, goal setting, coaching, motivating, and ongoing informal and formal feedback on employee performance. Performance evaluations provide the following positive opportunities:

- ✔ **A chance to summarize past performance and establish new performance goals:** All employees want to know whether they're doing a good job. Formal performance evaluations force managers to communicate performance results — both good and bad — to their employees and to set new goals. In many organizations, the annual performance evaluation is the only occasion when supervisors and managers speak to their employees about performance expectations and the results of employee efforts for the preceding evaluation period.

- ✔ **An opportunity for clarification and communication:** You need to constantly compare expectations with your employees. Performance evaluations help the employer and employee compare notes and make sure that assignments and priorities are in order.

Try this exercise with your own manager: List your ten most important activities, and then ask your manager to list your ten most important activities. Surprise! Chances are, your lists are quite different. On average, this exercise reveals that employee and manager lists overlap only 40 percent, at best.

- ✔ **A forum for planning goals and career development:** In many organizations, career development takes place as a part of the formal performance evaluation process. Managers and employees are all busy folks and often have difficulty setting aside the time to sit down and chart out the steps they must take to progress in an organization or career. Although career-development discussions should generally take place in a forum separate from the performance evaluation process, combining the activities does afford the opportunity to kill both birds with the same stone, or something like that.

- ✔ **A formal documentation to promote advancement or dismissal:** Most employees get plenty of informal performance feedback — at least, of the negative kind. "You did what? Are you nuts?" Most informal feedback is verbal and, as such, undocumented. If you're trying to build a case to give your employee a promotion, you can support your case much easier if you have plenty of written documentation (including formal performance evaluations) to justify your decision.

Many companies have paid a lot of money to employees and former employees who have successfully sued them for wrongful termination or for other biased employment decisions. In many cases, employees were able to successfully sue their employers because either they conducted no performance evaluations with them or their manager gave them good performance ratings when, in fact, their performance was not good.

Spelling Out the Performance Evaluation Process

Believe it or not, one of your most important jobs as a manager is to conduct accurate and timely performance evaluations of your employees. As the old saying goes, feedback is the breakfast of champions — make it a regular part of your management diet!

Many managers tend to see the performance evaluation process in narrow terms and want to get it done as quickly as possible so they can get back to their real jobs (whatever their "real" jobs are as managers). In their haste to get the evaluation done and behind them, many managers merely consider a few examples of recent performance and base their entire evaluation on them. And because few managers give their employees the kind of meaningful, ongoing performance feedback that they need to do their jobs better, the performance evaluation can become a dreaded event full of surprises and dismay. On the other hand, it can be so sugar-coated that it becomes a meaningless exercise in management. This scenario isn't the right way to evaluate your employees!

The performance appraisal process is much broader than just the formal, written part of it. Five steps can help you encompass the broader scope of the process. Follow them when you evaluate your employees' performance:

1. **Set goals, expectations, and standards.**

   Before your employees can achieve your goals or perform to your expectations, you have to set goals and expectations with them and develop standards to measure their performance. After you've done all this, you have to communicate the goals and expectations *before* you evaluate your employees — not afterward. In fact, the performance review really starts on the first day of work! Tell your employees right then how you evaluate them, show them the forms to be used, and explain the process. (We cover goal setting in detail in Chapter 6.)

Make sure that job descriptions are clear and unambiguous, and that you and your employees understand and agree to the standards you've set for them. This is a two-way process. Make sure that employees have a voice in setting their goals and standards, and that they're comfortable coming to you if anything is unclear or is a concern.

2. Give continuous and specific feedback.

Catch your employees doing things right — every day of the week — and tell them about it then and there. And if you catch them doing wrong (after all, nobody's perfect), let them know about that, too. Feedback is much more effective when you give it regularly and often than when you save it for a special occasion (known as *gunnysacking,* if the feedback is negative). The best formal performance evaluations contain the fewest surprises.

Not only does gunnysacking have little effect on getting the performance you want out of your employees, but it also can cost you their respect in the process.

3. Prepare a formal, written performance evaluation with your employee.

Every organization has different requirements for the formal performance evaluation. Some evaluations are simple, one-page forms that simply require checking off a few boxes; others are multipage extravaganzas that require extensive narrative support. The form often varies by organization and the level of the employee being evaluated. Regardless of the requirements of your particular organization, the formal performance evaluation should be a summary of the goals and expectations for the evaluation period — events that you have discussed previously (and frequently!) with your employees. Support your words with examples and make evaluations meaningful to your employees by keeping your discussion relevant to the goals, expectations, and standards that you developed in Step 1.

For a more collaborative process, have employees complete their own performance evaluation. Then compare your comments with the employee's comments. The differences that you find become topics of discussion and mutual goal setting.

4. Meet personally with your employees to discuss the performance evaluation.

Most employees appreciate the personal touch when you give the evaluation. Set aside some quality time to meet with them to discuss their performance evaluation. This doesn't mean five or ten minutes, but at least an hour — or maybe more! When you plan performance appraisal meetings, less is definitely not more. Pick a place that's comfortable and free of distractions. Make the meeting positive and upbeat. Even when you have to discuss performance problems, center your discussions on ways you and your employees can work together to solve them.

Often performance appraisals and discussions can become defensive as negative elements are raised and employees start to feel that they will get little or no raise. Start with letting the employee share how the job is going and what's working — and what's not. Then share your version, starting with the positive. Be sure to include feedback that they or their clients have given you as well.

5. **Set new goals, expectations, and standards.**

   The performance evaluation meeting gives you and your employees the opportunity to step back from the inevitable daily issues for a moment and take a look at the big picture. You both have an opportunity to review and discuss what worked well and what didn't. Based on this assessment, you can then set new goals, expectations, and standards for the next review period. The last step of the performance evaluation process becomes the first step, and you start all over again.

When it comes to conducting performance appraisals, managers have plenty of points to remember. Consider a few more:

- ✔ Frequently communicate with employees so there are no surprises (okay, *fewer* surprises). Give your employees informal feedback on their performance early and often.

- ✔ Keep the primary focus of performance appraisals on moving forward — setting new goals and improving future performance — more than looking back. Your employees can't change the past, but they can (and should) learn from it.

- ✔ Always include learning and development as part of the performance appraisal process (although sometimes a discussion about pay raises can be separate).

Doing the Right Prep Work

From our experience, employee evaluation rarely is done well. Not only do managers write evaluations that lack meaningful examples and insights, but they also fail to give the main process of the performance evaluation — the discussion — the time and attention it deserves. Furthermore, performance evaluation meetings often become one-way presentations, from manager to employee, instead of two-way discussions or conversations. As a result, performance evaluations often fail to have the kind of impact on employees that the managers and supervisors who gave them intended.

Real apprehension can surround the evaluation process from both sides of the equation. Often managers don't feel up to the task, and workers don't get the kind of timely and quality feedback they need to do the best job possible. In addition, an underlying tension often accompanies the performance evaluation process and comes from the fact that most companies tie money and pay raises to performance evaluations. Evaluations frequently focus on the pay — or the lack thereof — instead of on the performance.

The entire process consists of setting goals with your employees, monitoring their performance, coaching them, supporting them, counseling them, and providing continuous feedback on their performance — both good and bad. If you've been doing these things before you sit down for your annual or semiannual performance evaluation session with your employees, you'll find reviews to be a pleasant wrap-up and a look at past accomplishments instead of a disappointment for both you and your employees.

Preparing for the no-surprises evaluation

If you're doing your job as a manager, the evaluation holds no surprises for your employees. Follow the lead of the best managers: Keep in touch with your employees and give them continuous feedback on their progress. Then when you do sit down with them for their formal performance evaluation, the session becomes a recap of what you've already discussed during the evaluation period instead of an ambush. Keeping up a continuous dialogue lets you use the formal evaluation to focus on the positive points that you and your employees can work on together to get the best possible performance.

Above all, be prepared for your employee evaluations!

As with interviews, many managers leave their preparation for performance evaluation meetings till the last possible minute — often just before the employee is scheduled to meet with them. "Oh, no. Cathy is going to be here in five minutes. Now, what did I do with her file? I know it's here somewhere!" The average manager spends about one hour preparing for an employee review that required an entire year of performance.

Although the performance evaluation process itself is pretty simple, a lot more goes into it than filling out a three-page form that you get once a year to justify a salary action and then meeting with your employees for 15 minutes to give them the results of your assessment. Performance evaluation is a year-round job that doesn't end until, through transfer, promotion, or termination, employees move out of your sphere of responsibility. Whenever you recognize a problem with your employees' performance, mention it to them, make a note of it, and drop it in your employees' files. Similarly, whenever your employees do something great, mention it to them, make a note of it, and drop it in their files. Then when you're ready to do your employees' periodic performance evaluations, you can pull their files and have plenty of documentation available on which to base the evaluations. Not only does this practice make the process easier for you, but it also makes the evaluation a lot more meaningful and productive for your employees.

Don't be one of the many managers who fail to give their employees ongoing performance feedback and instead wait for the scheduled review. Despite your best intentions — and the best efforts of your employees — assignments can easily go astray. Schedules can stretch, roadblocks can stop progress, and confusion can wrap its ugly tentacles around a project. However, if you haven't set up systems to track the progress of your employees, you may not identify this oversight until it's too late. You end up mad, and your employees are forced to bear the brunt of it.

Avoiding common evaluation mistakes

Evaluators can easily fall into certain traps in the evaluation process. To avoid making a misstep that may result in getting your foot stuck in one of these traps, keep in mind these common mistakes:

- ✔ **The halo effect:** When an employee is so good in one particular performance area, you may be tempted to ignore problems in other areas of performance. For example, you may give your star salesperson (whom your firm desperately needs to ensure continued revenue growth) a high rating (a halo) despite the fact that she refuses to complete and submit company-required paperwork within required time limits.

- ✔ **The recency effect:** The opposite of the halo effect, the recency effect happens when you allow one instance of poor performance to adversely affect your assessment of an employee's overall performance. For example, your administrative assistant may have done a good job for you in the months preceding his evaluation, but last week he missed a customer's deadline for submitting a proposal to continue with their advertising account. Your firm lost the account, and you give your assistant a scathing performance evaluation as a result.

- ✔ **Stereotyping:** In this pitfall, you allow preconceived notions about your employees to dictate how you rate them. For example, you may be convinced that women make better electronic parts assemblers than do men. As a result, your stereotyping automatically gives female employees the benefit of the doubt and higher ratings, whereas men have to prove themselves before you take them seriously.

- ✔ **Comparing:** Often when you rate two employees at the same time, you can be tempted to compare their performances. If one of the employees is a particularly high performer, your other employee may look bad in comparison, regardless of the individual level of performance. Conversely, if one of the employees is a particularly low performer, the other employee may look really good in comparison. Make sure your assessment of an individual employee's performance can stand on its own two feet and isn't subject to how good or bad your other employees are.

✔ **Mirroring:** Everyone naturally likes people who are most like themselves. You can easily fall into the trap of rating highly employees who are most like you (same likes, dislikes, interests, hobbies, and so forth) and giving a lower rating to employees who are least like you. Although this is great for the employees you favor, the employees you don't favor understandably won't like it. Take some advice: Don't do it.

✔ **Nice guy/gal:** One reason many managers dread doing performance evaluations is that it forces them to acknowledge the failings of their employees and then talk to their employees about them. Few managers enjoy giving their employees bad news, but employees need to receive the bad news as well as the good (just be ready to duck when you give them the bad news). Otherwise, they won't know where they need to improve. And if they don't know where they need to improve, you can bet they won't.

Turning the tables: Upward and 360-degree evaluations

In recent years, a new kind of performance evaluation has emerged. Unlike the typical downward evaluation in which managers review their workers' performance, the upward evaluation process stands this convention on its head by requiring workers to evaluate their managers' performance. If you think that getting a performance evaluation from your manager is uncomfortable, you haven't seen anything yet. Nothing is quite like the feeling you get when a group of your employees gives you direct and honest feedback about the things you do that make it hard for them to do a good job.

However, despite the discomfort you may feel, the upward evaluation is invaluable — who better to assess your real impact on the organization than your employees? The system works so well that Fortune 500 companies such as Federal Express and others have institutionalized the upward evaluation and made it a part of their corporate cultures. More than 15 percent of American firms are using some form of the upward performance evaluation to assess the performance of their managers.

Also popular is the 360-degree evaluation, which companies such as Levi Strauss & Co. and Boeing Co use. Levi's 360-degree evaluation process dictates that all employees must be evaluated by their supervisors and by their underlings and peers. The results can be quite a surprise to the employee who is the subject of the evaluation, who may find that other employees see him as less caring and visionary than he initially thought.

Of course, 360-degree feedback needs to be confidential, and that's difficult in smaller departments or where unique feedback can be tracked directly back to its originator. If a company embarks on this approach, managers need to clearly communicate the need and value of 360-degree evaluations, and make the process a positive one. If you don't set your employees' expectations and tell them exactly how the feedback will be used, you run the risk of setting up the process to be a negative and scary one for your employees.

Chapter 14

Budgeting, Accounting, and Other Financial Stuff

. . . .

In This Chapter

▶ Creating your budget

▶ Applying professional budget tricks

▶ Understanding accounting basics

▶ Interpreting financial statements

. . . .

*I*n any organization, money makes the world go 'round. No matter how great your department is, how exciting your products are, or what a fabulous bunch of workers you employ, you and your group are in serious jeopardy if you don't have the money you need to keep your business in business. If profits are down and money is increasingly tight in your organization, you'd better take some immediate actions to correct the situation (or revise your résumé and warm up your personal network of business contacts).

As a manager, you need to understand the basics of budgeting and accounting. When your co-workers start throwing around terms such as "labor budget," "cash flow," "income statement," and "balance sheet," don't you want to do more than simply nod your head and respond with a blank stare? Here's some good news: You don't need an MBA to grasp these basics.

In this chapter, we cover the importance of budgeting in an organization, as well as putting together a budget by using some of the professional tricks of the budget trade. We then introduce the survival basics of accounting. We aren't going to make you an accountant, but this chapter can help remove that quizzical look that appears on your face every time someone starts talking balance sheets or cash flow.

Note: Although you may currently work for a governmental entity or non-profit organization, and some of these concepts may not directly apply to you right now, you never know when you may find yourself in a new, private-sector job.

Exploring the Wonderful World of Budgets

A *budget* is an itemized forecast of an individual or company's income and expenses expected for some period in the future. Budgets provide the baseline of expected performance against which managers measure actual performance. Accounting systems that generate reports to compare expected performance against actual performance provide financial information on an organization's actual performance. With this information, managers with budget responsibility act as physicians to assess the current financial health of their businesses.

Imagine that when you read the latest accounting report, it says that sales are too low compared to budget. As a responsible manager, you need to figure out what that means and why it has happened; identifying key trends is the duty of most managers. Are prices too high? Maybe your sales force is having problems getting the product delivered to your customers in a timely fashion. Or perhaps your competition developed a new thingamajig that is taking sales away from your product. Are labor costs exceeding your budget? Perhaps your employees are working too much overtime. Maybe a reduction in quality has led to an increase in the amount of rework required. Or perhaps the employee pay mix simply is too high for the work being done.

Because change is the norm in today's global business environment, why bother having budgets? You go through all that work and then your budget is out-of-date the day after you finish it, right? Sure, planning becomes more difficult as the world changes all around you, but plan you must. Without plans and goals — and the budgets necessary to support them — your organization lacks focus and its resources are wasted as employees wander without focus. A budget isn't just an educated guess that reflects your organization's plans and allows you to act on them; it's a manager's personal commitment to make a designated future happen. The best budgets are flexible, allowing for changes in different key assumptions, such as revenue results.

Experienced managers already know the importance of budgets. Budgets allow business plans to become realities, and creating and administering them is an essential part of most managers' jobs. Through interaction with frontline managers during the budgeting process, upper management can have a tremendous impact on the direction an organization and its employees take. Conversely, rank-and-file employees can also have a huge impact on the organization during the budgeting process by submitting budget requests to management for discussion and approval. And in an increasing number of enlightened organizations today, employees are given the authority they need to make decisions for themselves as issues and opportunities arise, along with the ability to create and monitor their own budgets.

Budgets determine how many people you have on your staff and how much you pay them. Budgets determine the financial resources you have to improve your workplace or to buy necessary office equipment, such as computers and copiers. And budgets determine how much money you have available to support key projects. Furthermore, budgets allow you to use all that expensive spreadsheet software that the company bought last year.

But budgets also fulfill another important purpose: They provide a baseline against which you can measure your progress toward business goals. For example, if you're 50 percent of the way through your fiscal year but have actually spent 75 percent of your budgeted operating funds, then you have an immediate indication that a potential problem exists if you don't see any significant change in your expenditures. Either you've underbudgeted your expenses for the year or you're overspending. Whenever budgeted performance and actual performance disagree, or are in *variance,* the job of the responsible manager is to ask why — and to then fix any problems.

Depending on your organization's size, the budgeting process may be quite simple or, alternatively, very complex. Regardless of an organization's size, however, you can budget for anything needed to run your department. Following are some examples:

- ✔ **Sales budget:** The sales budget is an estimate of the total number of products or services that will be sold in a given period. Determine the total revenues by multiplying the number of units by the price per unit.

- ✔ **Labor budget:** Labor budgets consist of the number and name of all the various positions in a company, along with the salary or wages budgeted for each position.

- ✔ **Production budget:** The production budget translates the figures from the sales budget and its estimate of quantities of units to be sold, and comes up with the cost of labor, material, and other expenses required to produce them.

- ✔ **Expense budget:** Expense budgets contain all the different expenses that a department may incur during the normal course of operations. You budget travel, training, office supplies, and more as expenses.

- ✔ **Capital budget:** This budget is a manager's plan to acquire *fixed assets* (anything your organization owns that has a long useful life), such as furniture, computers, facilities, physical plant, and so forth, to support the operations of a business.

Making a Budget

You have a right and a wrong way to create a budget. The wrong way is simply to make a photocopy of the last budget and submit it as your new budget. The right way is to gather information from as many sources as possible, review and check the information for accuracy, and then use your good judgment to make your best educated guess at what the future may bring. A budget is a *forecast* — a commitment to the future — and is only as good as the data that goes into it and the good judgment that you bring to the process.

So how do you actually put together a budget? Where does the information come from? With whom should you talk? The possibilities seem endless. However, experienced managers know that when you understand your costs of doing business — and where they come from — the budgeting process is actually quite simple. Make a few phone calls. Have a couple meetings. Look over some recent accounting reports. Crunch a few numbers. Bingo! Your budget is complete! Well, your budget may have a little more to it than that. Review these basic steps in putting together a budget:

1. **Closely review your budgeting documents and instructions.**

   Take a close look at the budgeting documents that you're working with and read any instructions that your accounting staff provides with them. Although your organization may have done something the same way for years, you never know when that procedure may change.

   Back when he used to work in a regular, 9-to-5 job (now he's a 24/7 kind of guy), Peter spent more hours than he likes to admit preparing an annual budget for his organization's liability and property insurance — something that he'd routinely done year after year. One year, he spent a lot of time preparing the budget as he always had, only to realize after finishing the job — and after reading the new budget instructions — that the responsibility for that particular task had moved to a different manager. *Oops!*

2. **Meet with staff.**

   When you're starting the budget process, meet with your staff members to solicit their input. In some cases, you need the specific input of your employees to forecast accurately. For example, you may need to know how many trips your salespeople plan to make next year and where they plan to go. In other cases, you can simply ask for employee suggestions. One employee may ask you to include a pay increase in the next budget. Another may inform you that the current phone system is no longer adequate to meet the needs of employees and customers and that a new one needs to be budgeted. Whichever the case, your staff can provide you with useful and important budget information.

3. **Gather data.**

   Pull copies of previous budgets and accounting reports, and then compare budgeted numbers to actual numbers. Were previous budgets managed effectively? If not, why? If no historical data is available, find other sources of information that can help guide the development of figures for your budget. How much business do you plan to bring in during the next budget period, and what will it cost you to bring it in? Consider whether you need to hire more people, lease new facilities, or buy equipment or supplies. Furthermore, consider the possibility of large increases or decreases in sales or expenses and what effect they may have on your budget.

4. **Apply your judgment.**

   Hard data and cold facts are important in the budgeting process; they provide an unbiased, factual source of information on which to base your decisions. However, data and facts aren't everything — not by a long shot. Budgeting is part science and part art. Gather the data and facts and then apply your own judgment to determine the most likely outcomes.

For example, Peter used to budget more for extraordinary maintenance of his office facility than he could ever justify on an item-by-item basis. He did so knowing that some unanticipated equipment breakdown or building failure would occur during the course of the year (and it always did), and he needed to have enough money available in his budget to accommodate it. So when the roof leaked or the big boss decided to redo the entire building in pink wallpaper, the money was available.

When you're new to management, you have little experience on which to draw, so you have a natural tendency to rely more heavily on data. However, as you become more accomplished in management and budgeting, your personal experience and judgment can prove very helpful.

5. **Run the numbers.**

   Depending on how your organization conducts business, either fill out your budget forms and send them to your finance group for processing, or enter them into the budget model yourself. The result is a budget draft that you can review and modify before you finalize it. Don't worry if the draft is rough or is missing information. You'll have a chance to fill in the gaps soon enough.

6. **Check results and run the budget again as necessary.**

   Check over your draft budget and see whether it still makes sense to you. Are you missing any anticipated sources of revenue or expenses? Are the numbers realistic? Do they make sense in a historical perspective? Are they too high or too low? Will you be able to support them when you present them to upper management? The fun part of budgeting is playing with your numbers and trying different scenarios and what-ifs. When you're satisfied with the results, sign off on your budget and turn it in. Congratulations! You did it!

The accuracy of your budget hinges on two main factors: the quality of the data that you use to develop your budget and the quality of the judgment that you apply to the data you're working with. Although judgment comes with experience, the quality of the data you use depends on where you get it. You can use three basic approaches to develop the data for building a budget:

- **Build it from scratch.** In the absence of historical data, when you're starting up a new business unit, or when you just want a fresh view, you want to develop your budgets based strictly on current estimates. In this process, widely known as *zero-based budgeting,* you build your budget from scratch — determining the people, facilities, travel, advertising, and other resources that are required to support it. You then cost out each need, and the budget is complete. Perhaps not too surprisingly, the answer that comes out of building a budget from scratch is often quite different from one that results from using historical data.

- **Use historical data.** One of the easiest ways to develop data for your budget is to use the actual results from the preceding budget period. Although the past isn't always an indication of the future — especially when an organization is undergoing significant change — using historical data can be helpful in relatively stable organizations, and it's interesting to track trends to see which numbers have gone up and which have gone down.

- **Use the combination approach.** Many managers use a combination of the two preceding methods to determine what data to include in their budgets. To use this approach, gather historical data and compare the figures to the best estimates of what you think performing a particular function will cost. You then adjust historical data up or down, depending on your view of reality.

Pulling Rabbits out of Hats and Other Budget Tricks

In any organization, a certain amount of mystery and intrigue — some would call it "smoke and mirrors" — hovers around budgets and the budgeting process. Indeed, whether your organization is a one-person operation, a large business, or the federal government, you can use many tricks of the budget trade to ensure that you get all the resources you need. *Note:* In these days of big-business scandals and shenanigans, we definitely aren't suggesting that you do anything illegal, immoral, or unethical. The tricks we suggest in this section are quite legal, and they're time-honored techniques for budgeting used every day in all kinds of organizations around the world.

The top ten excuses for being over budget

In the long history of modern business, managers have used a million and one excuses for exceeding their budgets. Admittedly, trying to predict the future of a business that is going through dynamic change is like trying to hit a gnat with a slingshot at 100 paces. Regardless, your boss expects you to manage your budget, just as you expect your employees to manage theirs. However, for those times when the future gets a little fuzzy, here are the top ten excuses for going over budget:

1. The accounting reports must be wrong.

2. Didn't you get my revised budget?

3. How was I supposed to know that it would rain (insert your own excuse here) this year?

4. You're not going to quibble over a measly couple million dollars, are you?

5. What we lose in margin we'll make up for in volume!

6. My assistant worked up that budget — he must have messed it up.

7. It's an investment in our future.

8. Cathy's (insert name of another manager here) department didn't come through with the support that I was promised.

9. We're doing better than last year!

10. Well, two years out of three isn't bad, is it?

The budget game is a long-standing tradition in business and government. Managers who discover how to play the game effectively get what they need, as do the people who work for them. Managers who fail to properly play the game, and the employees who work for them, are doomed to always have to make do with insufficient resources, facilities, and pay. If you're a manager, finding out how the game is played is definitely in your interest.

Generally, the goal of the budget game is to build in enough extra money to be able to get the entire job done well each year. In the worst case, you'll have enough funding available to protect your employees and vital operations when the business fails. If you manage your budget properly, you'll have money left over after you pay all your necessary expenses. You can turn the money back in to accounting, or you can apply the money to the purchase of some equipment or other department needs. Of course, if you work for the government, your goal is to spend every penny of your budgeted amount so that your budget won't decrease in the following year.

You can play the budget game up front, when you create the budget, or during the course of the budget period. The following sections tell you how to develop a solid budget.

Maneuvering up-front budgets

Although the following techniques that the pros use when they develop budgets are most appropriate for new or unpredictable departments or projects, you can use them when developing any budget. We may be exaggerating just a bit on some of these points, but most of them have a clear ring of truth.

- ✔ **Do some selective padding.** Simple, but effective. The idea is to slightly pad your anticipated expenses so that you can achieve your budget targets more easily. You end up looking like a hero when you come in under your budget, plus you get some extra money to use at the end of the year. This situation is win-win.

- ✔ **Tie your budget request to your organization's values.** This approach is the Mom and apple pie approach to budgeting. If you want to beef up your budget in a particular area, just pick one of your organization's values — for example, quality — and tie your request to it. When your boss asks you to justify why you've tripled your office furniture budget, just tell him that your employees can't do quality work without large, handcrafted desks.

- ✔ **Create more requests than you need, and give them up as you have to.** You don't want to appear unreasonable in your budget demands — don't forget, you're a team player! When you draft your budget, build in items that are of relatively low priority to you overall. When your boss puts on the pressure to reduce your budget (and bosses always do), give up the stuff you didn't care much about anyway. Doing so ensures that you get to keep the items that you really do want.

- ✔ **Shift the time frame.** Insist that the budget items are an investment in the company's future. The secret is to tie these investments to a big payoff down the road. "If we double our labor budget, we'll be able to attract the talent we need to expand our operations."

- ✔ **Be prepared.** The best defense is a good offense. Know your budget numbers well and be ready to justify each budget item in intimate detail. Don't rely on someone else to prepare for you — it can be your finest hour as a manager. Be a star and go for it!

Staying on budget

After your new department or project starts up, you need to closely monitor your budget to make sure you don't exceed it. If your actual expenditures start to exceed your budget, you need to take quick and decisive action. Following are some of the ways experienced managers make sure they stay on budget:

✔ **Freeze discretionary expenses.** Some expenses, such as labor, benefits, and electricity, are essential to an operation or project and can't be stopped without jeopardizing performance. Other expenses, such as purchasing new carpeting, upgrading computers, or traveling first-class, are discretionary and can be postponed without jeopardizing performance. Freezing discretionary expenses is the quickest and least painful way to get your actual expenditures back in line with your budgeted expenditures.

✔ **Freeze hiring.** Although you may have budgeted new hires, you can save money by freezing the hiring of new employees. Not only do you save on the cost of hourly pay or salaries, but you also save on the costs of fringe benefits such as medical care and overhead expenses like water, electricity, and janitorial services. And because you aren't decreasing your current employees' pay or benefits, most everyone will be happy with your decision. Of course, some critical positions in your organization may need to be filled, budget problem notwithstanding. You can determine which positions have to be filled if they become vacant and which positions other employees can cover.

✔ **Postpone products and projects.** The development and production phases of new products and projects can add significant costs. By postponing the start-up and rollout of these new products and projects, you can get your budget back on track. Sometimes it takes only a few weeks or months to make a difference.

✔ **Stretch payments to suppliers.** Instead of paying right on time, you can stretch out your payments over a longer period of time. If you choose to go this route, it's generally best to work it out with your suppliers in advance (that is, if you want them to continue to be your suppliers in the future).

✔ **Freeze wages and benefits contributions.** These kinds of savings directly affect your employees, and we can guarantee that they aren't going to like it one bit. Most employees are used to regular wage and benefits increases. Although increases aren't as generous as they were a decade ago, employees still expect them. However, if you've made cuts and still need to cut more, you may not have any choice but to freeze your employees' wages and benefits contributions — medical insurance, 401(k) matching, and so on — at their current levels.

✔ **Lay off employees and close facilities.** You're in business to make money, not to lose money. When sales aren't sufficient to support your expenses — even after enacting the cost-savings measures just mentioned — you must take drastic action. Action doesn't get much more drastic than laying off employees and closing facilities. However, if your budget has significant gaps, then cut you must. See Chapter 19 for more information on conducting employee layoffs.

Whether or not you're responsible for budgeting as a part of your managerial duties, you need to have a basic understanding of the process your business goes through to account for the money it makes and the money it spends. In the section that follows, we present all the information you need to know about accounting to achieve a basic level of comprehension.

Understanding the Basics of Accounting

The accounting system that takes up gigabytes of storage space on your company's network server depends on a few basic assumptions. These assumptions determine how every dollar and cent that flows into and out of your organization is assigned, reported, and analyzed. (If you ever want to drive your accounting staff nuts, tell them that you noticed a two- or three-cent mistake in your accounting reports and that you want them to find the source.)

Some managers believe that they can skate by with little or no knowledge of accounting and finance. This attitude is a mistake. As a manager, you must be just as familiar with these accounting basics as are the employees who work in your accounting department. Not only does this knowledge help ensure that you understand and support your organization's financial initiatives, but if you understand the financial side of your business as well as the technical side, you're also much more likely to survive the next round of corporate layoffs.

Figuring out the accounting equation

Daily events affect every business's financial position. A manager spends cash to buy a stapler and is reimbursed out of the petty cash fund. The company taps its bank line of credit to pay vendor invoices. Customers pay bills and those payments are deposited. Employees receive paychecks. Each of these *financial transactions* and many more has its place in the accounting equation.

The accounting equation states that an organization's *assets* are equal to its *liabilities* plus its *owners' equity*. The accounting equation looks like this:

Assets = Liabilities + Owners' equity

This simple equation drives the complex system of accounting used to track every financial transaction in a business; provide reports to managers for decision making; and provide financial results to owners, shareholders, lenders, the government, and other stakeholders.

So what exactly does each part of the accounting equation represent? Take a look at each part and what it comprises.

Assets

Assets are generally considered to be anything of value — primarily financial and economic resources — that a company owns. The most common forms of assets in a business include the following:

- ✔ **Cash:** This asset encompasses money in all its forms, including cash, checking accounts, money market funds, and marketable securities, such as stocks and bonds.

- ✔ **Accounts receivable:** This asset represents the money that customers who buy goods and services on credit owe to your company. For example, if your business sells a box of computer memory chips to another business and then bills the other business for the sale instead of demanding immediate payment in cash, this obligation becomes an account receivable until your customer pays it. Accounts receivable are nice to have unless the companies or individuals that owe you money skip town or decide to delay their payments for six months.

- ✔ **Inventory:** Inventory is the value of the merchandise your business holds for sale, the finished goods that you have manufactured but not yet sold, and the raw materials and work in process that are part of the manufacture of finished goods. Inventory usually becomes cash or an account receivable when sold. Inventory that sits on a shelf forever isn't the best way to tie up your company's assets. Keeping your inventory moving all the time is much better because you're generating sales.

- ✔ **Prepaid expenses:** Prepaid expenses represent goods and services that your firm has already paid for but not yet used. For example, your company may pay its annual liability insurance premium at the beginning of the year, before the insurance policy actually goes into effect. If the policy is canceled during the course of the year, part of the premium is refunded to your business.

- ✔ **Equipment:** Equipment is the property — machinery, desks, computers, phones, and similar items — that your organization buys to carry out its operations. For example, if your company sells computer supplies to individuals and other businesses, you need to purchase shelves on which to store your inventory of computers, forklifts to move it around, and phone systems on which to take orders from your customers. As equipment ages, it loses value. You account for this loss through *depreciation,* which spreads the original cost of a piece of equipment across its entire useful lifetime. When in doubt, depreciate.

- ✔ **Real estate:** Real estate includes the land, buildings, and facilities that your organization owns or controls. Examples include office buildings, manufacturing plants, warehouses, sales offices, mills, farms, and other forms of real property.

Assets are divided into two major types: *current* assets and *fixed* assets.

- ✔ **Current assets** can be converted into cash within one year. Such assets are considered to be *liquid*. In the preceding list of assets, cash, accounts receivable, inventory, and prepaid expenses are considered current assets. Liquid assets are nice to have around when your business is in trouble and you need to raise cash quickly to make payroll or pay your vendors.

- ✔ **Fixed assets** require more than one year to convert to cash. In the preceding list of assets, equipment and real estate are classified as fixed assets. If your business gets into trouble and you need cash, fixed assets probably won't do you much good unless you can use them as collateral for a loan.

Liabilities

Liabilities are generally considered to be debts that you owe to others — individuals, other businesses, banks, and so on — outside the company. In essence, liabilities are the claims that outside individuals and organizations have against a business's assets.

The most common forms of business liabilities include the following:

- ✔ **Accounts payable:** Accounts payable are the obligations that your company owes to the individuals and organizations from which it purchases goods and services. For example, when you visit your local office supply store to buy a couple pencils and you bill the purchase to your company's account, this obligation becomes an account payable. You can conserve your company's cash in times of need by slowing payments to your vendors and suppliers, although you have to be careful not to jeopardize your credit in the process.

- ✔ **Notes payable:** Notes payable are the portion of loans made to your organization by individuals, financial institutions, or other organizations that are due to be paid back within one year. For example, if your firm takes a 90-day loan to increase its inventory of computer memory chips to satisfy a rapid increase in customer demand, the loan is considered a note payable.

- ✔ **Accrued expenses:** Accrued expenses are miscellaneous expenses that your company incurs but that aren't reimbursed. Examples include obligations for payroll, sick leave due to employees, taxes payable to the government, and interest due to lenders.

- ✔ **Bonds payable:** Some large companies issue bonds to raise money to finance expansion or achieve other goals. Bonds payable represent the money that a company owes to the individuals and organizations that purchase the bonds as an investment.

✔ **Mortgages payable:** When organizations purchase real estate, they often do so by incurring long-term loans known as *mortgages*. Mortgages differ from standard loans because they're usually secured by the real estate that the mortgage finances. For example, if your company defaults in its payments on the mortgage used to purchase your office building, ownership of the office building reverts to the entity that originally issued the mortgage — usually a bank or investment group. .

Like assets, liabilities are divided into two major types: *current* liabilities and *long-term* liabilities.

✔ **Current liabilities** are repaid within one year. In the preceding list of liabilities, accounts payable, notes payable, and accrued expenses are considered current liabilities.

✔ **Long-term liabilities** are repaid in a period greater than one year. In the preceding list of liabilities, bonds payable and mortgages payable are both classified as long-term liabilities.

Owners' equity

All businesses have owners. In some cases, the owners are a few individuals who founded the company. In other cases, the owners are the many thousands of individuals who buy the company's stock through public offerings. Owners' equity is the owners' share of the assets of a business after all liabilities have been paid.

The most common forms of owners' equity include the following:

✔ **Paid-in capital:** Paid-in capital is the investment — usually paid in cash — that the owners make in a business. For example, if your firm sells common stock to investors through a public offering, the money that your firm obtains through the sale of the stock is considered paid-in capital.

✔ **Retained earnings:** These earnings are reinvested by a business, not paid out in dividends to shareholders. A certain amount of earnings are retained in hopes of increasing the firm's overall earnings and also to increase the dividends paid to owners.

Knowing double-entry bookkeeping

Double-entry bookkeeping is the standard method of recording financial transactions that forms the basis of modern business accounting. Invented in 1494 by Luca Pacioli, a bored Franciscan monk (he must have been *really* bored to invent accounting!), double-entry bookkeeping recognizes that every financial transaction results in a record of a *receipt* (also known as an asset) and a record of an *expense* (also known as a liability).

Consider this example: Your company buys $1,000 worth of computer memory chips from a manufacturer to resell to your customers. Because your company has established an account with the memory chip manufacturer, the manufacturer bills you for the $1,000 instead of demanding immediate cash payment. Do you remember the accounting equation we discuss earlier in this chapter? Here's the double-entry version of the accounting equation illustrating the $1,000 purchase of memory chips to stock in your inventory:

Assets	=	**Liabilities**	+	**Owners' equity**
$1,000	=	$1,000	+	$0
(Inventory)		(Accounts payable)		

In this example, assets (inventory) increase by $1,000 — the cost of purchasing the memory chips to stock your shelves. At the same time, liabilities (accounts payable) also increase by $1,000. This increase represents the debt that you owe to your supplier of memory chips. In this way, the accounting equation always stays balanced. Now, imagine the effect of the several hundreds or thousands of financial transactions that hit your accounting system on a daily, weekly, or monthly basis. Whew! And you wondered why your information systems manager is always complaining that the company's computer system isn't big enough or fast enough.

Identifying the Most Common Types of Financial Statements

An accounting system is nice to have, but the system is worthless unless it can produce data that's useful to managers, employees, lenders, vendors, owners, investors, and other individuals and firms that have a financial stake in your business. And believe us, a lot of people have a financial interest in your business.

Does it surprise you to hear that almost everyone wants to know the financial health of your business? Well, they do. Managers want to know so that they can identify and fix problems. Employees want to know because they want to work for a company that's in good financial health and that provides good pay, benefits, and job stability. Lenders and vendors need to know your company's financial health to decide whether to extend credit. And owners and investors want to know because this knowledge helps them determine whether their investment dollars are being used wisely.

TIP

The make-or-buy decision

One of the most common decisions made in business is whether to make — that is, build or perform with in-house staff — or buy goods and services that are necessary for the operation of a business. For example, suppose you decide that you need to assign a security guard to your reception area to ensure the safety of your clients. Do you hire someone new as an employee, or does contracting with a company that specializes in providing security services make more sense?

When you consider such a make-or-buy decision, the first point to consider is the cost of each alternative to your firm. Say that, in Case A, you hire your security guard as a full-time employee for $10 an hour. In Case B, a security services firm provides a guard for $12 an hour. On the surface, hiring a security guard as an employee seems to make the most sense. If the guard works 2,000 hours a year, then in Case A, you spend $20,000 a year for your guard, and in Case B, you spend $24,000 a year. By employing the guard yourself, you stand to save $4,000 a year. Right?

Maybe not. See why.

Case A: Hire in-house security guard

Hourly pay rate	$10.00
Fringe benefits rate @ 35%	3.50
Overhead rate @ 50%	5.00
Total effective pay rate	**$18.50**
Hours per year	× 2,000
Total annual labor cost	**$37,000**
Annual liability insurance increase	4,000
Uniforms/cleaning	1,000
Miscellaneous equipment	500
Total annual cost	**$42,500**

Case B: Contract with security firm

Hourly pay rate	$12.00
Total effective pay rate	**$12.00**
Hours per year	× 2,000
Total annual cost	**$24,000**

Surprise, surprise. Instead of saving $4,000 per year by hiring an in-house security guard, you're actually going to spend almost $18,500 more each year because more costs are involved in hiring an in-house employee than just hourly pay. You have to add all the fringe benefits, such as life insurance, medical and dental plans, and more, plus the employee's share of overhead — facilities, electricity, air conditioning, and so forth — to the basic wage rate to get a true picture of the cost of the employee to your organization. Furthermore, you need to purchase additional liability insurance, uniforms, uniform cleaning, and miscellaneous equipment such as a flashlight, Mace, and handcuffs.

On the other hand, when you contract with a security services firm, the firm bears the cost of fringe benefits, overhead, insurance, uniforms, and equipment. You simply pay the hourly fee and forget it. Furthermore, if the guard doesn't work out for some reason, you just make a phone call, and a replacement is sent immediately. No messy employee terminations or unemployment benefits to worry about.

Now, which deal do you think is the better one?

Accountants invented *financial statements* to measure the financial health and performance of a company.

Financial statements are nothing more than reports — intended for distribution to individuals outside the accounting department — that summarize the amounts of money contained within selected accounts or groups of accounts at a selected point or period of time. Each type of financial statement has a unique value to the people who use them, and different individuals may use some or all of an organization's financial statements during the normal course of business. The following sections review the financial statements you're most likely to encounter during your career as a manager.

The balance sheet

The *balance sheet* is a report that illustrates the value of a company's assets, liabilities, and owners' equity — the company's financial position on a specific date. Think of it as a snapshot of the business. Although it can be prepared at any time, a balance sheet, like the one shown in Figure 14-1, is usually prepared at the end of a definite accounting period — most often a year, quarter, or month.

As you can see, the balance sheet provides values for every major component of the three parts of the accounting equation. By reviewing each item's value in the balance sheet, managers can identify potential problems and then take action to solve them.

The income statement

Assets, liabilities, and owners' equity are all very nice, thank you, but many people really want to see the bottom line. Did the company make money or lose money? In other words, what was its profit or loss? This job belongs to the *income statement.*

An income statement, shown in Figure 14-2, adds all the sources of a company's revenues and then subtracts all the sources of its expenses to determine its net income or net loss for a particular period of time. Whereas a balance sheet is a snapshot of an organization's financial status, an income statement is more like a movie.

Revenues

Revenue is the value received by a company through the sale of goods, services, and other sources such as interest, rents, royalties, and so forth. To arrive at net sales, total sales of goods and services are offset by returns and allowances.

Sample Balance Sheet

	January 31, 20xx
ASSETS	
CURRENT ASSETS	
Cash and cash equivalents	$458,000
Accounts receivable	$11,759,000
Inventory	$154,000
Prepaid expenses and other current assets	$283,000
Refundable income taxes	$165,000
TOTAL CURRENT ASSETS	$12,819,000
EQUIPMENT AND FURNITURE	
Equipment	$4,746,000
Furniture, fixtures, and improvements	$583,000
	$5,329,000
Allowance for depreciation and amortization	($2,760,000)
	$2,569,000
COMPUTER SOFTWARE COSTS, NET	$3,199,000
NET DEPOSITS AND OTHER	$260,000
	$18,847,000
LIABILITIES AND SHAREHOLDERS' EQUITY	
CURRENT LIABILITIES	
Notes payable to bank	$1,155,000
Accounts payable	$2,701,000
Accrued compensation and benefits	$2,065,000
Income taxes payable	$0
Deferred income taxes	$990,000
Current portion of long-term debt	$665,000
TOTAL CURRENT LIABILITIES	$7,576,000
LONG-TERM DEBT, less current portion	$864,000
DEFERRED RENT EXPENSE	$504,000
DEFERRED INCOME TAXES	$932,000
STOCKHOLDERS' EQUITY	
Common stock	$76,000
Additional paid-in capital	$803,000
Retained earnings	$8,092,000
	$8,971,000
	$18,847,000

Figure 14-1:
A typical balance sheet.

Expenses

Expenses are all the costs of doing business. For accounting purposes, expenses are divided into two major classifications:

- ✔ **Cost of goods sold:** For a firm that retails or wholesales merchandise to individuals or other companies, this figure represents the cost of purchasing merchandise or inventory. By subtracting the cost of goods sold from revenue, you end up with the company's *gross margin,* also known as *gross profit.*

- ✔ **Operating expenses:** Operating expenses are all the other costs of doing business that aren't already part of the cost of goods sold. Operating expenses are usually further subdivided into *selling expenses,* which include marketing, advertising, product promotion, and the costs of operating stores; and *general and administrative expenses,* which are the actual administrative costs of running the business. General and administrative costs typically include salaries for accounting, data processing, and purchasing staff; and the cost of corporate facilities, including utilities, rent payments, and so on.

The difference between revenues and expenses (after adjustment for interest income or expense and payment of income taxes) is a company's net income (profit) or net loss. Also commonly known as a company's *bottom line,* net income or loss is the cash you have on hand after you've paid all the bills, and it's the one number most often of interest to people who want to assess the firm's financial health. Many corporate executives and managers have found themselves on the street — sometimes literally overnight — when their companies' bottom lines dipped too far into the loss side of the equation.

Top five accounting Web sites

Wondering where to find the best information on the Web about the topics addressed in this chapter? Here are our top five favorites:

- ✔ *Business Finance* magazine: www. businessfinancemag.com
- ✔ CFO.com: www.cfo.com

- ✔ *Strategic Finance* magazine: www. strategicfinancemag.com
- ✔ AccountingWEB: www.accounting web.co.uk
- ✔ SmartPros Accounting: finance. pro2net.com

Sample Income Statement

Twelve months ended

January 31, 20xx

REVENUES

Gross sales	$58,248,000	
Less: Returns	$1,089,000	
Net Sales		$57,159,000

COST OF GOODS SOLD

Beginning inventory		$4,874,000
Purchases	$38,453,000	
Less: Purchase discounts	$1,586,000	
Net purchases		$36,867,000
Cost of goods available for sale		$41,741,000
Less: Ending inventory		$6,887,000
Cost of Goods Sold		$34,854,000

GROSS PROFIT — $22,305,000

OPERATING EXPENSES

Total selling expenses		$8,456,000
Total general expenses		$1,845,000
Total operating expenses		$10,301,000
Operating income		$12,004,000
Other income and expenses		
Interest expense (income)		$360,000
Total other income and expenses		$360,000
Income before taxes		$11,644,000
Less: Income taxes		$3,952,000
Net Income		$7,692,000
Average number of shares		3,500,000
Earnings per share		$2.20

Figure 14-2:
A simple income statement.

The cash-flow statement

What's the old saying? "Happiness is a positive cash flow." Cash-flow statements show the movement of cash into and out of a business. It doesn't take an Einstein to realize that when more cash is moving out of a business than is moving into the business for a prolonged period of time, the business may be in big trouble.

Net income or loss

Cash is sort of like gasoline. Your car requires a plentiful supply of gasoline to run. If you run out of gas, your car is going to stop dead on the highway. One minute you're going 65 miles an hour, and the next you're at a standstill. Similarly, if your company runs out of cash, the company is going to stop dead, too. Without cash to pay employees' salaries, vendors' invoices, lenders' loan payments, and so forth, operations quickly cease to exist. Cash-flow statements come in three varieties:

- **Simple cash-flow statement:** The simple cash-flow statement arranges all items into one of two categories: cash inflows and cash outflows.

- **Operating cash-flow statement:** The operating cash-flow statement limits analysis of cash flows to only items related to the operations of a business, not its financing.

- **Priority cash-flow statement:** The priority cash-flow statement classifies cash inflows and outflows by specific groupings chosen by the manager or other individual who requests preparation of the statement.

Using financial ratios to analyze your business

If you don't know exactly what you're looking for, analyzing a company's financial records can be a daunting task. Fortunately, over a period of many years, expert business financial analysts have developed ways to quickly assess the performance and financial health and well-being of an organization by comparing the ratios of certain key financial indicators to established standards and to other firms in the same industries.

Current ratio: This ratio is the capability of a company to pay its current liabilities out of its current assets. A ratio of 2 or more is generally considered good. Consider this example:

Current ratio = Current assets ÷ Current liabilities

= \$100 million ÷ \$25 million

= 4.00

Quick ratio: The quick ratio (also known as the *acid-test* ratio) is the same as the current ratio, with the exception that inventory is subtracted from current assets. This ratio provides a much more rigorous test of a firm's capability to pay its current liabilities quickly than does the current ratio, because inventory can't be liquidated as rapidly as other current assets. A ratio of 1 or better is acceptable.

Quick ratio = (Current assets − Inventory) ÷ Current liabilities

= ($100 million − $10 million) ÷ $25 million

= $90 million ÷ $25 million

= 3.60

Receivables turnover ratio: This ratio indicates the average time it takes a firm to convert its receivables into cash. A higher ratio indicates that customers are paying their bills quickly, which is good. A lower ratio reflects slow collections and a possible problem that management needs to address, which is bad. Your boss isn't going to like it.

Receivables turnover ratio = Net sales ÷ Accounts receivable

= $50 million ÷ $5 million

= 10.00

You can gain one more interesting piece of information quickly from the receivables turnover ratio. By dividing 365 days by the receivables turnover ratio, you get the average number of days that it takes your firm to turn over its accounts receivable; this number is commonly known as the *average collection period.* The shorter the average collection period is, the better the organization's situation is — and the better your job security is.

Average collection period = 365 days ÷ Receivables turnover ratio

= 365 days ÷ 10.00

= 36.5 days

Debt-to-equity ratio: This ratio measures the extent to which the organization depends on loans from outside creditors versus resources provided by shareholders and other owners. A ratio in excess of 1 is generally considered unfavorable because it indicates that the firm may have difficulty repaying its debts. And nobody — especially cranky bankers or vendors — wants to loan money to companies that have problems repaying their debts. A particularly low ratio indicates that management may be able to improve the company's profitability by increasing its debt.

Debt-to-equity ratio = Total liabilities ÷ Owners' equity

= $50 million ÷ $150 million

= 0.33 or 33 percent

Return on investment: Often known by its abbreviation, *ROI,* return on investment measures the capability of a company to earn profits for its owners. Don't forget: Profit is good and loss is bad. Because owners — shareholders and other investors — prefer to make money on their investments, they like an organization's ROI to be as high as possible.

Return on investment = Net income ÷ Owners' equity

= $50 million ÷ $150 million

= 0.33 or 33 percent

Chapter 15

Harnessing the Power of Technology

- -

- -

*Y*ou've gotta love technology. Unfortunately, like everything else in life, technology has its good and bad points. On the upside, computers make our work lives much easier and more efficient. As long as your computer doesn't crash, it remembers everything you've done forever and makes completing repetitive tasks (like merging a letter with a 1,000-person mailing list) a snap. On the downside, computers can be an enormous waste of time. Instead of working, some people spend a significant portion of their workdays checking their Facebook accounts, bidding on items on eBay, and keeping track of the latest celebrity gossip.

You may automatically assume that your employees are more productive because they have computers at their fingertips, but are you (and your organization) really getting the most out of this innovative and expensive technology? Given how much money most companies invest in their information technology systems, hardware, and software, that can be a million-dollar question. Or more.

In this chapter, we explain how to harness information technology — technology used to create, store, exchange, and use information in its various forms. We examine the technology edge and consider how technology can help or hinder an organization. We look at how technology can improve efficiency and productivity, and how to get the most out of it. Finally, we describe how to create a technology plan.

Weighing the Benefits and Drawbacks of Technology in the Workplace

Think for a moment about the incredible progress of information technology just in your lifetime. With so many tools at your fingertips, can you believe that, only about three decades ago, the personal computer hadn't yet been introduced commercially? Word processing used to mean a typewriter and a lot of correction fluid or sheets of messy carbon paper; computers have revolutionized the way businesspeople can manipulate text, graphics, and other elements in their reports and other documents. Mobile telephones, fax machines, the Internet, broadband wireless connections, and other business technology essentials are all fairly recent innovations.

You can't turn back the clock on technology. To keep up with the competition — and beat it — you must keep pace with technology and adopt tools that can make your employees more productive, while improving products and services, customer service, and the bottom line. You really have no other choice.

Making advances, thanks to automation

Information technology can have a positive impact on your business in two important ways, both related to the practice of automation:

- **By automating processes:** Not too many years ago, business processes were manual. For example, your organization's accounting and payroll departments may have calculated payroll entirely by hand with the assistance of only a ten-key adding machine. What used to take hours, days, or weeks can now be accomplished in minutes or even seconds. Other processes that are commonly automated are inventory tracking, customer service, call analysis, and purchasing.

- **By automating personal management functions:** More managers than ever are moving their calendars and personal planners onto computers. Although paper-based planners aren't going to die completely, many managers are finding that computers are much more powerful management tools than their unautomated counterparts. Managers also use computers to schedule meetings, track projects, analyze numbers, manage business contact information, conduct employee performance evaluations, and more.

However, before you run off and automate everything, keep this piece of information in mind: If your manual system is inefficient or ineffective, simply automating the system isn't necessarily going to make your system perform any better. In fact, automating it can make your system perform worse than the manual version. When you automate, review the process in detail. Cut out any unnecessary steps and make sure your system is optimized for the new, automated environment. Believe us, the time you take now to improve your processes and functions is going to pay off when you automate.

Improving efficiency and productivity

The recent explosion of information technology accompanies the shift in industry from old-line standards, such as steel mills and petroleum refineries, to companies producing semiconductors, computers, and related products. The personal computer industry, which was still in its infancy three decades ago, has quickly grown into a market worth many billions of dollars in annual sales.

The idea that businesspeople who best manage information have a competitive advantage in the marketplace seems obvious enough. The sooner you receive information, the sooner you can act on it. The more effectively you handle information, the easier you can access that information when and where you need it. The more efficiently you deal with information, the fewer expenses you incur for managing and maintaining your information.

Management often cites the preceding reasons, and others like them, as justification for spending obscenely huge amounts of corporate resources to buy computers, install e-mail and voice-mail systems, and train employees to use these new tools of the Information Age. But have all these expenditures made your own workers more productive? If not, perhaps you aren't taking the right approach to implementing information technology within your business.

Before spending the money, a manager should take time to identify the questions that need an answer:

- ✔ Who needs the answer? (customer, supplier, employee, management)
- ✔ How fast do they need the answer? (real time, one minute, one hour, one day)
- ✔ How frequently do they need the answer? (daily, weekly, monthly)

When the answers to these questions become clear, you have a rational basis for evaluating alternate technologies based on how well they meet the criteria needed for your "answers." A lot of technology seems to be designed to provide a real-time answer to a question that needs to be asked only once a month.

When planned and implemented wisely, information technology can improve an organization's efficiency and productivity. Recent studies are beginning to show a relationship between the implementation of information technology and increased productivity. Examples like the following bear out this relationship:

✔ Implementing a computerized inventory-management system at Warren, Michigan–based Duramet Corporation — a manufacturer of powdered metal and now a part of the Cerametal Group — helped the company double sales over a three-year period without hiring a single new salesperson.

✔ By using information technology to provide employees with real-time information about orders and scheduling that cuts through the traditional walls within the organization, M.A. Hanna, a manufacturer of polymers that merged with Geon Company to form PolyOne Corporation, reduced its working capital needs by a third to achieve the same measure of sales.

✔ At Weirton Steel Corporation — now Mittal Steel USA, based in Weirton, West Virginia — the company found that it needed only 12 people to run the hot mill that once required 150 people to operate, all because of the efficiencies gained as a result of new technology installed in the production line.

Although evidence is beginning to swing toward productivity gains, studies indicate that merely installing computers and other information technology doesn't automatically lead to gains in employee efficiency. As a manager, you must take the time to improve your work processes before you automate them. If you don't, office automation can actually lead to decreases in employee efficiency and productivity. Instead of the usual lousy results that you get from your manual, unautomated system, you end up with something new: garbage at the speed of light. Don't let your organization make the same mistake!

Taking steps to neutralize the negatives

Just as information technology can help a business, it can also hinder it. Consider a few examples of the negative side of information technology:

✔ Widespread worker abuse of Internet access has reduced worker productivity by 10 to 15 percent. According to Forrester Research, 20 percent of employee time on the Internet at work doesn't involve their jobs. A recent study by Nucleus Research found that employee use of Facebook at work causes a 1.5 percent decrease in employee productivity all by itself.

✔ Hackers have sent periodic waves of computer viruses and malicious attacks through the business world, leaving billions of dollars of damage and lost productivity in their wake.

✔ E-mail messages can be unclear and confusing, forcing workers to waste time clarifying their intentions or covering themselves in case of problems.

✔ Employees are forced to wade through an ever-growing quantity of spam and junk e-mail messages.

✔ The slick, animated, and sound-laden computer-based full-color presentations so common today can take longer to prepare than the simple text and graphs that were prevalent a few years ago — especially if you're not technologically savvy.

You have to take the bad with the good. But don't take the bad lying down. You can maximize the positives of information technology while minimizing the negatives:

✔ **Stay current on the latest information innovations and news.** You don't need to become an expert on how to install a network server or configure your voice-mail system, but you do need to become conversant in the technology behind your business systems.

✔ **Hire experts.** Although you must have a general knowledge of information technology, plan to hire experts to advise you in the design and implementation of critical information technology–based systems.

✔ **Manage by walking around.** Make a habit of dropping in on employees — wherever they're located — and observe how they use your organization's information technology. Solicit their feedback and suggestions for improvement. Research and implement changes as soon as you discover the need.

Using Technology to Your Advantage

Information technology is all around us today, and it touches every aspect of our lives — at home and at work. Computers and telecommunications technology are essential tools for any business. Even the most defiant, old-school CEOs have finally taken the plunge and are wirelessly telephoning and surfing the Web on their Blackberrys in ever-increasing numbers. Information technology can give you and your business tremendous advantages. As a manager, you must capitalize on them — before your competition does.

Before you act, you must become technology savvy. In the next sections, we recommend the four basic ways for doing just that.

Know your business

Before you can design and implement information technology in the most effective way, you have to completely understand how your business works. What work is being done? Who's doing it? What do employees need to get their work done?

One way to know your business is to approach it as an outsider. Pretend you're a customer and see how your company's people and systems handle you. Do the same with your competitors to see how their people and systems handle you. What are the differences? What are the similarities? How can you improve your own organization using information technology as a result of what you've discovered?

Create a technology-competitive advantage

Few managers understand how technology can become a competitive advantage for their businesses. They may have vague notions of potential efficiency gains or increased productivity, but they're clueless when dealing with specifics.

Information technology can create real and dramatic competitive advantages over other businesses in your markets, specifically by doing the following:

- Competing with large companies by marketing on a level playing field (the Internet)
- Helping to build ongoing, loyal relationships with customers
- Connecting with strategic partners to speed up vital processes, such as product development and manufacturing
- Linking everyone in the company, as well as with necessary sources of information both inside and outside the organization
- Providing real-time information on pricing, products, and so forth to vendors, customers, and original equipment manufacturers (OEMs)

Now is the time to create advantages over your competition. Keep in mind that the winner isn't the company that *has* the most data, but the company that *manages* that data best.

Develop a plan

If you're serious about using information technology as an edge, you must have a plan for its implementation. When it comes to the fast-changing area of technology, having a *technology plan* — a plan for acquiring and deploying information technology — is a definite must. Many businesses buy bits and pieces of computer hardware, software, and other technology without considering the technology that they already have in place and without looking very far into the future. Then when they try to hook everything together, they're surprised that their thrown-together system doesn't work.

Managers who take the time to develop and implement technology plans aren't faced with this problem, and they aren't forced to spend far more money and time fixing the problems with their systems.

Technology is no longer an optional expense; it's a strategic investment that can help push your company ahead of the competition. And every strategic investment requires a plan. In their book *eBusiness Technology Kit For Dummies* (Wiley), Kathleen Allen and Jon Weisner recommend that you take the following steps in developing your technology plan:

1. **Write down your organization's core values.**

   For example, some of your core values might be to provide customers with the very best customer service possible, or to always act ethically and honestly.

2. **Picture where you see your business ten years from now. Don't limit yourself.**

   Will you be in the same industry or perhaps some new ones? What products and services will you offer, and to whom will you offer them? Will you be a small business or a large multinational corporation with global reach and influence? How many employees will you have? 1,000? 10,000? 100,000?

3. **Set a major one-year goal for the company that is guided by your vision.**

   This goal might be to create a system that tracks customer service complaints and gets them in front of the company's management team in real time.

4. **List some strategies for achieving the goal.**

   A strategy to achieve the preceding one-year goal might be to assign an employee team to work with your IT department to develop a set of recommended solutions within three months.

5. **Brainstorm some tactics that can help you achieve your strategies.**

   Specific tactics to achieve the preceding strategy might include assigning responsibility for the project to a specific employee or manager, and setting milestones and deadlines for completion and reporting of results.

6. **Identify technologies that support your strategies and tactics.**

   Provide some guidance by bounding the technologies to use in achieving the one-year goal, strategies, and tactics. For example, you may require that any new system work with existing systems or that the new system be Web based.

Gather your thoughts — and your employees' thoughts — and write them down. Create a concise document — perhaps no more than five to ten pages — that describes your information technology strategies as simply and exactly as possible. After you create your plan, screen and select vendors that can help you implement your plan. Close out the process by monitoring performance and adjusting the plan as needed to meet the needs of your organization and employees, and to produce optimal performance.

Keep the following points in mind as you navigate the planning process:

✔ **Don't buy technology just because it's the latest and greatest thing.** It's always fun shopping for the latest whiz-bang gizmo. Unfortunately, just because an item is new, has lots of flashing lights, and makes cool noises doesn't mean that it's right for your business. It could be too big or too small, too fast or too slow, too expensive or too cheap. Or it might not even be compatible with the systems you've already got. Be sure that whatever technology you include in your plan makes sense for your business.

✔ **Check in with your IT department.** It's important to make sure your planned purchase will be compatible with existing systems. You also want to find out if your IT department is planning to change directions on funding how the company infrastructure is set up. You don't want to buy a program in your department that will be obsolete within a couple months.

✔ **Plan for the right period of time.** Different kinds of businesses require different planning *horizons,* the time periods covered by their plans. If you're in a highly volatile market such as wireless communications, your planning horizon may be only six months or so out. If you're in a stable market such as a grocery chain, your planning horizon may extend three to five years into the future.

✔ **Consider the benefits of outsourcing.** You may be able to save significant amounts of money by outsourcing appropriate functions to further streamline systems and create efficiencies.

✔ **Make the planning process a team effort.** You're not the only one who's going to be impacted by all this new technology that you bring into your company. Make employees, customers, and vendors a part of your planning team. If you take time to involve them in the process and get their buy-in ahead of time, your technology rollout will go much more smoothly.

✔ **Weigh the costs of upgrading your old system versus going to a new system.** Every system eventually comes to the end of its useful life. Instead of continuing to patch a system that's becoming increasingly expensive to maintain, start fresh. Run the numbers and see what alternative makes the most sense for your organization before you finalize your plans.

Get some help

If you're a fan of technology and pretty knowledgeable in it, that's great — you have a head start on the process. But if you're not, get help from people who are experts in information technology. Does your company have knowledgeable people? Can you hire a technician or technology consultant to fill in the gaps? Whatever you do, don't try it alone. Even if you're a full-fledged techno-geek, recruit others for your cause. Technology is changing incredibly fast and on every front. No one person can be an expert in every aspect of the information technology necessary to run and grow your business.

PC versus Apple

Only a few years ago, business managers took the question of whether to buy a PC (IBM-compatible personal computer) or an Apple computer very seriously. Although Apple's products — with their intuitive and easy-to-learn operating interface, graphical icons, and computer mouse — were once vastly superior to their PC rivals, Microsoft Windows software changed all that. PCs using Microsoft Windows are virtually indistinguishable from their Apple equivalents in their ease of use, and they generally cost less, to boot.

Although Apple almost crashed and burned some years ago, the return of Steve Jobs to the company has led to a resurgence both in Apple and in the popularity of its hardware. And although the Macintosh is still the standard for specific applications such as video, graphics and design, and musical composition, the Mac is increasingly finding its way back into business — especially now that Apple prices its machines much more competitively than it did in past years.

Now that computer networks can simultaneously accommodate both PCs and Apple computers, you have really no reason to limit yourself to a certain one. Your accounting employees can be blazing away on their multigigahertz PCs while the graphics department happily designs and creates on their super-charged Apples.

Who says that we can't all coexist peacefully? PC or Apple — the choice is yours.

Getting the Most Out of Company Networks

The personal computer began revolutionizing business a decade ago, shifting the power of computing away from huge mainframes and onto the desks of individual users. Now computer networks are bringing about a new revolution in business. Although the personal computer is a self-sufficient island of information, when you link these islands in a network, individual computers have the added benefit of sharing with every computer on the network.

So does networking have any benefits? You bet it does! See what you think about these reasons:

- **Networks improve communication:** Computer networks allow anyone in an organization to communicate with anyone else quickly and easily. With the click of a button, you can send messages to individuals or groups of employees. You can send replies just as easily. Furthermore, employees on computer networks can access financial, marketing, and product information to do their jobs from throughout the organization.

- **Networks save time and money:** In business, time is money. The faster you can get something done, the more tasks you can complete during the course of your business day. Computer e-mail allows you to create messages, memos, and other internal communications; to attach work files; and then to transmit them instantaneously to as many co-workers as you want. Even better, these co-workers can be located across the hall or around the world.

- **Networks improve market vision:** Information communicated via computer networks is, by nature, timely and direct. In the old world of business communication, many layers of employees filtered, modified, and slowed the information as it traveled from one part of the organization to another. With direct communication over networks, no one filters, modifies, or slows the original message. What you see is what you get. The sooner you get the information that you need and the higher its quality is, the better your market vision can be.

Top five information technology Web sites

Wondering where to find the best information on the Web about the topics addressed in this chapter? Here are our top five favorites:

- *Wired* magazine: www.wired.com

- Computerworld: www.computer world.com

- cNet.com: www.cnet.com

- PCWorld.com: www.pcworld.com

- Internet.com: www.internet.com

Surfing the old intranet

If you think that the Internet is the greatest thing since sliced bread in business computing, guess again. Establishing a presence on the Internet is old news for most corporations. Now the big addition in business is the *intranet*. With few exceptions, America's largest corporations, including Federal Express, AT&T, Levi Strauss, and Ford Motor Company, have built internal versions of the Internet *within* their organizations. For example, employees at DreamWorks SKG, the entertainment conglomerate created by Steven Spielberg, Jeffrey Katzenberg, and David Geffen, use their company's intranet to produce films and to take care of production details such as tracking animation objects, coordinating scenes, and checking the daily status of projects.

Intranets bring the basic tools of the Internet — Web servers, browsers, and Web pages — inside the organization. Intranets are designed to be accessible strictly by employees and aren't available to outside Internet users.

For companies that have already invested in Web hardware and software, they're an inexpensive and powerful way to pull together an organization's computers — and its employees.

Intranets are also a valuable way to communicate effectively across companies with satellite offices and those whose employees are on the road. Companies are also able to remind employees of key goals/mission statements and other initiatives for greater awareness.

Not only are intranets revolutionizing the development of computer networks within organizations, but they're also democratizing them. Where most company computer networks are the sole province of a small staff of computer systems administrators and programmers, intranets allow novices and experts alike to create Web pages. At Federal Express, for example, employees created many of the company's Web pages.

Chapter 16

Embracing Corporate Social Responsibility and Ethics

Corporate social responsibility — CSR, for short — is a way of doing business that's rapidly gaining in popularity both in the United States and around the world. *Corporate social responsibility* is conducting your business in a way that has a positive impact on the communities you serve. As you discover in this chapter, CSR affects many different aspects of operating a business — from recycling, to ethics, to environmental laws, and much more.

Ethics and office politics are powerful forces in any organization. *Ethics* is the framework of values that employees use to guide their behavior. You've seen the devastation that poor ethical standards can lead to — witness the string of business failures attributed to less than sterling ethics in more than a few large, seemingly upstanding businesses. Today more than ever, managers are expected to model ethical behavior, to ensure that their employees follow in their footsteps, and to purge the organization of employees who refuse to align their own standards with the standards of their employer.

At its best, *office politics* means the relationships that you develop with your co-workers — both up and down the chain of command — that allow you to get tasks done, stay informed about the latest goings-on in the business, and form a personal network of business associates for support throughout your career. Office politics help ensure that all employees work in the best interests of their co-workers and the organization. At its worst, office politics can degenerate into a competition, with employees concentrating their efforts on trying to increase their personal power at the expense of other employees — and their organizations.

This chapter looks at adopting a corporate social responsibility strategy, building an ethical organization, and determining the nature and boundaries of your political environment.

Understanding Socially Responsible Practices

CSR has been gaining traction within businesses of all kinds in recent years. At one time, CSR was the sole province of socially progressive companies like ice cream maker Ben & Jerry's and organic yogurt manufacturer Stonyfield Farm, but this is no longer the case. Today even the largest, most conservative companies — including Walmart, ExxonMobil, General Electric, and McKesson — have adopted CSR practices and strategies.

Depending on the exact approach you take and how you implement it, you may have to spend a significant amount of money to conduct your business in a socially responsible way, but the benefits nearly always outweigh the costs. People want to buy products and services from companies that are socially responsible and that are making a positive impact on their communities. What's more, they want to *work for* companies that are socially responsible and that are making a positive impact on their communities. Finally, becoming a socially responsible company can actually reduce costs. For these reasons and others like them, CSR is taking the business world by storm.

Figuring out how you can employ CSR

As we mention at the beginning of this chapter, CSR involves conducting your business in a way that has a positive impact on the communities you serve. But what exactly does that look like in the real world? Consider some of the traits of a socially responsible business:

- Takes responsibility for the conditions in which its products are manufactured, whether in this country or internationally, and whether by the company itself or by subcontractors.

- Promotes recycling, environmental responsibility, and natural resources used in more efficient, productive, and profitable ways.

- Views employees as assets instead of costs and engages them in their jobs by involving them in decision making. In the event of layoffs or job eliminations, they are viewed as a company that treats people fairly.

✔ Is committed to diversity in hiring and selection of vendors, board members, and advisers.

✔ Adopts strong internal management and financial controls.

✔ Meets or exceeds all applicable social and environmental laws and regulations.

✔ Supports its communities through volunteerism, philanthropy, and local hiring.

✔ Promotes sustainability — that is, meeting the needs of the present without compromising the ability of future generations to meet their needs.

As a manager, you may be tasked with helping to develop your company's CSR goals. If that's the case, the exact goals you select must be aligned with both your company's core business objectives and its core competencies. Some of the traits in the preceding list may or may not fit with your company's culture, objectives, or competencies. To be effective, your approach to CSR must make sense for your company and its employees, customers, and other stakeholders.

Consider for a moment the six Guiding Principles that coffee purveyor Starbucks embraces. As you can see, the company's CSR strategy strongly influences these Guiding Principles:

✔ Provide a great work environment and treat each other with respect and dignity.

✔ Embrace diversity as an essential component in the way we do business.

✔ Apply the highest standards of excellence to the purchasing, roasting, and fresh delivery of our coffee.

✔ Develop enthusiastically satisfied customers all the time.

✔ Contribute positively to our communities and our environment.

✔ Recognize that profitability is essential to our future success.

Enjoying net benefits of socially responsible practices

The best corporate social responsibility is tightly integrated into a company's business operations; this strong connection can have a positive impact on the bottom line. Many CSR activities can reduce the cost of doing business while drawing new customers into the company's orbit, increasing the top line. The younger generation of employees now entering the workplace wants to make a difference in the world, too. Companies that practice CSR are more attractive to these talented men and women, who will remain loyal to their employers as long as they continue to have an opportunity to make a difference.

Starbucks presents a strong business case for adopting a corporate social responsibility strategy in its Corporate Social Responsibility Annual Report:

- ✔ **Attracting and retaining our partners (employees):** We believe Starbucks' commitment to CSR contributes to overall retention and higher-than-usual levels of partner satisfaction and engagement. The company's comprehensive benefits package also motivates partners to stay at Starbucks.

- ✔ **Customer loyalty:** Studies have revealed that customers prefer to do business with a company they believe to be socially responsible, when their other key buying criteria are met. In 2007, we surveyed our customers and found that 38 percent associate Starbucks with good corporate citizenship. The vast majority (86 percent) of customers surveyed indicated being extremely or very likely to recommend Starbucks to a friend or family. Our customers' loyalty has been instrumental to the company's ability to grow.

- ✔ **Reducing operating costs:** Many environmental measures, such as energy-efficient equipment or lighting, involve initial investments but deliver long-term environmental and cost-saving benefits.

- ✔ **Creating a sustainable supply chain:** We have made significant investments in our supply chains, with the long term in mind. Our focus has been to ensure that our suppliers of today will have the capacity to supply Starbucks business tomorrow. Their sustainability is critically linked to our growth and success. This is especially true of those who supply our core products or ingredients, such as coffee, tea, and cocoa.

- ✔ **License to operate:** Having a strong reputation as a socially responsible company makes it more likely we will be welcomed into a local community. In a recent customer survey, nearly half of the respondents indicated extremely or very positive attitudes about having a Starbucks in their neighborhood, while only 7 percent expressed negative attitudes.

Long story short, adopting socially responsible business practices is a net benefit to the companies that adopt them. Why not try them in your organization and see what happens? We think you'll be pleasantly surprised with the results.

Developing a CSR strategy for implementation

Adopting corporate social responsibility in an effective manner requires developing a strategy for its implementation. The spectrum of possible CSR initiatives available to a company is mind boggling. You can start with a barebones approach — say, replacing disposable (and environmentally unfriendly) Styrofoam coffee cups with washable and infinitely reusable porcelain coffee mugs — or you can go all the way to a multiphase international CSR strategy that touches every part of your organization and has a direct and significant impact on the world.

Kellie McElhaney is the faculty director of the Center for Responsible Business at the Haas School of Business, University of California, Berkeley. In her book *Just Good Business: The Strategic Guide to Aligning Corporate Social Responsibility and Brand* (Berrett Koehler), Kellie describes seven rules to consider when developing an effective CSR strategy:

- **Know thyself.** Your CSR strategy must be authentic and must ring true for your organization. The best way to ensure that this is the case is to closely match it to your company's mission, vision, and values. Employees, customers, and others will know when it's not authentic, and your CSR strategy won't have the desired effect.

- **Get a good fit.** The goals you select for your CSR strategy must fit your company and its products and services. For example, if your company manufactures women's clothing, then actively supporting Susan G. Komen for the Cure — which raises money for breast cancer research — is a good fit.

- **Be consistent.** Be sure that everyone in your organization knows what your CSR strategy and goals are and that they can express them consistently to one another — and to the general public. Your CSR efforts are multiplied when everyone in your company has a clear understanding of their role and is completely aligned with the program.

- **Simplify.** In developing and implementing a CSR strategy, simpler is usually better. Organic yogurt maker Stonyfield Farm's mantra is simple: "Healthy food, healthy people, healthy planet." Anyone can understand what the company is committed to accomplishing, and customers feel tremendous brand loyalty because they want to be a part of what Stonyfield is doing. Of course, it also doesn't hurt that Stonyfield's yogurt is a great product!

- **Work from the inside out.** Your CSR strategy isn't worth the paper it's written on if you haven't engaged your employees in the process of developing and implementing it. Instead of forcing a CSR strategy on your employees, invite their active participation in creating it and then rolling it out. You'll get better results and your employees will be pleased that you thought highly enough about them to involve them in the process.

✔ **Know your customer.** When developing a CSR strategy, it's better to address the immediate needs of your customers before you try to solve all the problems of the world. These customer needs often boil down to the most basic of human needs: safety, love and belonging, self-esteem, and self-actualization. If you can address these customer needs, you'll have a customer for life.

✔ **Tell your story.** When you have your CSR strategy in place, don't be afraid to publicize your efforts to be socially responsible along with your successes. Again, many people (including prospective customers, clients, and employees) are attracted to companies that operate in a socially responsible way. If you don't get out the word about your programs, you'll lose this powerful advantage. So tell your story — as often as you can — to your employee and to the general public. Use company newsletters and brochures, your Web site, and online social media such as Twitter, Facebook, and YouTube.

Above all, don't spend hours, days, or weeks laboring over a CSR strategy, only to file it away and forget all about it. Integrate your strategy into your everyday business operations. In this way, you'll gain the full benefit of corporate social responsibility — a benefit that can give you a distinct competitive advantage in the marketplace.

Evaluating the Political Side of Your Workplace

How political is your office or workplace? As a manager, having your finger on the political pulse of the organization is particularly important. Truth be told, although it may make perfect sense to do something new or different in an organization, you often have to convince a decision maker to make a change. This task is easier if you're politically savvy and have a good handle on your political environment.

Embarking on the path of corporate social responsibility may make good sense for a variety of different reasons, but you've got to sell it to your boss. And she has to sell it to her boss. Getting in touch with the office politics at play can make you more effective, and it can help your department and your employees have a greater impact within the organization.

Assessing your organization's political environment

Asking insightful questions of your co-workers is one of the best ways to quickly assess your organization's political environment. You can often get the "inside scoop" from co-workers who have been around for awhile. You'll also quickly discover whether you need to avoid organizational taboos or hot buttons. Give these questions a try:

- ✔ "What's the best way to get a nonbudget item approved?"

- ✔ "How can I get a product from the warehouse that my client needs today when I don't have time to do the paperwork?"

- ✔ "Can I do anything else for you before I go home for the day?"

Although asking savvy questions gives you an initial indication of the political lay of the land in your organization, you can do more to assess the office politics. Watch for the following signs while you're getting a sense of how your organization really works:

- ✔ **Find out how others who seem to be effective get tasks done.** How much time do they spend preparing before sending through a formal request for a budget increase? Which items do they delegate and to whose subordinates? When you find people who are particularly effective at getting tasks done in your organization's political environment, model their behavior.

- ✔ **Observe how others are rewarded for the jobs they do.** Does management swiftly and enthusiastically bestow warm and personal rewards in a sincere manner to clearly show what behavior is important? Does management give credit to everyone who helped make a project successful, or does only the manager get his picture in the company newsletter? By observing your company's rewards, you can tell what behavior management expects of employees in your organization. Practice this behavior.

- ✔ **Observe how others are disciplined for the jobs they do.** Does management come down hard on employees for relatively small mistakes? Are employees criticized in public or in front of co-workers? Is everyone held accountable for decisions, actions, and mistakes even if they had no prior involvement? Such behavior indicates that management doesn't encourage risk taking. If your organization is risk averse, maintain an outwardly reserved political style as you work behind the scenes.

✔ **Consider how formal the people in the organization are.** When you're in a staff meeting, for example, you definitely show poor form if you blurt out, "That's a dumb idea. Why would we even consider doing such a thing?" Instead, buffer and finesse your opinions like so: "That's an interesting possibility. Could we explore the pros and cons of implementing that?" The degree of formality you find in your company indicates how you need to act to conform to the expectations of others.

Identifying key players

When you've discovered that you work in a political environment (did you really have any doubt in your mind?), you need to determine who the key players are. Why? They are the individuals who can help you move your corporate social responsibility goals forward. They can also provide positive models of ethical behavior for you and your employees to follow and emulate. Key players are the politically astute individuals who make things happen in an organization.

Some key players are at the top of the organization, as you may expect. However, you'll find key players at every level — not just the top. For example, as the department head's assistant, Jack may initially appear to be nothing more than a gofer. However, you may later find out that Jack is responsible for scheduling all his boss's appointments, setting agendas for department meetings, and vetoing actions on his own authority. Jack is an informal leader in the organization, and because you can't get to your boss without going through Jack, you know that Jack has much more power in the organization than his title indicates.

All the following factors are indicators that can help you identify the key players in your organization:

✔ Which employees in your organization do others seek out for advice?

✔ Which employees do others consider to be indispensable?

✔ Whose office is located closest to those of the organization's top management, and whose is located miles away?

✔ Who eats lunch with the president, the vice presidents, and other members of the upper management team?

As you figure out who the key players in your organization are, you start to notice that they have different office personalities. Use the following categories to figure out how to work with the different personality types of your organization's key players. Do you recognize any of these players in your organization?

✔ **Movers and shakers:** These individuals usually far exceed the boundaries of their office positions. For example, you may find a mover and shaker who's in charge of purchasing but who's also helping to negotiate a merger. Someone in charge of the physical plant may have the power to designate a wing of the building to the group of her choosing.

✔ **Corporate citizens:** These employees are diligent, hardworking, company-loving people who seek slow but steady, long-term advancement through dedication and hard work. Corporate citizens are great resources for getting information and advice about the organization. You can count on them for help and support, especially if your ideas are in the best interest of the organization.

✔ **The town gossips:** These employees always seem to know what's going on in the organization — usually before the individuals who are actually affected by the news know it. Assume that anything you say to these individuals will get back to the person about whom you say it.

✔ **Firefighters:** These individuals relish stepping into a potential problem with great fanfare at the last conceivable moment to save a project, client, deadline, or whatever. Keep these people well informed of your activities so that you aren't the subject of the next "fire."

✔ **Vetoers:** These people in your organization have the authority to kill your best ideas and ambitions with a simple comment such as, "We tried that and it didn't work." The best way to deal with vetoers is to keep them out of your decision loop. Try to find other individuals who can get your ideas approved, or rework the idea until you hit upon an approach that satisfies the vetoer.

✔ **Techies:** Every organization has technically competent workers who legitimately have a high value of their own opinions. Experts can take charge of a situation without taking over. Get to know your experts well — you can trust their judgments and opinions.

✔ **Whiners:** A few employees are never satisfied with whatever is done for them. Associating with them inevitably leads to a pessimistic outlook, which you can't easily turn around. Worse, your boss may think that you're a whiner, too. In addition, pessimistic people tend to be promoted less often than optimists. Be an optimist: Your optimism makes a big difference in your career and in your life.

Redrawing your organization chart

Your company's organization chart may be useful for determining who's who in the formal organization, but it really has no bearing on who's who in the informal political organization. What you need is the real organization chart. Figure 16-1 illustrates a typical official organization chart.

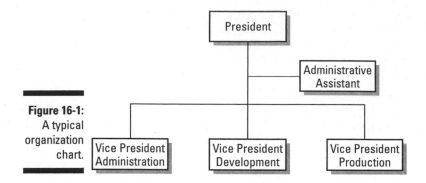

Figure 16-1:
A typical
organization
chart.

Start by finding your organization's official organization chart — the one that looks like a big pyramid. Throw it away. Now, from your impressions and observations, start outlining the real relationships in your organization. Begin with the key players whom you've already identified. Indicate their relative power by level and relationships by approximation. Use the following questions as a guideline:

- ✔ **Whom do these influential people associate with?** Draw the associations on your chart and connect them with solid lines. Also connect friends and relatives.

- ✔ **Who makes up the office cliques?** Be sure that all members are connected, because talking to one is like talking to them all.

- ✔ **Who are the office gossips?** Use dotted lines to represent communication without influence and solid lines for communication with influence.

- ✔ **Who's your competition?** Circle those employees likely to be considered for your next promotion. Target them for special attention.

- ✔ **Who's left off the chart?** Don't forget about these individuals. The way today's organizations seem to change every other day, someone who is off the chart on Friday may be on the chart on Monday. Always maintain positive relationships with all your co-workers, and never burn bridges between you and others within and throughout the company. Otherwise, you may find yourself left off the chart someday.

The result of this exercise is a chart of who really has political power in your organization and who doesn't. Figure 16-2 shows how the organization really works. Update your organization chart as you find out more information about people. Of course, understand that you may be wrong. You can't possibly know the inner power relationships of every department. Sometimes individuals who seem to have power may have far less of it than people who have discovered how to exhibit their power more quietly.

Finally, be genuine and respectful in your quest to understand your company's politics. If you're seen as someone who's two-faced or untrustworthy, someone who aligns only with the power players for a while and then moves on, you ultimately won't be trusted or rewarded for your political savvy.

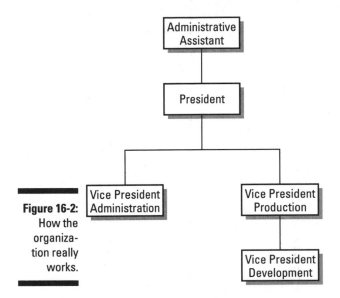

Figure 16-2:
How the organization really works.

Doing the Right Thing: Ethics and You

Each year or two, the leaders of some company somewhere trigger a huge scandal due to some ethical lapse. These lapses are often so egregious that you often wonder whether anyone in charge knows the difference between right and wrong — or, if they do know the difference, whether they really care.

Despite appearances to the contrary, many business leaders do know the difference between right and wrong. Now more than ever, businesses and the leaders who run them are trying to do the right thing, not just because the right thing is politically correct, but also because it's good for the bottom line.

Defining ethics on the job

Do you know what ethics are? In case you're a bit rusty on the correct response, the long answer is that ethics are standards of beliefs and values that guide conduct, behavior, and activities — in other words, a way of thinking that provides boundaries for our actions. The short answer is that ethics are simply doing the right thing.

Although all people come to a job with their own sense of ethical values — based on their own upbringing and life experiences — organizations and leaders are responsible for setting clear ethical standards.

When you have high ethical standards on the job, you generally exhibit some or all of the following personal qualities and behaviors:

- ✔ Accountability
- ✔ Dedication
- ✔ Fairness
- ✔ Honesty
- ✔ Impartiality
- ✔ Integrity
- ✔ Loyalty
- ✔ Responsibility

Ethical behavior starts with you. As a manager, you're a leader in your organization, and you set an example — both for other managers and for the many workers who are watching your every move. When others see you behaving unethically, you're sending the message loud and clear that ethics don't matter. The result? Ethics won't matter to them, either.

However, when you behave ethically, others follow your example and behave ethically, too. And if you practice ethical conduct, it also reinforces and perhaps improves your own ethical standards. As managers, we have a responsibility to try to define, live up to, and improve our own set of personal ethics.

Creating a code of ethics

Although most people have a pretty good idea about what kinds of behavior are ethical and what kinds of behavior aren't, ethics are somewhat subjective and open to interpretation by the individual employee. For example, one worker may think that making unlimited personal phone calls from the office is okay, while another worker may consider that to be inappropriate.

So what's the solution to ethics that vary from person to person in an organization? A code of ethics.

A sample code of ethics

Because of the nature of the public trust they are charged with (they're spending our tax dollars, after all!), government workers have long been held to a higher standard of ethical behavior than employees in private industry. The U.S. Congress adopted this Code of Ethics for Government Service on July 11, 1958 (and it's still just as valid today).

Any person in government service should:

1. Put loyalty to the highest moral principles and to country above loyalty to Government persons, party, or department.

2. Uphold the Constitution, laws, and legal regulations of the United States and of all governments therein and never be a party to their evasion.

3. Give a full day's labor for a full day's pay; giving to the performance of his duties his earnest effort and best thought.

4. Seek to find and employ more efficient and economical ways of getting tasks accomplished.

5. Never discriminate unfairly by the dispensing of special favors or privileges to anyone, whether for remuneration or not; and never accept for himself or his family, favors or benefits under circumstances which might be construed by reasonable persons as influencing the performance of his governmental duties.

6. Make no private promises of any kind binding upon the duties of office, since a Government employee has no private word, which can be binding on public duty.

7. Engage in no business with the Government, either directly or indirectly, which is inconsistent with the conscientious performance of his governmental duties.

8. Never use any information coming to him confidentially in the performance of governmental duties as a means for making private profit.

9. Expose corruption wherever discovered.

10. Uphold these principles, ever conscious that public office is a public trust.

By creating and implementing a code of ethics, you clearly and unambiguously spell out for all employees — from the very top to the very bottom — your organization's ethical expectations. A code of ethics isn't a substitute for company policies and procedures; the code complements them. Instead of leaving your employees' definition of ethics on the job to chance — or someone's upbringing — you clearly spell out that stealing, sharing trade secrets, sexually harassing a co-worker, and engaging in other unethical behavior is unacceptable and may be grounds for dismissal. And when you require your employees to read and sign a copy acknowledging their acceptance of the code, your employees can't very well claim that they didn't know what you expected of them. The ethics policy should be reviewed and agreed to annually so that it remains top-of-mind for all employees.

What's in a comprehensive code of ethics?

According to the Ethics Resource Center Web site (www.ethics.org), a comprehensive code of ethics has the following seven parts:

- **A memorable title:** Examples include Price Waterhouse's *The Way We Do Business* and the World Bank Group's *Living Our Values*.

- **Leadership letter:** A cover letter that briefly outlines the content of the code of ethics and clearly demonstrates commitment from the very top of the organization to ethical principles of behavior.

- **Table of contents:** The main parts within the code, listed by page number.

- **Introduction/prologue:** Why the code is important, the scope of the code, and to whom it applies.

- **Statement of core values:** Detailed description of the organization's primary values.

- **Code provisions:** The meat of the code, the organization's position on a wide variety of issues, including such topics as sexual harassment, privacy, conflicts of interest, gratuities, and so forth.

- **Information and resources:** Places employees can go for further information or for specific advice or counsel.

Four key areas form the foundation of a good code of ethics:

- Compliance with internal policies and procedures
- Compliance with external laws and regulations
- Direction from organizational values
- Direction from individual values

Of course, a code of ethics isn't worth the paper it's printed on if it doesn't address some very specific issues, as well as the more generic ones listed previously. The following are some of the most common issues addressed by typical codes of ethics:

- Conflicts of interest
- Diversity
- Employee health and safety
- Equal opportunity
- Gifts and gratuities
- Privacy and confidentiality
- Sexual harassment

In addition to working within an organization, a well-crafted code of ethics can be a powerful tool for publicizing your company's standards and values to people outside your organization, including vendors, clients, customers, investors, potential job applicants, the media, and the general public. Your code of ethics tells others that you value ethical behavior and that it guides the way you and your employees do business.

Of course, simply having a code of ethics isn't enough. You and your employees must also live it. Even the world's best code of ethics does you no good if you file it away and never use it.

Making ethical choices every day

You may have a code of ethics, but if you never behave ethically in your day-to-day business transactions and relationships, what's the purpose of having a code in the first place? Ethical challenges abound in business — some are spelled out in your company's code of ethics, or in its policies and procedures, and some aren't. For example, what would you do in these situations?

- One of your favorite employees gives you tickets to a baseball game.

- An employee asks you not to write her up for a moderate infraction of company policies.

- You sold a product to a client that you later found out to be faulty, but your boss wants you to forget about it.

- Your department's financial results are actually lower than what appears in your boss's presentation to the board of directors.

- You find out that your star employee actually didn't graduate from college, as he claimed in his job application.

- You know that a product you sell doesn't actually do everything your company claims it does.

We all make ethical choices on the job every day — how do you make yours? Consider this framework comprising six keys to making better ethical choices:

- **Evaluate** circumstances through the appropriate filters. (Filters include culture, laws, policies, circumstances, relationships, politics, perception, emotions, values, bias, and religion.)

- **Treat** people and issues fairly within the established boundaries. *Fair* doesn't always mean *equal*.

✔ **Hesitate** before making critical decisions.

✔ **Inform** those affected of the standard or decision that has been set.

✔ **Create** an environment of consistency for yourself and your working group.

✔ **Seek** counsel when you have any doubt (but from those who are honest and whom you respect).

Part IV
Tough Times for Tough Managers

The 5th Wave   By Rich Tennant

"I assume everyone on your team is on board with
the proposed changes to the office layout."

In this part . . .

No one ever said being a manager is easy. Rewarding? Yes. Easy? No. In this part, we present strategies for managing change in the workplace, disciplining employees easily and effectively, and conducting employee terminations. Understanding the processes and being well prepared can help you smooth transitions and ease your way through these often unpleasant tasks.

Chapter 17

Managing Change and Morale

. . . .

In This Chapter

▶ Dealing with crisis

▶ Putting up roadblocks to change

▶ Helping others through change

▶ Inspiring initiative in others

▶ Moving on with your life

. . . .

*N*othing stays the same, in business or in life. Change is all around us — it always has been and always will be. Many people view change as something to be feared and avoided, but you can embrace change because it brings excitement, new opportunities, and personal growth.

So what does change mean to you as a manager? The world of business is constantly changing, and the pressures on managers to perform are greater than they've ever been. In addition, most organizations have gone from being bastions of stability and status quo in the stormy seas of change to being agile ships, navigating the fluid and ever-changing seas in which they float.

The words *business* and *change* are quickly becoming synonymous. And the more things change, the more everyone in an organization is affected. This chapter is about managing and thriving on change, and helping your employees find ways to take advantage of it — instead of letting change take advantage of them!

Understanding Urgency and Crisis

Although it sometimes seems like everything is a crisis at work, a difference really does exist between what is truly a crisis and what isn't. In this section, we help you divine the two.

What's your typical business day like? Maybe you get into the office, grab a cup of coffee, and scan your appointment calendar. Looks like a light day for meetings — two in the morning and only one in the afternoon. Maybe you can finally get a chance to work on the budget goal you've been meaning to complete for the past few months, plus have some extra time to go for a walk at lunch to unwind. Doesn't that sound nice? Next, you pick up your telephone to check your voice mail. Of the 25 messages that have stacked up since you last checked, 10 are urgent. When you check your e-mail, you find much the same thing.

As you begin to think about how you can respond to these urgent messages, an employee arrives with his own crisis that needs your immediate attention. He tells you that the computer network has broken down, and until someone fixes it, the entire corporate financial system is on the fritz. While you're talking to your employee, your boss calls to tell you to drop everything because you've been selected to write a report for the president that absolutely has to be done by the close of business today.

So much for working on your budget goal. And you can forget that relaxing walk at lunch. On the surface, your day may appear to have been turned upside down, but is that really true? Perhaps not. To determine whether that's the case, first you need to separate what's truly a crisis from what's not.

When urgency is really poor planning

Urgency has its place in an organization. The rate of change in the global business environment demands it. The revolutions in computer use, telecommunications systems, and information technology demand it. The need to be more responsive to customers than ever demands it. In these urgent times, companies that provide the best solutions faster than anyone else are the winners. The losers are the companies that wonder what happened as they watch their competitors streak by.

However, an organization has a real problem when its managers fall into the behavior of managing by crisis. When every problem in an organization becomes a drop-everything-else-that-you're-doing crisis, the organization isn't showing signs of responsiveness to change in its business environment. Instead, the business is showing signs of poor planning and lousy execution. Someone (perhaps a manager?) isn't doing his job.

Recognizing and dealing with crises

Sometimes outside forces cause crises. For example, suppose that a vital customer requests that all project designs be submitted by this Friday instead of next Friday. Or perhaps the city sends you a notice that a maintenance crew plans to cut off the power to your plant for three days while the crew performs needed maintenance on switching equipment. Or a huge snowstorm in the Northeast cuts off all flights, in and out, for the rest of the week.

On the other hand, many crises occur because someone in your organization drops the ball, and now you (the manager) have to fix everything. The following are avoidable crisis situations:

- Hoping that the need will go away, you avoid making a necessary decision. Surprise! The need didn't go away, and now you have a crisis to deal with.

- An employee forgets to relay an important message from your customer. Your customer gets mad, and you're about to lose the account as a result. Another crisis. (See Chapter 18 for details about disciplining an employee.)

- A co-worker decides that informing you about a major change to a manufacturing process isn't all that important. Because of your experience, you would have quickly seen that the change would lead to quality problems in the finished product. When manufacturing grinds to a halt, you come in after the fact to clean up the mess. One more crisis to add to your list.

You have to be prepared to deal with externally generated crises. You have to be flexible, you have to work smart, and you have to work hard. But your organization can't afford to become a slave to internally generated crises. Managing by crisis forgoes one of the most important elements in business management: *planning.*

You establish plans and goals for a reason: to make your company and your employees as successful as possible, creating great products and happy customers. However, if you continually set your plans and goals on a back burner because of today's crisis, why waste your time making the plans? And where does your organization go then? (See Chapter 6 for a discussion on the importance of having plans and goals.)

When you, as a manager, allow everything to become a crisis through your own inaction or failure to anticipate change, not only do you sap the energy of your employees, but eventually they lose the ability to recognize when a real crisis is upon them. Remember the old fable about the boy who cried "Wolf"? After the boy issued several false alarms in jest, the villagers didn't bother to respond to his cries when some wolves actually appeared to attack his sheep. After responding to several manufactured crises, your employees begin to see the crises as routine, and they may not be there for you when you really need them.

Accepting that Change Happens

Change happens, and you can't do anything about it. You can try to ignore it, but does that stop change? No, you only blind yourself to what's really happening in your organization. You can try to stop it, but does that keep change from happening? No, you're only fooling yourself if you think that you can stop change — even for a moment. You can try to insulate yourself and the employees around you from the effects of change, but can you really afford to ignore it? No, to ignore change is to sign a death warrant for your organization and, quite possibly, for your career.

Unfortunately, from our personal observations, most managers seem to spend their entire careers trying to fight change — to predict, control, and harness change and its effects on the organization. But why? Change is what allows organizations to progress, products to get better, and people to advance — both personally and in their careers.

When Bill Taylor, owner of Lark In The Morning (a seller of musical instruments located in Ft. Bragg, California), discusses the topic of change with his employees, he likes to tell the following story about swinging on a trapeze — inspired by an essay published in *The Essene Book of Days* (Earthstewards Publications) by Danaan Parry: You have a good grip on the trapeze. You get some confidence, and maybe you even do a pike or hang by your ankles. This position begins to feel really comfortable. Then, off in the darkness, you see another trapeze bar swinging toward you, and you get that old familiar feeling in your stomach. You have to completely let go of this trapeze, fly through the air, and grab the next trapeze. You've done this before. You know you can do it again. But it always creates anxiety and uncertainty, maybe even a sense of dread. So you let go and start flying through the air. Remember that the very uncomfortable place in midair is the only place personal growth takes place. Maybe you don't get comfortable with being in the air, but at least you recognize the value it adds to your life. When you grab the new trapeze, personal growth is over.

Identifying the four stages of change

Change is no picnic. Despite the excitement change can bring to your working life — both good and bad — you've probably had just about all the change you can handle right about now, thank you very much. But as change continues, both you and your employees go through four distinct phases in response to change:

1. **Deny change.** When change happens, the first response you have (if you're like most people) is one of immediate denial. "Whose dumb idea was that? That idea is never going to work here. Don't worry, they'll see

their mistake and go back to the old way of doing things!" Operating with this attitude is acting like an ostrich sticking its head in the sand: If you can't see it, it'll go away. Of course, it never works this way — change happens regardless of whether you acknowledge it.

2. **Resist change.** At some point, you realize that the change isn't just a clerical error; however, this realization doesn't mean that you have to accept the change lying down! "Nope, I'm sticking with the old way of doing that job. If that way was good enough then, why isn't it good enough now?" Resistance is a normal response to change — everyone goes through it. Just don't let your resistance get you stuck. The quicker you get with the program, the better it'll be for your organization and your career.

3. **Explore change.** By now, you know that further resistance is futile and the new way just may have some good points. "Well, maybe that change actually does make sense. I'll see what opportunities can make the change work *for* me instead of *against* me." During this stage, you examine both the good and the bad that come from the change, and you decide on a strategy for managing the change. You're finally beginning to make some progress.

4. **Accept change.** The final stage of change is acceptance. At this point, you've successfully integrated the change into your routine. "Wow, this new system really works well. It beats the heck out of the old way of doing things!" Now the change that you so vigorously denied and resisted is part of your everyday routine; the change has become the status quo.

At the end of your change responses, you come full circle, and you're ready to face your next change.

Are you (or your employees) fighting change?

You or the employees you manage may be fighting change and not even know it. Besides watching the number of gray hairs on your head multiply, how can you tell? Look out for these seven deadly warning signs of resistance to change:

✔ **Still using the old rules to play a new game:** Sorry to be the ones to bring you this bad news, but the old game and its rules are gone. The pressures of global competition have created a brand new game with a brand new set of rules. For example, if you're one of those increasingly rare managers who refuses to use e-mail (don't laugh, they do exist!), you're playing by the old rules. Computer literacy and information proficiency are the new rules. If you're not playing with the new rules, not only is this a warning sign that you're resisting change, but you can bet on being left behind as the rest of your organization moves along the path to the future.

- **Ducking new assignments:** Usually, two basic reasons cause you to avoid new assignments. First, you may be overwhelmed with your current job and can't imagine taking on any more duties, no matter how simple they may be. If you're in this situation, remember that new ways often make your work more efficient or even wipe out many old things that you do. Second, you may simply be uneasy with the unknown, so you resist change.

Ducking new assignments to resist change is a definite no-no. Not only are you interfering with the progress of the organization, but you're also effectively putting your own career on hold.

- **Trying to slow things down:** Trying to slow down is a normal reaction for most people. When something new comes along — a new way of doing business, a new assignment, or a new wrinkle in the marketplace — most people tend to want to slow down, to take the time to examine, analyze, and then decide how to react. The problem is that the newer something gets, the slower some people go — bringing their organizations to a grinding halt.

As a manager, you want to remain competitive in the future. You don't have the luxury of slowing down every time something new comes along. From now on, the amount of new that you have to deal with will greatly outweigh the old. Instead of resisting the new by slowing down (and risking an uncompetitive and obsolete organization), you need to keep up your pace. How? When you're forced to do more with less, focus on less.

- **Working hard to control the uncontrollable:** Have you ever tried to keep the sun from rising in the morning? Or tried to stop the dark clouds that drop rain, sleet, and snow on your house during a storm? Or tried to stay 29 years old forever? We didn't think so. Face it, you just can't control many parts of life — you waste your time when you try.

Are you resisting change by trying to control the uncontrollable at work? Perhaps you want to try to head off a planned corporate reorganization, stop your foreign competitors from having access to your domestic markets, or delay the acquisition of your firm by a much larger company. Don't bother. The world of business is changing all around you, and you can't do anything about it. You have a choice: You can continue to resist change by pretending that you're controlling it (believe us, you can't), or you can concentrate your efforts on figuring out how to most effectively respond to change to leverage it to your advantage.

✔ **Playing the role of victim:** Oh, woe is me! This response is the ultimate cop-out. Instead of accepting change and finding out how to respond to it (and using it to the advantage of your organization and yourself), you choose to become a victim of it. Playing the role of victim and hoping that your co-workers feel sorry for you is easy to do. ("Poor Samantha, she's got a brand new crop of upstart competitors to handle. I wonder how she can even bring herself to come to work every morning?")

But today's successful businesses can't afford to waste their time or money employing victims. If you're not giving 110 percent each day you go to work, your organization will find someone who can.

✔ **Hoping someone else can make things better:** In the old-style hierarchical organization, top management almost always took responsibility for making the decisions that made things better (or worse) for workers. We have a news flash: The old-style organization is changing forever, and the new-style organization taking its place has empowered every employee to take responsibility for decision making.

The pressures of global competition and the coming of the Information Age require that decisions be made quicker than ever. In other words, the employees closest to the issues must make the decisions — and right now; a manager who is seven layers up from the front line and 3,000 miles away can't do it. You hold the keys to your future. You have the power to make things better for yourself. If you wait until someone else makes things better for you, you're going to be waiting an awfully long time.

✔ **Acting absolutely paralyzed, like a deer in the headlights:** This condition is the ultimate sign of resistance to change and is almost always terminal. Sometimes change seems so overwhelming that the only choice is to give up. When change paralyzes you, not only do you fail to respond to change, but you can no longer perform your current duties and responsibilities. In today's organization, such resistance means certain career death.

Instead of allowing change to paralyze you, become a leader of change. Consider these ideas:

- Embrace the change. Become its friend and its biggest cheerleader.

- Be flexible and responsive to the changes that swirl all around you and through your organization.

- Be a model to the employees around you who continue to resist change. Show them that they can make change work *for* them instead of *against* them.

- Focus on what you can do, not what you can't do.

- Recognize and reward employees who have accepted the change and who have succeeded as a result.

If you notice any of these seven warning signs of resistance to change — in yourself or in your employees — you can do something about it. As long as you're willing to embrace change instead of fight it, you hold incredible value for your organization. You can take advantage of change instead of fall victim to it. Make responsiveness to change your personal mission: Be a leader of change, not a follower of resistance.

Guiding Employees through Change

When your organization finds itself in the midst of change — whether because of fast-moving markets, changing technology, rapidly shifting customer needs, or some other reason — you need to remember that change affects everyone, not just you as a manager. And although some of your employees can cope with these changes with nary a hiccup, others may have a difficult time adjusting to their new environment and the expectations that come along with it. Be alert for employees who are resisting or having a hard time dealing with change, and help them transition through the process.

Helping employees cope

Change can be traumatic for some people. Stay alert to the impact of change on your employees and help them work their way through it. Not only will your employees appreciate your support — showing their appreciation with loyalty to you and your organization — but morale will improve and your employees will be more productive as a result.

The following tips can help your employees cope with change on the job:

✔ **Show that you care.** Managers are busy people, but never be too busy to show your employees that you care — especially when they're having difficulties on the job. Take a personal interest in your employees and offer to help them in any way you can.

✔ **Widely communicate the potential for change.** Nothing is more disconcerting to employees than being surprised by changes that they didn't expect. As much as possible, give your employees a heads-up on potential changes in the business environment, and keep them up-to-date on the status of the changes as time goes on.

✔ **Seek feedback.** Let your employees know that you want their feedback and suggestions on how to deal with potential problems resulting from change, or how to capitalize on any opportunities that may result. And when your employees give you feedback, do your best to respond to it in a positive way.

✔ **Be a good listener.** When your employees are in a stressful situation, they naturally want to talk about it — this part of the process helps them cope with change. Set aside time to chat informally with employees, and encourage them to voice their concerns about the changes that they and the organization are going through.

✔ **Don't give false assurances.** Although you don't want to needlessly frighten your employees with tales of impending doom and gloom, also avoid sugarcoating the truth. Be frank and honest with your employees; treat them like the adults they are.

✔ **Involve employees.** Involve employees in planning for upcoming changes and, whenever practicable, delegate to them the responsibility and authority for making decisions.

✔ **Train employees.** Consider offering training in change management for your employees, or bring in an outside change-management consultant to help bring them along.

✔ **Look to the future.** Paint a vision for your employees that emphasizes the many ways in which the organization will be a better place as everyone adapts to change and begins to use it to their benefit.

Encouraging employee initiative

One of the most effective ways to help employees make it through the change process in one piece is to give them permission to take charge of their own work. You can encourage your employees to take the initiative to come up with ideas to improve the way they do their work and then to implement those ideas.

The most successful organizations are the ones that actively encourage employees to take initiative; the least successful ones are organizations that stifle initiative.

Consider how these companies reward employee initiative:

✔ Federal Express, based in Memphis, Tennessee, awards the Golden Falcon to employees who go above and beyond to serve their customers. For example, one winner took the initiative to order new shipping forms for a regular customer after noticing that the customer had not thought to change his area code on a return address.

✔ At least one All-Star is chosen monthly at each D'Agostino supermarket location. The chain, based in Larchmont, New York, chooses winners based on employees who go "beyond the call of duty" to help co-workers or customers.

✔ At El Torito Restaurants, based in Irvine, California, employees receive a "Be a Star" award for going above and beyond their job description. Winners receive Star Bucks, which are entered for a monthly drawing for up to $1,000 worth of merchandise.

As a manager, you need to make your employees feel safe enough to take initiative in their jobs. Not only will your employees better weather the change that swirls all around them, but they also will create a more effective organization and provide better service to customers in the process. Ask your employees to do the following:

✔ Look for ways to make improvements to the status quo, and follow through with an action plan.

✔ Focus suggestions on areas that have the greatest impact on the organization.

✔ Follow up suggestions with action. Volunteer to help implement suggestions.

✔ Step outside the box. Look for areas of improvement throughout the organization, not just within their department or business unit.

✔ Don't make frivolous suggestions. They degrade your credibility and distract you from more important areas of improvement.

Keeping employees' spirits high

When a company is downsizing or going through other dramatic changes, employee morale may plummet. Not only does much uncertainty hang in the air, but employees may be required to pick up the slack when other employees are laid off or reassigned, essentially getting paid the same amount of money (or less) to do more work. Keeping employee morale and loyalty high is critically important during times of change. Consider a few tips for doing just that:

✔ **Have fun.** Don't allow your office to become a morgue, with everyone walking around like zombies. Have a costume contest with employee judges or sponsor an impromptu ice cream social. Telecommunications giant Sprint once turned a regular workday into Beach Day at their Kansas City headquarters. The company turned its parking lot into a beach by trucking in sand, and it provided sunglasses, plastic leis, and live music to the "vacationing" employees.

✔ **Be honest.** Don't sugarcoat the truth; employees don't like it, and they'll lose respect for anyone who isn't giving them the straight scoop. If a change in your business will impact them — whether in a good or a bad way — tell them sooner rather than later.

✔ **Put people first.** It's far too easy to forget that your employees make your business what it is. When you make employees number one on your list of priorities, they will pay you back many times over in increased loyalty, perseverance, and quality of work. Show your employees that they are important by always putting them and their concerns at the top of your list.

✔ **Set a good example.** When you set a positive example for your employees, they naturally follow. Don't wait for others to make the first move; be a leader of change and inspire your employees to give their all to the cause, whatever it may be.

Making a Change When All Else Fails

If you've done everything you can to deal with change at work and take control of your business life, but you're still feeling lost, you may be facing a deeper issue that's not readily apparent on the surface.

When you read a book, do you ever wish you had written it? When you go to a seminar, do you ever think you could teach it? Have you ever wondered what owning your own business is like — to be your own boss and be completely responsible for your company's profits or losses?

If you answered "yes" to any of these questions, you may not be truly happy until you pursue your dream. Maybe you want to start a new career or move to a new company. Or perhaps you have an opportunity with your current employer to make a job change that can take you to your dream. Maybe you want to go back to school to pursue an advanced degree. Or maybe you just want to take a vacation or short leave of absence. The change you need to make may well be within yourself.

Top five change management Web sites

Wondering where to find the best information on the Web about the topics in this chapter? Well, you've come to the right place! These sites are our top five favorites:

✔ Change Management: `www.the manager.org/Knowledgebase/ Management/Change.htm`

✔ Change Management Toolbook: `www. change-management-toolbook. com`

✔ Wharton Center for Leadership and Change Management: `leadership.wharton. upenn.edu`

✔ Change Management Learning Center: `www.change-management.com`

✔ HDI Managing Change Library: `www. hdinc.com/library.html`

Chapter 18

Employee Discipline for Improving Performance

· ·

In This Chapter

▶ Disciplining your employees

▶ Eyeing performance

▶ Following the twin tracks of discipline

▶ Writing a script

▶ Developing an improvement plan

▶ Putting an improvement plan into action

· ·

*W*ouldn't it be nice to have all your employees always carrying out their tasks perfectly? Wouldn't it be nice to have them all love the organization as much as you do? Winning the lottery would be nice, too, but don't quit your day job just yet.

The fact is, your employees will make mistakes, and some of them will exhibit attitudes that don't reflect well on themselves, their department, or their company. Every organization has employees (and managers) who exhibit varying degrees of these behaviors, but don't worry too much about it. No one is perfect. However, when your employees make repeated, serious mistakes; when they fail to meet their performance goals and standards; or when it seems that they'd rather be working somewhere else (anywhere but where they are now!) and they prove that by ignoring company policies, you have to take action to stop the offending behaviors — immediately and decisively.

When employees aren't performing up to standard, or when they allow a poor attitude to overcome their ability to pull with the rest of the team, these employees cost your organization more than do the employees who are working at or above standard and pulling their share of the load. Poor performance and poor attitudes directly and negatively affect your work unit's efficiency and effectiveness.

If other employees see that you're letting their co-workers get away with poor performance, they have little reason to maintain their own standards. "Hey! If Marty can get away with it, I can, too!" Not only do you create more management headaches, but the morale and performance of your entire work unit decreases as a result.

In this chapter, you discover the importance of dealing with employee performance issues before they become major problems. You find out why you need to focus on performance, not personality. You also discover how to implement a consistent system of discipline that can work for you, regardless of your line of business.

Getting to the Root of Employee Discipline

Employee discipline has lately gotten something of a black eye. For many workers, the word *discipline* conjures up visions of crazed management tirades, embarrassing public scolding, and worse. And, unfortunately, because of the abuses that more than a few overzealous supervisors and managers in a wide variety of organizations have committed over the years, this expectation is often not far off target.

But it doesn't have to be that way. Consider the following questions for a moment: What does *discipline* mean to you? What does it mean in your organization? Do your employees look forward to being disciplined? Do you?

The reality is that far too many employees confuse the terms *discipline* and *punishment,* considering them to be one and the same. This belief can't be further from the truth — at least, when discipline is done well. The word *discipline* comes from the Latin *disciplina,* meaning "teaching" or "learning." *Punishment,* on the other hand, is derived from the Latin root *punire,* which itself is derived from the Latin word *poena,* or "penalty." Interestingly, the English word *pain* also found its beginnings in the Latin *poena.*

The whole point of this little digression is that employee discipline can (and should) be a positive experience — at least, it should be when you do it the right way. Through discipline, you bring problems to your employees' attention so that they can take actions to correct them before they become major problems. You can even provide them with the additional guidance and training they need to do their jobs better. Remember, however, to build a strong foundation of positives and trust that you can draw upon when dealing with the negatives. The primary goal of discipline isn't to punish your employees;

you want to guide them back to a satisfactory job performance. Of course, sometimes this step isn't possible and you have no choice but to terminate employees who can't perform satisfactorily. If that's the case, be sure to check out Chapter 19 for a complete discussion on terminating employees.

You generally discipline your employees for two main reasons:

- ✔ **Performance problems:** All employees must meet goals as a part of their jobs. For a receptionist, a goal may be to always answer the telephone on the second ring or sooner. For a sales manager, a goal may be to increase annual sales by 15 percent. When employees fail to meet their performance goals, administering some form of discipline is required.

- ✔ **Misconduct:** Sometimes employees behave in ways that are unacceptable to you as a manager and to the organization. For example, if an employee abuses the company sick leave policy, you have a valid reason for disciplining that employee. In some cases, employee misconduct can cross the line into violations of the law, such as when an employee sexually harasses or threatens other employees, or when an employee steals or engages in physical violence.

Discipline ranges from simple verbal counseling ("William, you turned in the report a day late. I expect future reports to be submitted on time.") to termination ("Sorry, Mary, I warned you that I wouldn't tolerate any further insubordination. You're fired."). A wide variety of options lies between these two extremes, depending on the nature of the problem, its severity, and the work history of the employee involved. For example, if the problem is an isolated incident and the employee normally performs well, the proper discipline is less severe than if the problem is repeated and persistent.

Always carry out discipline as soon after the incident as possible — it's best to deal with problems before they escalate. As with rewarding employees, your message is much stronger and more relevant when it has the immediacy of a recent event. If too much time elapses between an incident and the discipline that you conduct afterward, your employee may forget the specifics of the incident. If you wait, you also send the message that the problem isn't that serious because you didn't bother doing anything about it for so long.

Managers practice effective discipline by noticing performance shortcomings or misconduct before these problems become serious. Effective managers help guide their employees along the right path. Managers who don't discipline their employees have only themselves to blame when poor performance continues unabated or acts of misconduct escalate and get out of hand. Employees need the active support and guidance of their supervisors and managers to know what's expected of them. Without guidance, employees sometimes find it easy to stray from the right path.

And don't forget the Greatest Management Principle in the World: You get what you reward. Take a close look at the behavior you're rewarding in your employees. You may be surprised to find that you're inadvertently reinforcing negative behaviors and poor performance instead of creating the good behavior and performance you're actually trying so hard to get from your employees.

Don't put off discipline. Don't procrastinate. Don't look the other way and hope that your employees' bad behavior disappears. In many cases, it won't just disappear. And if you do decide to look the other direction (or think you just don't have the time), you're doing a disservice to the employees who need your guidance, to the employees who are working at or above standard, and to your organization. Discipline your employees before you run out of time. Do it now.

Focusing on Performance, Not Personalities

You're a manager (or a manager-to-be). You're probably not a psychiatrist or psychologist — even if you feel that you sometimes do nothing but counsel your employees. Your job isn't to analyze your employees' personalities or attempt to understand why they act the way they do — it's impossible to read minds about things like attitude. Your job is to assess your employees' performance against the standards that you and your employees agree to and be alert to employee violations of company policy. If your employees are performing above standard, reward them for their efforts. (See Chapter 3 for more information on rewarding and motivating your employees.) On the other hand, if they're performing below standard, you need to find out why (possibly a process, motivation, or training problem is out of your employees' control) and, if necessary, discipline them.

We're not saying that you shouldn't be compassionate. Sometimes performance suffers because of family problems, financial difficulties, or other pressures unrelated to the job. Although you can give your employees the opportunity to get through their difficulties — you may suggest some time off or a temporary reassignment of duties — they eventually have to return to meeting their performance standards. Allowing certain employees to perform at a lower standard than their co-workers' is a sure path to unhappy employees and a dysfunctional organization.

If an employee is overwhelmed by personal problems or other difficulties, encourage him to seek confidential help from a professional source through your organization's employee assistance program (EAP), a therapist, or other professional counselor.

To be fair, and to be sure that discipline focuses on performance and not on personalities, ensure that all employees fully understand company policies and that you communicate performance standards clearly. When your organization hires new employees, the new hires should get an orientation to key company policies. When your human resources representative drops off new employees at your door, you or someone in your department should take the time to discuss your department's philosophy and practices. And you should periodically sit down with your employees to review and update their performance standards.

When you apply discipline, use it consistently and fairly. Although you must always discipline your employees soon after a demonstrated shortfall in performance or act of misconduct, rushing to judgment before you have a chance to get all the facts is a mistake. Proving that an employee submitted a report a week late is simple, but uncovering the facts in a case of sexual harassment may not be so simple. When you discipline employees, know the facts and act impartially and without favoritism for certain employees. If one employee does something wrong, you can't ignore the same behavior in your other employees. To do so certainly risks the loss of employee respect for your management, and it invites lawsuits and other such unpleasantness.

Remember, although your job is to point out your employees' shortcomings and to help guide your employees in their performance efforts, your employees are ultimately responsible for their performance and their behavior. You can't, and shouldn't, do their work for them. You also can't cover for their mistakes and misdeeds. Sure, you can excuse an occasional mistake, but you must deal with an ongoing pattern of substandard performance or misconduct.

Identifying the Two Tracks of Discipline

As the beginning of this chapter explains, two key reasons for disciplining employees exist: performance problems and misconduct. The two-track system of discipline includes one set of discipline options for performance problems and another for misconduct. These tracks reflect the fact that misconduct, usually an employee's willful act, is considered a much more serious transgression than a shortfall in performance. Performance problems often aren't the employee's direct fault and can usually be corrected with proper training or motivation.

These two tracks reflect the concept of *progressive discipline.* In progressive discipline, you always select the least severe step that results in the behavior you want. For example, if your employee responds to a verbal warning and improves as a result, you can move on to your next management challenge. However, if the employee doesn't respond to a verbal warning, you progress to the next step — a written warning — and give that step a try. The hope is that your employee gets the hint and corrects the behavior before you get to heavy-handed steps, such as reductions in pay, demotions, or terminations.

As you prepare to discipline your employees, first decide whether you're trying to correct performance-related behaviors or misconduct. After you figure that out, decide the best way to get your message across. If the transgression is minor — a lack of attention to detail, for example — you may need only conduct a verbal counseling. However, if you catch an employee sleeping on the job, you may decide to suspend your employee without pay for some period of time. The choice is yours.

In any case, make sure that the discipline takes place as soon as possible after the transgression occurs. You want to correct your employee's performance before the problem becomes significant. If you wait too long, it's probably already too late. And you definitely don't want to make discipline only an annual event by saving all your employee's problems for a periodic performance appraisal.

Your organization's system for disciplining employees may be somewhat different from the one that we outline in this chapter. If you're dealing with union-represented employees, you're likely required to work within the system proscribed by the contract between the union and your firm. For example, you may be required to allow a union representative to sit in on any discipline sessions that you conduct with union-represented employees. Whatever the case, review your organization's policies and labor relations practices and procedures before you embark on the task of disciplining your employees.

Dealing with performance problems

If you've done your job right, each of your employees has a job description and a set of performance standards. The job description is simply an inventory of all the different duties that accompany a particular position. You should have a job description in place for every different position in your company, preferably *before* you actually hire someone to fill the position. Performance standards, on the other hand, are the measurements you and your employees agree to use in assessing your employees' performance. Performance standards form the basis of periodic performance appraisals and reviews. They also make great filler for your personnel files.

Although every organization seems to have its own unique way of conducting performance assessments, employees usually fall into one of three broad categories:

  ✔ Outstanding performance

  ✔ Acceptable performance

  ✔ Unacceptable performance

When it comes to employee discipline, you're primarily concerned with correcting unacceptable performance. You always want to help your good employees become even better employees, but your first concern has to be to identify employees who aren't working up to standard and to correct their performance shortcomings.

As you work your way down the list — from least to most severe — be sure to keep your human resources department in the loop. You may not need to consult them if you conduct a simple verbal counseling, but you definitely need to consult them if you decide to demote or terminate an employee. In general, when it comes to deciding when to get human resources involved, sooner is usually better than later.

The following steps are listed in order of least to most severe. Don't forget: Use the least severe step that results in the behavior you want. If that step doesn't do the trick, move down the list to the next step.

1. **Verbal counseling:** This form of discipline is certainly the most common, and most managers take this step first when they want to correct an employee's performance. A typical manager verbally counsels a variety of employees in any given day. Verbal counseling can range from a simple, spontaneous correction performed in the hallway ("Marge, you need to let me know when our clients call with a service problem.") to a more formal, sit-down meeting in your office ("Sam, I'm concerned that you don't understand the importance of checking the correct address prior to shipping orders. Let's discuss what steps you can take to correct this problem and your plan to implement them."). *Note:* You usually don't document verbal counseling in your employees' files.

2. **Written counseling:** When an employee doesn't respond favorably to verbal counseling, or when the magnitude of performance problems warrants its use, consider written counseling. Written counseling formalizes the counseling process by documenting your employee's performance shortcomings in a written memo. Written counseling is presented to the employee in one-on-one sessions in the supervisor's office. After the employee has an opportunity to read the document, verbal discussions regarding the employee's plan to improve performance ensue. This documentation becomes a part of your employee's personnel file.

3. **Negative performance evaluation:** If verbal and written counseling fail to improve your employee's performance, the situation warrants a negative performance evaluation. Of course, because performance evaluations

are generally given only annually in many organizations, if at all, they're not usually useful for dealing with acute situations. However, if you give verbal and written counseling to no avail, negative performance evaluations are another option to consider, particularly if you can accelerate the process.

4. **Demotion:** Repeated negative performance evaluations or particularly serious performance shortcomings may warrant demoting your employee to a lower rung on the organizational ladder. Often, but not always, the pay of demoted employees is also reduced at the same time, making for a very unhappy employee. Face it: Some employees are hired or promoted into positions that they just can't handle. This situation isn't their fault, but you can't let your employees continue to fail if you have no hope of bringing performance up to an acceptable level with further training or guidance. Although demoralizing, demotions at least allow your employees to move into positions that they can handle. Before you resort to demotion, first try to find a position at an equivalent level that the employee can handle. This step may help improve your employee's motivation and self-confidence and result in a "win" for both the employee and the organization.

5. **Termination:** When all else fails, termination is the ultimate form of discipline for employees who are performing unsatisfactorily. As any manager who has fired an employee knows, terminating employees isn't fun. Consider it as an option only after you exhaust all other avenues. Perhaps needless to say, in these days of wrongful termination lawsuits and multimillion-dollar judgments, you must document employees' performance shortcomings well and support them with the facts. For further information on the ins and outs of this important form of discipline, see Chapter 19.

Dealing with misconduct

Misconduct is a whole different animal from performance problems, so it has its own discipline track. Although both misconduct and performance problems can have negative effects on a company's bottom line, misconduct is usually considered a much more serious offense than performance shortcomings because it indicates a problem with your employees' attitudes or ethical beliefs. And modifying performance behaviors through the use of discipline is a great first step in eventually modifying workers' attitudes or belief systems.

Even the terminology of the different steps in the second track indicates that something serious is going on. For example, although the first step on the first track is called verbal *counseling,* the first step on the second track is called verbal *warning*. You need to deal with misconduct more severely than you deal with performance problems.

The discipline that results from misconduct also has much more immediate consequences to your employees than does the discipline that results from performance problems. Although performance may take some time to bring up to standard — with preparing a plan, scheduling additional training, and so forth — misconduct has to stop immediately. When you discipline your employees for misconduct, you put them on notice that you won't tolerate their behavior. Repeated misconduct can lead quickly to suspension and termination.

Involve your human resources department whenever an employee is to be disciplined for misconduct. Depending on the specific offense the employee committed, such misconduct can have serious legal implications for your company and perhaps for you personally. Now is not the time to try to wing it on your own.

As in the first track, the following discipline steps are listed from least severe to most severe. Your choice depends on the severity of the misconduct and the employee's work record.

1. **Verbal warning:** When employee misconduct is minor or a first offense, the verbal warning provides the least severe option for putting your employees on notice that their behavior won't be tolerated. ("John, I understand that you have continued to pressure Susan into going to lunch with you, even though she has told you on numerous occasions that she isn't interested. This isn't acceptable. I expect you to stop this harassing behavior immediately.") In many cases of misconduct, a verbal warning that demonstrates to your employees that you're aware of the misconduct is all the situation requires, and the negative behavior stops.

2. **Written warning:** Unfortunately, not all your employees get the message when you give them a verbal warning. The magnitude of the offense also may require that you skip the verbal warning and proceed directly to the written warning. Written warnings signal to your employees that you're serious and that you're documenting their behavior for their personnel files. The employee's immediate supervisor gives the written warning.

3. **Reprimand:** Repeated or serious misconduct results in a reprimand. A reprimand is generally constructed in the same format as a written warning. However, a manager higher up in the organization gives the reprimand instead of the employee's immediate supervisor. The reprimand is the employee's last chance to correct the behavior before suspension, demotion, or termination.

4. **Suspension:** A *suspension,* or mandatory leave without pay, is used in cases of serious misconduct or repeated misconduct that hasn't been corrected as a result of other, less severe attempts at employee discipline. You may have to remove an employee from the workplace for a period of time, to ensure the safety of your other employees or to repair your work unit's morale. An employee may also be given nondisciplinary suspensions while being investigated on charges of misconduct. During a nondisciplinary suspension, an employee is usually paid while the manager, human resources representative, or other company official reviews the case.

5. **Termination:** In particularly serious cases of misconduct, termination may be your first choice in disciplining a worker. This rule is particularly true for extreme violations of safety rules, theft, gross insubordination, and other serious misconduct. Termination may also be the result of repeated misconduct that less severe discipline steps don't correct. See Chapter 19 for more information about terminating employees.

Disciplining Employees: A Suite in Five Parts

A right way and many wrong ways to discipline employees exist. Forget the many wrong ways for now and focus on the right way.

Regardless of which kind of discipline you select for the particular situation, the approach you take with your employees remains the same whether you conduct verbal counseling or give a suspension or demotion (because of their finality, terminations are an exception here). Five steps must always form the basis of your discipline script. By following these simple steps, you can be sure that your employees understand the problem, their role in creating the problem, and how to correct it.

Step 1: Describe the unacceptable behavior

Exactly what is your employee doing that is unacceptable? When describing unwanted behavior to an employee, make sure that you're excruciatingly specific. You don't have time for mushy, vague statements such as "You have a bad attitude," or "You make a lot of mistakes," or "I don't like your work habits."

Always relate unacceptable behaviors to specific performance standards that haven't been met or to specific policies that have been broken. Specify exactly what the employee did wrong and when the unacceptable behavior occurred. Don't forget to focus on the behavior and not on the individual.

Following are some examples for you to consider:

- "Your performance last week was below the acceptable standard of 250 units per week."
- "You failed the drug test that you took on Monday."
- "The last three analyses that you submitted to me contained numerous computational errors."
- "You've been late to work three out of four days this week."

Step 2: Express the impact to the work unit

When an employee engages in unacceptable behavior — whether her work doesn't meet standards or she engages in misconduct — the behavior typically affects a work unit negatively. When an employee is consistently late to work, for example, you may have to assign someone else to cover your employee's position until the tardy employee arrives. Doing so takes your other employee away from the work she should be doing, reducing the efficiency and effectiveness of the work unit. And if an employee engages in sexual harassment, the morale and effectiveness of the workers who are subjected to the harassment unnecessarily suffer.

Continuing with the examples in the preceding section, following are the next steps in your discipline script:

- "Because of your below-standard performance, the work unit didn't meet its overall targets for the week."
- "This violation specifically breaks our drug-free workplace policy."
- "Because of these errors, I now have to take extra time to review your work much more thoroughly before I can forward it up the chain."
- "Because of your tardiness, I had to pull Marge from her position to cover yours."

Step 3: Specify the required changes

Telling your employee that he did something wrong does little good if you don't also tell that employee what he needs to do to correct the behavior. As a part of your discipline script, tell your employee the exact actions that you want him to adopt. Tell the employee that his behavior must be in accordance with an established performance standard or company policy.

Following are some examples of the third part of your discipline script:

- ✔ "You must bring up your performance to the standard of 250 units per week or better immediately."

- ✔ "You will be required to set an appointment with the company's employee assistance program for drug counseling."

- ✔ "I expect your work to be error free before you submit it to me for approval."

- ✔ "I expect you to be in your seat, ready to work, at 8:00 a.m. every morning."

Step 4: Outline the consequences

Of course, if the unacceptable behavior continues, you need to have a discussion with your employee about the consequences of his actions. Make sure that you get the message across clearly and unequivocally and that your employee understands it.

Consider these possibilities for the fourth part of your script:

- ✔ "If you can't meet the standard, you'll be reassigned to the training unit to improve your skills."

- ✔ "If you refuse to undergo drug counseling, you'll be suspended from work without pay for five days."

- ✔ "If the accuracy of your work doesn't improve immediately, I'll have to issue a written counseling to be placed in your employee file."

- ✔ "If you're late again, I will request that the general manager issue a formal reprimand in your case."

Step 5: Provide emotional support

Give your employee an emotional boost by expressing your support for his efforts. Make this support sincere and heartfelt — you do want your employee to improve, right?

Finally comes the icing on the pineapple upside-down cake that is employee discipline:

✔ "But let's try to avoid that — I know you can do better!"

✔ "I really want this to work out — let's find you the help you need."

✔ "Is there anything I can do to help you avoid that outcome?"

✔ "There's no reason we can't avoid that situation — I'm counting on you to turn this around!"

Putting it all together

After you develop the five parts of your discipline script, combine them into a unified statement that you deliver to your wayward employee. Although you'll undoubtedly discuss the surrounding issues in some detail, make the script be the heart of your discipline session.

The five parts of the script work together to produce the final product as follows:

✔ "Your performance last week was below our standard of 250 units per week. Because of your below-standard performance, the work unit didn't meet its overall targets for the week. You must bring up your performance to the standard of 250 units per week or better immediately. If you can't meet the standard, you'll be reassigned to the training unit to improve your skills. But let's try to avoid that — I know you can do better!"

✔ "You failed the drug test you took on Monday. This violation specifically breaks our drug-free workplace policy. You'll be required to set an appointment with the company's employee assistance program for drug counseling. If you refuse to undergo drug counseling, you'll be suspended from work without pay for five days. I really want this to work out — let's find you the help you need."

✔ "The last three analyses you submitted to me contained numerous computational errors. Because of these errors, I now have to take extra time to review your work much more thoroughly before I can forward it up the chain. I expect your work to be error free before you submit it to me for approval. If the accuracy of your work doesn't improve immediately, I'll have to issue written counseling to be placed in your employee file. Is there anything I can do to help you avoid that outcome?"

> ✔ "You've been late to work three out of four days this week. Because of your tardiness, I had to pull Marge from her position to cover yours. I expect you to be in your seat, ready to work, at 8:00 a.m. every morning. If you're late again, I will request that the general manager issue a formal reprimand in your case. There's no reason we can't avoid that situation — I'm counting on you to turn this around!"

Making a Plan for Improvement

Managers love plans: plans for completing projects on time, plans for meeting the organization's financial goals in five years, and plans to develop more plans. In the case of employee discipline, one more plan exists. The *performance improvement plan* is a crucial part of the discipline process because it sets definite steps for the employee to take to improve performance within a fixed period of time.

If your employee's performance transgressions are minor and you're giving only verbal counseling, working up a performance plan is probably overkill. Also, because most instances of misconduct must, by nature, be corrected right now or else, performance improvement plans generally aren't appropriate for correcting employee misconduct. However, if your employee's poor performance is habitual and you've selected counseling or more severe discipline, a performance plan is definitely what the doctor ordered. *Take two and call me in the morning!*

A performance improvement plan consists of the following three parts:

1. **Goal statement:** The goal statement provides clear direction to your employees about exactly what it takes to make satisfactory improvement in their performance. The goal statement, which is tied directly to an employee's performance standards, may be something along the lines of "Completes all his assignments on or before agreed deadlines" or "Is at her workstation ready to work at exactly 8:00 a.m. every day."

2. **Schedule for attainment:** What good is a plan without a schedule? Not having a schedule is like eating an ice cream cone without the ice cream or like watching TV with the sound turned off. Every good plan needs a definite completion date with fixed milestones along the way if the plan for goal attainment is complex.

3. **Required resources/training:** The performance improvement plan must also contain a summary of any additional resources or training to help your employee bring performance up to snuff.

Figure 18-1 shows a sample performance improvement plan for a worker who makes repeated errors in typed correspondence.

Performance Improvement Plan

Jack Smith

Goal statement:
- Complete all drafts of typed correspondence with two or fewer mistakes per document.

Schedule for attainment:
- Jack must meet this goal within three months of the date of this plan.

Required resources/training:
- Jack will be enrolled in the company refresher course in typing and reviewing correspondence. This training must be successfully completed no later than two months after the date of this plan.

Figure 18-1:
A sample performance improvement plan.

Implementing the Improvement Plan

After you put the performance improvement plan in place, your job is to ensure that it doesn't just gather dust on your employee's shelves. Follow up with your employee to make sure he's acting on the plan and making progress toward the goals you both agreed to. Yes, following up on improvement plans takes time, but that time is well spent. Besides, if you can't find the time to check your employees' progress on their improvement plans, don't be surprised if they can't find the time to work on them.

Are your employees following through with the goal statements you agreed to? Do they even have the goal statements you agreed to? Are they keeping to their schedules, and are they getting the training and other resources that you agreed to provide? If not, you need to emphasize the importance of the improvement plans with your employees and work with them to figure out why they haven't been implemented as agreed.

To assist your employees in implementing their improvement plans, schedule regular progress reporting meetings with them on a daily, weekly, or monthly basis. More extensive improvement plans necessitate more frequent follow-up. Progress meetings serve two functions:

- ✔ They provide you with the information you need to know to assess your employees' progress toward meeting their plans.

- ✔ They demonstrate to your employees — clearly and unequivocally — that their progress is important to you. If you demonstrate that the plans are important to you, your employees can make the plans a priority in their busy schedules.

Top five discipline Web sites

Wondering where to find the best information on the Web about the topics addressed in this chapter? Here are our top five favorites:

✔ Dummies.com: Giving Constructive Feedback: `www.dummies.com/how-to/content/giving-constructive-feedback.html`

✔ Business Owner's Toolkit: `www.toolkit.com/tools/bt.aspx?tid=coach_m`

✔ HRhero: How to Discipline and Document Employee Behavior: `www.hrhero.com/sample/trialdiscipline.pdf`

✔ EHow: How to Discipline Employees: `www.ehow.com/how_2076755_discipline-employees.html`

✔ Career Lab: `www.careerlab.com/art_confrontation.htm`

Set up performance improvement plans with your employees and stick with them. One of the most difficult challenges of management is dealing with a poor performer who improves under scrutiny and then lapses again. Stick with your plan. If an employee can't maintain necessary performance standards, you may want to consider whether that employee is really suited for continued employment. Unfortunately, not every employee is.

Chapter 19

Terminating Employees When All Else Fails

. . . .

In This Chapter

▶ Understanding the various kinds of termination

▶ Carrying out layoffs

▶ Taking necessary precautions before terminating an employee

▶ Firing employees: A step-by-step approach

▶ Determining the proper time to terminate employees

. . . .

*B*eing a manager is a tough job. If people tell you that the job is easy, they're joking, lying, or totally confused. Challenging? Yes. Constantly changing? Yes. Satisfying? Yes — for the most part. Easy? No. And of all the tough jobs managers have to do routinely, firing employees has to be the absolute toughest. Take our word for it: No matter how many times you fire someone, terminating an employee is never a pleasant thing to do.

The mechanics of terminating employees — setting goals, gathering data, assessing performance, carrying out discipline, and completing the paper-work — aren't so tough. The tough part is all the emotional baggage that goes along with firing someone — especially someone you've worked with for some time and have shared good and bad times with. However, no matter how difficult, taking an employee aside and telling him that his services are no longer needed is sometimes your only option.

No matter how much you try to help someone succeed in your organization, sometimes that person's employment at your firm just isn't meant to be. This forces the questions, what's the best way for you to deal with the problem, and what's the best way for you to deal with the person?

You see, terminations aren't limited only to your discretion. Sometimes employees "fire" themselves: "I quit!" If you're lucky, they give you two weeks. If you're not so lucky, you get less time to handle the transition. In any case, you're going to be awfully busy for a while as you work your way through the hiring process. (See Chapter 5 for more information about hiring good employees.)

This chapter deals with why employees are terminated, the different kinds of terminations, and exactly how you can carry them out. You discover the difference between a layoff and a firing, as well as the importance of documentation to support your actions.

Understanding the Types of Terminations

When you say the word *termination,* most people immediately think of the process of firing a worker who isn't doing her job. Although firing is the most dramatic and potentially volatile form of termination (just ask any manager who has had to deal with an employee who exploded during a termination), terminations come in many different flavors, depending on the situation.

Two major categories of employee termination exist: voluntary and involuntary. The key difference between the two is that an employee undertakes a voluntary termination of his own free will, while involuntary terminations are carried out against the will of the employee — often with the employee kicking and screaming all the way out the door. The following sections describe each category of termination.

Voluntary terminations

Employees have many reasons to terminate their own employment. Yeah, we know — that anyone would voluntarily choose to leave your particular brand of workers' paradise is hard to believe, but leave they do, and for all kinds of reasons. Sometimes employees find better promotional or pay opportunities with another firm. Sometimes employees find themselves in dead-end work situations or leave because of personality conflicts with their manager or other employees. Sometimes employees leave because of emotional stress, family needs, chemical dependency, or other personal reasons.

In some cases of voluntary termination, you don't want your employees to leave; in others, you're happy to see them go. And every once in a while, an employee actually stays with your firm long enough to retire. Because so few people seem to stay anywhere long enough to retire anymore — or to truly retire — this phenomenon is always a novel experience for the employees who witness it.

The following are the main reasons employees voluntarily leave:

✔ **Unprompted resignation:** Some resignations occur when an employee decides to quit his position with your firm with no prodding or suggestion to do so from you. Unfortunately, the best employees always seem to be the ones who resign. Although you can't force someone to stay with your organization forever (nor would you want to), you can make sure that people aren't leaving because your organization isn't adequately addressing problems. If a certain department is experiencing a lot of turnover, it may be a warning sign of a problem. Perhaps work conditions are too stressful or a supervisor or manager isn't treating the employees fairly or well. You may be able to save a good employee by addressing the organizational problem before he actually leaves. If not, conducting exit interviews with these employees as they are processing out of your organization can be a particularly useful tool in uncovering problems that need to be addressed. Don't let employees get away without first asking them why they decided to leave and what the organization could do better.

✔ **Encouraged resignation:** An encouraged resignation occurs when you suggest to an employee that she quit her job. Such resignations are often used as face-saving measures for employees who are about to be fired. Instead of firing your employees, you can offer them the opportunity to resign. This approach can help dampen the hurt of being fired, plus it keeps a potentially damaging employment action off the employee's record.

✔ **Retirement:** Some employees reach the end of their career and decide to terminate their employment finally and forever. Occasionally, organizations working to quickly cut costs offer certain employees early retirement, extending the benefits of regular retirement to those who are willing to retire from the company before they've reached the normal age of retirement. Retirement is generally a happy time for all involved, marked with celebrations and tokens of the organization's affection and gratitude (such as plaques, proclamations from company executives, and a nice luncheon).

Involuntary terminations

Of course, not all terminations are as easy to deal with as the voluntary forms we mention in the preceding section. Involuntary terminations are seldom pleasant experiences — for either manager or employee — and you really have to be at the end of your rope before you invoke this ultimate sanction against an employee. Involuntary terminations come in two types:

- **Layoffs:** A *layoff,* also known as a *reduction in force,* occurs when an organization decides to terminate a certain number of employees for financial reasons. For example, your company loses several key contracts and the revenue that was projected to come with them. To stay afloat, your firm may have no choice but to reduce payroll costs through layoffs.

    Every company has its own policy for determining the order of layoffs. In some organizations, the last employee hired is the first to go. In others, employee performance determines layoffs. Most organizations give hiring preference to laid-off employees if and when financial health is restored.

- **Firing:** Employees are fired when they have no hope of improving their performance, when job descriptions need to evolve and the people in the jobs aren't able to evolve along with them, or when they commit an act of misconduct that is so serious that termination is the only choice.

An 1884 Tennessee court decision (*Payne* v. *Western & A.R.P. Co.,* 81 Tenn. 507) established the termination-at-will rule within the United States. This rule said that employers have the right to terminate employees for any reason whatsoever — including no reason — unless a contract between employer and employee expressly prohibits such an action. However, more than 100 years of court decisions, union agreements, and state and federal laws have eroded the ability of employers to terminate employees at will. The federal government, in particular, has had the greatest effect on the termination-at-will rule, particularly in cases of discrimination against employees for a wide variety of reasons.

At-will still exists on a state-by-state basis, and some companies require prospective employees to sign a statement confirming termination-at-will when they're hired. Be sure to check your local regulations.

Federal regulations, such as the Civil Rights Act of 1964, the Equal Employment Opportunity Act of 1991, the Age Discrimination in Employment Act, and others, prohibit terminating employees specifically because of their age, race, gender, color, religion, national origin, and other federally mandated exclusions. Double-check any local and state regulations, too. To ignore these prohibitions is to invite a nasty and expensive lawsuit. Even the mere appearance of discrimination in the termination process (or anywhere else in your firm) can get you into trouble. In fact, most former employees — by some estimates, up to 90 percent — who bring wrongful termination cases to court today win their cases.

Good reasons for firing your employees

As long as you aren't discriminating against your employees when you terminate them, you have a lot of discretion as a manager. Although you generally have the right to terminate employees at will, you may find yourself on thin legal ice, depending on the specific grounds you select for firing your employees.

People generally agree, however, on certain behaviors that merit firing. Some of these behaviors are considered *intolerable offenses* that merit immediate action — no verbal counseling, no written warning, and no reprimand or suspension. Just immediate and unequivocal termination. They generally include these behaviors:

- **Verbal abuse of others:** Verbal abuse includes cursing, repeated verbal harassment, malicious insults, and similar behaviors. Your employees have the right to do their jobs in a workplace that is free of verbal abuse. And verbal abuse of customers and other business associates is just plain bad for business. If an employee continues to verbally abuse others after you give him fair warning, you can fire him without fear of legal repercussions. (And keep in mind that if you don't take action by quickly firing a repeated offender, you put yourself and your company at risk of a lawsuit by the employees being harassed!)

- **Incompetence:** Despite your continued efforts to train them, some employees just aren't cut out for their jobs. If you've tried to help an employee and she still can't perform her duties at an acceptable level of competence, parting ways is clearly in the best interest of both the employee and the firm.

- **Repeated, unexcused tardiness:** You depend on your employees to get their jobs done as scheduled. Not only does tardiness jeopardize the ability of your employees to complete their tasks on time, but it also sets a bad example for employees who are punctual. If an employee continues to be late to work after you warn him that you won't tolerate this behavior, you have clear grounds for termination.

- **Insubordination:** *Insubordination* — the deliberate refusal to carry out one's duties — is grounds for immediate termination without warning. Although supervisors commonly encourage their employees to question why a decision is made, after the decision is made, the employees must carry it out. If an employee is unwilling to follow your direction, the basic employer-employee relationship breaks down, and you don't have to tolerate it.

- **Physical violence:** Most companies take employee-initiated physical violence and threats of violence very seriously. Employees have the right to do their jobs in a safe workplace; employers have the duty to provide a safe workplace. Physical violence jeopardizes your employees' safety and distracts them from doing their jobs. Never let an employee think that you don't take a physical threat seriously; the best way to communicate that is to call law enforcement immediately, along with your human resources department. The workplace is no place for violence or threats of violence. If the employee has a need to act tough, call security or law enforcement.

✔ **Theft:** Theft of company property and the property of co-workers or clients is another big no-no. Most companies that catch employees engaging in this nasty little practice terminate them immediately and without warning. If you decide to terminate an employee for theft, and you have concrete proof that she carried out the crime, you can do so knowing that you're on firm legal ground.

✔ **Sexual harassment:** Unwelcome sexual advances, requests for sexual favors, and other verbal or physical conduct of a sexual nature on the job are intolerable offenses in many organizations and subject to immediate termination. Just say no!

✔ **Intoxication on the job:** Although being drunk or under the influence of drugs on the job is sufficient grounds for immediate termination, many companies nowadays offer their employees the option of undergoing counseling with an employee assistance program or enrolling in a program such as Alcoholics Anonymous. In many cases, employees can rehabilitate themselves and return to regular service.

✔ **Falsification of records:** Falsifying records is another big no-no that can lead to immediate dismissal. This category includes providing fraudulent information during the hiring process (fake schools, degrees, previous jobs, and so on) and producing other fraudulent information during the course of employment (faking expense reports, falsifying timecards, cheating on examinations, and so on).

Keep in mind that just because you *can* terminate an employee immediately for any of these offenses doesn't mean you *should.* For example, if an employee doesn't know how to do his job, you may decide to provide additional training opportunities instead of terminating him. Or if an employee is verbally abusive, you may provide a warning that if it happens again, the employee will be terminated immediately.

Regardless of whether you decide to terminate an employee immediately when one of these intolerable offenses occurs, you do need to take some sort of action that puts the employee on notice. If you don't, you're sending a clear signal to the offending employee — and to all your employees, customers, vendors, and other associates — that such behavior is acceptable. That message is one you don't want to send.

Reasons some managers avoid the inevitable

Terminating an employee isn't a pleasant way to spend an afternoon; most managers prefer doing most anything else. ("John, maybe we should go for a quick swim in the shark tank.") Although the reasons for terminating employees listed in the preceding section are clear cut and relatively easy for managers to use as leverage in a termination, having that leverage doesn't make the task any easier. But always keep in mind this old saying: Hire slow, fire quick. Few managers end up regretting firing a wayward employee too soon; far more regret not taking action more quickly when the writing is on the wall.

Some managers avoid carrying out a termination for the following reasons:

✔ **Fear of the unknown:** Terminating an employee can be a frightening prospect — especially if you're getting ready to do it for the first time. Is your employee going to cry? Have a heart attack or stroke? Get mad? Punch you out? Don't worry, every manager has to experience a first time.

The best way to get past this fear is to sit in on the termination of another employee, conducted by another manager or executive in your organization. If you can't make that happen, read up on the firing process and check in with human resources before you do it, to get both logical and emotional support.

✔ **Emotional involvement:** Considering that you likely spend from one-fourth to one-third of your waking hours at work, becoming friends with some of your employees is natural. Doing so is fine until you have to discipline or terminate one or more of your friends. Letting any employee go is tough enough, much less an employee with whom you have developed an emotional attachment.

✔ **Fear of a negative reflection upon yourself:** If you have to terminate one of your employees, what are you saying about yourself as a manager? In the case of a layoff, is it your fault that the organization didn't attain its goals? If you're firing an employee, did you make the wrong choice when you decided to hire that person? Many managers decide to put up with performance problems in their employees rather than draw attention to their own shortcomings — whether real or perceived.

✔ **Possibility of legal action:** The fear of legal action is often enough to stop a bull moose in his tracks at 50 paces. In these days of runaway, sue-at-the-drop-of-a-hat litigation, managers sometimes are afraid to terminate their employees and avoid it as long as they can, letting the problems fester and even grow.

✔ **Hope that the problem just goes away:** Yeah, right. Don't hold your breath.

Firing someone humanely, no matter what the reason

One of the hardest tasks any manager ever has to do is to fire an employee. Can you terminate an employee humanely? We'd like to think so. If you focus on being fair and keeping the person whole, you stand a good chance of minimizing the negative impact while making the best of a situation that's not working. These guidelines can help you make this difficult transition a little easier.

✔ **Give your employee the benefit of the doubt.** Be sure you're giving the employee a fair chance to succeed — not necessarily an endless number of chances, but a fair chance. This idea is especially important when the employee is new. You can say something like, "I don't know how you've been managed in the past, but I want to make it clear what's expected of you in this position so that we can agree on some mutual goals for your job." Summarize your expectations in writing and set up a time frame for reviewing progress on the employee's goals. Ask the employee to come to you if he has questions or needs help in meeting the expectations, and acknowledge when the employee has done good work. Don't expect employees to know what you want without open, two-way communication.

✔ **Make it clear when expectations aren't being met.** You have a much easier time dealing with problems when they're small than when they become huge. Bring up your concerns and the reasons behind them. You can use a disclaimer, such as, "I know you're capable of improving in this area of your job," but you also at some point need to be clear that if improvement isn't forthcoming, the employee could lose his job. Document these discussions for clarity, for reinforcement, and — if necessary — to provide evidence that you have made an honest attempt to manage the employee fairly.

✔ **Exhaust alternative approaches to dismissal.** Some managers find it useful to try one or more attempts to get through to an employee who isn't performing well. You can discuss other opportunities that may better match the employee's abilities, for example. Or you can offer the employee a "career day": "Tom, I'd like you to take a career day tomorrow. Take the day off and don't come to work. I'm still going to pay you, but I want you to go to the beach, a museum, or your kid's school — or even watch TV all day — and simply focus on one question: 'Is this job really what I want to be doing with my life right now?' Come back and give me your answer, and if you do really want to stay in your position, we have to talk about what needs to change in order for you to keep your job."

✔ **Offer a 0 percent increase.** Typically, in this approach, the person quickly falls in line or ends up leaving of his own accord. Either way, your problem is solved. For example, your conversation may go something like this: "Joe, we have some mutually agreed-upon goals, but I haven't seen where you've actually changed your behavior or achieved any of the results we've discussed. I don't like surprises, and I'm sure you don't, either. So I wanted to make it clear that your next performance review is in a few months, and if you haven't shown a substantial improvement in your performance, you won't be getting any salary increase."

✔ **Act quickly to dismiss.** When all is said and done, if someone isn't working out well, the sooner you deal with the situation, the better it'll be — for the employee, yourself, and the workgroup. You have to move from hoping that your employee improves to looking at the evidence as if he is, in fact, improving. Remember, sometimes the biggest motivator for your workgroup is to get rid of the people who aren't performing, thereby sending a clear message to everyone else that the group can't afford to have anyone who isn't contributing per their level of responsibility and compensation. In reality, the reaction from other employees — who often know more about a co-worker's performance than anyone else in the organization could ever hope to — is "What took you so long?" Even at dismissal, you can still be gracious: "I thought things would work out, but they haven't and we're going to let you go."

Conducting a Layoff

Call it what you like: a reduction in force, a downsizing, a rightsizing, a re-engineering, or whatever. The causes and results are still the same. Your organization needs to reorganize its operations, or cut payroll and related personnel and facilities costs, and some of your employees need to go.

Although they're understandably traumatic for the employees involved, lay-offs are different from firings because the employees who are terminated in a layoff generally aren't at direct fault. They're usually good employees who follow the rules. They're productive and do their jobs. They're loyal and dedicated workers. They may even be your friends. The real culprits are usually external factors, such as changes in markets, mergers and acquisitions, and pressures of a more competitive global marketplace.

When it's time to conduct a layoff, use the following step-by-step guide to help you through the process:

1. **Get your human resources department in the loop.**

   Remember these words: No manager is an island. Whenever you make plans to terminate any employee, get your human resources department involved at the outset. HR involvement helps ensure that the termination is done as smoothly as possible and that it complies with the law.

2. **Determine the extent of the problem and figure out what departments will be affected.**

   How deep is the financial hole your organization finds itself in? Will fortunes change anytime soon? If certain products or services aren't selling, what departments are affected?

3. Freeze hiring.

Hiring employees during a layoff process doesn't make sense unless the position is absolutely critical. For example, if a receptionist quits, you still need someone to answer the phones and receive visitors. Not only do you risk laying off a new hire, but hiring at this time sends the wrong message to your employees that you don't care about your current employees. If you do have to hire, be sure to first consider previously laid-off employees before you go outside the organization.

4. Prepare tentative lists of employees to be laid off.

To identify which employees to lay off, start by determining which employees have the most skill and experience in the areas the organization needs and which employees have the least. The first employees to go in a layoff are usually employees whose skills and experience don't mesh with the organization's needs. Review age, gender, and ethnicity of proposed affected employees with human resources and your legal department.

5. Notify all employees of planned layoffs in advance.

When the need for a layoff seems certain, get the word out to all employees immediately and well in advance of the planned layoff. Fully disclose the financial and other problems your organization faces and solicit employee suggestions for ways to cut costs or improve efficiency. Sometimes employee suggestions can save you enough money to avert the layoff or at least soften its blow on the organization. Err on the side of overcommunication.

6. Prepare a final list of employees to be laid off.

After you turn the organization upside down to find potential savings, you need to prepare a list of employees to be laid off. Write the list in rank order, in the event of a change that allows you to remove employees from the list. Most companies have standard procedures for ranking employees for layoff — especially if a union represents workers. These procedures generally give preference to permanent employees over temporary ones and include seniority and/or performance in the formula for determining who stays and who goes. If you don't have a policy, you need to determine the basis for laying off employees. In this case, you want to consider your employees' experience and how long they've been with the organization. Be particularly careful not to discriminate against protected workers — people protected by law from firings based purely on, for example, age or race — who are good performers.

7. Notify affected employees.

By now, many employees are probably paralyzed with the fear that they'll be let go. As soon as you finish developing the layoff list — updating it to account for employees who may have already found new jobs on their own — notify the affected employees that they will be laid off at some future time. Private, one-on-one meetings are the best way to handle notification. This step often occurs days, weeks, or sometimes even months before the actual layoff occurs, but you may opt to skip it in favor of immediate terminations.

8. **Provide outplacement services to terminated employees.**

If time and money permit, provide outplacement and counseling support to the employees who have been selected for termination. Your organization can provide training in subjects such as résumé writing, financial planning, interviewing, and networking, and allow the employees to use company-owned computers, fax machines, and telephones in their job searches. If you can help your employees by providing job leads or contacts, by all means do so.

9. **Terminate.**

Conduct one-on-one termination meetings with employees to finalize arrangements and complete termination paperwork. Explain the severance package, continuation of benefits, and any other company-sponsored termination programs, as appropriate. Collect keys, identification badges, and any company-owned equipment and property. Keep in mind that in group layoff situations in the United States, the WARN Act may require up to 45 days notice before employment ends.

10. **Rally the "survivors."**

Rally your remaining employees together in an "all-hands" meeting to let them know that, now that the layoffs are completed, the firm is back on the road to good financial health. Tell the team that, to avoid future layoffs, you have to pull together to overcome this momentary downturn in the business cycle.

Following Procedure to Fire an Employee

Although your job is to point out your employees' shortcomings and help them perform to standard, the employees are ultimately responsible for their performance and behavior. When you arrive at the last disciplinary step before firing an employee, letting her know that the responsibility and choice are hers alone is important; you can't do this critical step for her. Your employee either improves her performance or leaves. And if she decides to leave, have her express his choice in writing.

Assuming that the employee has chosen to continue the misconduct or below-standard performance, the choice is then yours. And your choice must be to terminate before the employee does any more damage to your organization.

Taking steps to protect yourself prior to firing

Firing an employee is unpleasant enough without having to get dragged through the courts on a charge of wrongful termination. The problem is that, although most organizations have clear procedures for disciplining employees, some managers still ignore these procedures in the heat of the moment. A manager's minor oversight can lead to major monetary damage awards in favor of former employees.

Before you fire an employee for cause, make sure you meet the following criteria and line up your ducks in a nice, neat row. Take our word for it, you'll be glad you did!

- **Documentation:** Remember the rule: Document, document, and then document some more. If you're firing an employee because of performance shortcomings, you'd better have the performance data to back up your assertions. If you're firing an employee for stealing, have proof that this employee is the thief — real proof, not just a suspicion. You can never have too much documentation. This rule is always true when you take personnel actions, particularly when you terminate an employee.

- **Fair warning:** Were your employee's performance standards spelled out clearly in advance? Did you explain company policies and practices along with your expectations? Did you give your employee fair warning of the consequences of continued performance problems? Because of the American legal tradition of due process, terminating an employee without warning for performance-related behaviors is generally considered unfair. However, certain kinds of employee misconduct, including physical violence, theft, and fraud, are grounds for immediate termination without warning. See the complete list of these intolerable offenses earlier in this chapter.

- **Response time:** Did you give your employee enough time to rectify his performance shortcomings? The amount of time considered reasonable to improve performance depends on the nature of the problem to be addressed. For example, if the problem were tardiness, you expect the behavior to be corrected immediately. However, if the employee is to improve performance on a complex and lengthy project, demonstrating improvement may take weeks or months.

- **Reasonableness:** Are your company's policies and practices reasonable? Can the average worker achieve the performance standards that you set with your employees? Does the penalty match the severity of the offense? Put yourself in your employee's shoes. If you were being terminated, would you consider the grounds for termination to be reasonable? Be honest!

✔ **Avenues for appeal:** Does your firm offer employees ways to appeal your decision to higher-level management? Again, due process requires an avenue for terminated employees to present their cases to higher management. Sometimes a direct supervisor is too close to the problem or too emotionally involved, which can cause errors in judgment that someone not personally involved in the situation can see easily.

Planning the meeting and stating the facts

When you've made the fateful decision to fire an employee, it's time to get your human resources department involved. This ensures that the termination is done as smoothly as possible and that it complies with the law. If you try to freelance a termination — without the help or involvement of your human resources department — you may end up creating more problems that you solve.

Keep two key goals in mind when firing employees:

✔ **Provide a clear explanation for the firing.** According to legal experts, many employees file wrongful termination lawsuits simply in hopes of discovering the real reason they were fired.

✔ **Seek to minimize resentment against your company and yourself by taking action to maintain your employee's dignity throughout the termination process.** The world is a dangerous enough place without incurring the wrath of potentially unstable former employees. If you have any concern that the employee might not leave the workplace willingly, make arrangements ahead of time for a security guard or someone from human resources to escort the employee out of the office. In many cases, however, this step is unnecessary. You can help employees maintain their dignity by allowing them to work through their end dates, turn in property, and leave without escort. Refer to the earlier section "Firing someone humanely, no matter what the reason" for more ideas.

Fire an employee in a meeting in your office or other private location. Make the meeting concise and to the point; figure on setting aside approximately five to ten minutes for the meeting. Termination meetings aren't intended to be discussions or debates. Your job is to inform your employee that he is being fired. This meeting isn't going to be fun, but keep in mind that you're taking the best course of action for all concerned. One more thing: Have a witness with you when you terminate an employee — especially when the person being terminated is of a different gender or other protected class. Ideally, bring someone from human resources whom you can have step in with a discussion of the administrative details of the termination, such as turning in keys and equipment, continuing benefits, receiving severance pay, and so forth.

Here, then, are the three steps for firing an employee:

1. **Tell the employee that he's being terminated.**

   State simply and unequivocally that you've made the decision to fire him. Be sure to note that you considered all relevant evidence, that you reviewed the decision with all levels of your organization's management, and that the decision is final. If you did your homework and used a system of progressive discipline (see Chapter 18) in an attempt to correct your employee's behavior, the announcement should come as no surprise. Of course, regardless of the circumstances, a firing shakes anyone to the core.

2. **Explain exactly why the employee is being terminated.**

   If the firing is the result of misconduct, cite the policy that was broken and exactly what your employee did to break it. If the firing is due to a failure to meet performance standards, remind him of past attempts to correct his performance and the subsequent incidents that led to the decision to fire him. Stick to the facts.

3. **Announce the effective date of the termination and provide details on the termination process.**

   A firing is normally effective on the day you conduct your termination meeting, except in the case of group layoffs. Keeping a fired employee around is awkward for both you and your employee, so avoid it at all costs. If you're offering a severance package or other termination benefits, explain them to your employee, along with how he should make arrangements to gather personal effects from his office. Go through the termination paperwork with the employee and explain the handling of final wages due.

 You may find it helpful to prepare a *termination script* to read during the termination meeting. A script is beneficial because it keeps you from forgetting to mention an important piece of information, and it provides instant documentation for your employee's personnel file (which you should retain for at least seven years after terminating the employee). Practice it before you go into the termination meeting.

Here is a sample termination script for an employee with ongoing performance problems:

> Tom, we've decided that today is your last day of employment with the firm. The reason for this decision is that you can't maintain the performance standards that we agreed to when you were hired last year. We have discussed your failure to meet standards on many occasions over the past year. Specifically, the written counseling that I gave you on October 5 notified you that you had one month to bring your performance up to standard or you could be terminated. You didn't achieve this goal, and I therefore have no other choice but to terminate your employment, effective today. Jenny from Personnel is here to discuss your final pay and benefits and to collect your office keys and voice-mail password.

Defusing tense firing meetings

Termination can be quite traumatic for the employee on the receiving end of the news. Expect the unexpected. One employee may become an emotional wreck; another may become belligerent and verbally abusive. And every once in a great while, one may become physically violent. To help defuse these situations and others, consider applying the following techniques:

- ✔ **Empathize with your employee.** Don't try to sugarcoat the news, but be understanding of your employee's situation. The news you've just delivered is among the worst news anyone can get. If your employee becomes emotional or cries, don't try to stop it — offer a tissue and go on.

- ✔ **Be matter-of-fact and firm.** Even if your employee becomes unglued, you must maintain a calm, businesslike demeanor throughout the termination meeting. Don't lead your employee to believe that she's participating in a negotiating session or that she can do something to change your mind. Be firm in your insistence that the decision is final and not subject to change.

- ✔ **Keep the meeting on track.** Although letting your employee vent is appropriate, don't allow her to steer the meeting from the main goal of informing her about the termination. If the employee becomes abusive, inform her that you'll end the meeting immediately if she can't maintain control. If you have reason to believe that an employee may become abusive or physically violent, have security nearby.

Determining the Best Time to Terminate

Every manager likely has an idea of what day of the week and time of the day you should select to terminate your employees (through a layoff or firing). Monday terminations are the way to go because of A, B, and C. Or Friday terminations are best because of X, Y, and Z. And is it better to carry out a termination the first task in the morning, or should you wait until the close of business?

 We think that terminating an employee as soon as you decide it's necessary — regardless of what day of the week it may be — makes the most sense. When you've decided that an employee needs to go, every additional day is a drain on the organization — and on yourself.

So what time is the best to terminate? The best approach is when his co-workers aren't there to witness the termination, either prior to starting work, when everyone's out to lunch, or at the end of the business day when most employees have already gone home. The idea is to minimize the embarrassment for the terminated employee.

If you terminate an employee earlier in the day, he has to face co-workers and explain why he's packing up his belongings and why the security guard is preparing to escort him off the premises. Your intent isn't to punish or embarrass your employee — you want to make the termination process as painless and humane as possible. Allow him to save face by scheduling the termination meeting at a time when you can avoid public display.

Top five termination Web sites

Wondering where to find the best information on the Web about the topics addressed in this chapter? Here are our top five favorites:

✔ Nolo: Firing Employees and Employee Resignations: `www.nolo.com/legal-encyclopedia/firing-resignations`

✔ Business Owner's Toolkit: Firing and Termination: `www.toolkit.com/small_business_guide/sbg.aspx?nid=P05_8101`

✔ BusinessTown.com: Firing Employees: `www.businesstown.com/people/firing.asp`

✔ Fast Company: Losing or Firing Employees: `www.fastcompany.com/guides/lose.html`

✔ *Inc.* Magazine: Firing and Employee Resignations: `www.inc.com/firing-and-layoffs`

Part V
The Part of Tens

The 5th Wave   By Rich Tennant

"... and remember - a posse ain't a posse until it's good and riled up. Which is why I've brought one of the country's foremost rilers to speak with you today."

In this part . . .

Because you don't always have a lot of time to devote to an issue, the three chapters in this part are packed with quick ideas and advice to help you become a better manager. We start with ten common management mistakes to avoid, move on to advice for managers new to the position, and close with guidance on achieving a healthy work-life balance.

Chapter 20

Ten Common Management Mistakes

Managers make mistakes — it's part of the job. Mistakes are nature's way of showing you that you're learning. And this truism doesn't apply to only you, the manager — it also applies to employees in every position throughout your organization. Everyone in the company makes mistakes from time to time. So we say that you need to encourage your employees to take risks with innovative new approaches to doing their jobs that might result in better customer service, cost savings, increased revenues and profits, and other positive outcomes.

This chapter lists ten traps that new and experienced managers alike can — and do — fall victim to.

Not Making the Transition from Worker to Manager

When you're a worker, you have a job and you do it. Although your job likely requires you to join a team or to work closely with other employees, you're ultimately responsible only for yourself. Did you attain your goals? Did you get to work on time? Did you do your work correctly? When you become a manager, everything changes. Suddenly, you're responsible for the results of a group of people, not just for yourself. Did your employees attain their goals? Are your employees highly motivated? Did your employees do their work correctly?

Many accomplished employees are comfortable being responsible only for the work or tasks they've been assigned to do, but they may feel uncomfortable when they're made responsible for the work of others. Ultimately, it's up to you to make sure your employees are doing their jobs well. If they fail, you'll fail, too — unless you take immediate action to help get them back on the right path.

Becoming a manager requires developing a whole new set of business skills: people skills. Some of the most talented employees from a technical perspective become the worst managers because they fail to make the transition from worker to manager.

Not Setting Clear Goals and Expectations for Your Employees

Do the words "rudderless ship" mean anything to you? They should. Effective performance starts with clear goals. If you don't set goals with your employees, your organization often has no direction and your employees have few challenges. Therefore, your employees have little motivation to do anything but show up for work and collect their paychecks.

Your employees' goals begin with a vision of where they want to be in the future. Meet with your employees to develop realistic, attainable goals that guide them in their efforts to achieve the organization's vision.

The key in setting goals and expectations is to work with your employees in setting them. Despite rumors to the contrary, goal setting is not a one-way street; it should always be an interactive, two-way discussion between manager and employee that takes into account the wants and needs of both. Don't leave your employees in the dark. Help them to help you, and your organization, by setting goals and then working with them to achieve those goals.

Failing to Delegate

Some surveys rank "inability to delegate" as the number one reason managers fail. Despite the ongoing efforts of many managers to prove otherwise, you really can't do everything by yourself. Even if you could, doing everything by yourself isn't the most effective use of your time or talent as a manager.

For example, you may be the best statistician in the world, but when you become the manager of a team of statisticians, your job changes. Your job is no longer to perform statistical analyses, but to manage and develop a group of employees who are experts at performing statistical analyses — and a wide variety of other tasks that you may or may not be an expert at doing.

When you delegate work to employees, you multiply the amount of work that you can do many times over. A project that seems overwhelming on the surface is suddenly quite manageable when you divide it among 12 different employees. Furthermore, when you delegate work to employees, you create opportunities to develop their work and leadership skills. Whenever you take on a new assignment or work on an ongoing job, ask yourself whether one of your employees can do it instead (and if the answer is yes, then delegate it!).

But don't forget to keep a close eye on results. Just because you delegate a task doesn't mean it's going to get done. You're still ultimately responsible for the performance of your work unit. When you delegate a task, create measurable performance milestones so both you and the employees know whether they're performing according to plan.

Failing to Communicate

In some organizations, many employees don't have a clue about what's going on. Information is power, and some managers use information — in particular, the control of information — to ensure that they're the most knowledgeable and, therefore, most valuable individuals in an organization. Some managers shy away from social situations and naturally avoid communicating with their employees, especially when the communication is negative in some way. Other managers are just too busy to communicate well. They simply don't make efforts to communicate information to their employees on an ongoing basis, letting other, more pressing business take precedence by selectively "forgetting" to tell their employees.

The health of today's organizations — especially during times of great change, as has become the norm today — depends on the widespread dissemination of information throughout an organization and the communication that enables this dissemination to happen. Employees must be empowered with information so that they can make the best decisions at the lowest possible level in the organization, quickly and without the approval of higher-ups.

Not Making Time for Employees

To some of your employees, you're a resource. To others, you're a trusted associate. Still others may consider you to be a teacher, coach, parent, or mentor, whereas others see you as just The Boss. However your employees view you, they have one thing in common: They need your time and guidance during the course of their careers. Managing is a people job — you need to make time for people. Some workers may need your time more than others. You must assess your employees' individual needs and address them.

Although some of your employees may be highly experienced and require little supervision, others may need almost constant attention when they're new to a job or task. When an employee needs to talk, make sure that you're available. Put aside your work for a moment, ignore your phone, and give your employee your undivided attention. Not only do you show your employees that they're important, but when you focus on them, you hear what they have to say.

Some managers find it effective to have an open-door policy — that is, whenever their door is open, employees are invited to drop in to talk. Other managers find that scheduling regular meetings — say, every Tuesday at 2 p.m. — works best. The approach you take isn't important; the important point is that you make time for your employees.

Not Recognizing Employee Achievements

In these days of constant change and increased worker uncertainty, finding ways to recognize your employees for the good work they do is more important than ever. The biggest misconception is that managers don't want to recognize employees. Most managers agree that rewarding employees is important; they just aren't sure how to do so and don't take the time or effort to recognize their employees.

Although raises, bonuses, and promotions have decreased in many organizations as primary motivators, you can take many steps that require little time to accomplish, are easy to implement, and cost little or no money. In fact, the most effective reward — personal and written recognition from one's manager — doesn't cost anything. Don't be so busy that you can't take a minute or two to recognize your employees' achievements. Their morale, performance, and loyalty will surely improve as a result.

Failing to Learn from Change

Most managers are accustomed to success, and they initially learned a lot to make that success happen. Many were plucked from the ranks of workers and promoted into positions as managers for this very reason. Often, however, they catch a dreaded disease — *hardening of the attitudes* — after they become managers, and they want things done only their way.

Successful managers find the best ways to get tasks done and accomplish their goals, and then they develop processes and policies to institutionalize these effective approaches to doing business. This method is great as long as the organization's business environment doesn't change. However, when the business environment does change, if the manager doesn't adjust — that is, doesn't *learn* — the organization suffers as a result.

This situation can be particularly difficult for a manager who has found success by doing business a certain way. The model of a manager as an unchanging rock that stands up to the storm is no longer valid. Today managers have to be ready to change the way they do business as their environments change around them. They have to constantly learn, experiment, and try new methods. If managers don't adapt, they are doomed to extinction — or, at least, irrelevance.

Resisting Change

The scope, breadth, and speed of change in business today are breathtaking. Consider the global marketplace. Sudden, unpredictable, and fundamental change swirls all around us — changing technology (especially *information* technology), economic conditions, competitive landscapes, political environments, ethical and belief systems, fashions, modes of communication, and ways of relating to others.

Today's high-stress business environment is dominated by simultaneous and often contradictory actions, colliding with each other at blinding speed even as they interact with a vast array of overlapping forces and conflicting players. Of course, the faster change occurs, the more disorienting it can be to lose your familiar landmarks and frames of reference. Instead of being able to rely on a predictable, ordered future, you find that the future is increasingly unknowable and the present is unstable.

Welcome to life as a manager today.

If you think that you can stop change, you're fooling yourself. You may as well try standing in the path of a hurricane to make it change its course. Good luck! The sooner you realize that the world — your world included — will change whether you like it or not, the better. Then you can concentrate your efforts on taking actions that make a positive difference in your business life. You must discover how to adapt to change and use it to your advantage instead of fighting it.

Instead of reacting to changes after the fact, proactively anticipate the changes coming your way and make plans to address them before they hit your organization. Ignoring the need to change doesn't make that need go away. The best managers are positive and forward looking.

Choosing the Quick Fix over the Lasting Solution

Every manager loves to solve problems and fix the broken parts of an organization. The constant challenge of the new and unexpected (and that second-floor corner office) attracts many people to management in the first place. Unfortunately, in their zeal to fix problems quickly, many managers neglect to take the time to seek out long-term solutions to the problems of their organizations.

Instead of diagnosing cancer and performing major surgery, many managers perform merely what amounts to slapping on a bandage. Although the job isn't as fun as being a firefighter, you have to look at the entire system and find the cause if you really want to solve a problem. After you find the cause of the problem, you can develop real solutions that have lasting effects. Anything less isn't really solving the problem, but merely treating the symptoms.

Taking It All Too Seriously

Yes, business is serious business. If you don't think so, just see what happens if you blow your budget and your company's bottom line goes into the red as a result. You quickly learn just how serious business can be. Regardless — indeed, *because* — of the gravity of the responsibilities managers carry on their shoulders, you must maintain a sense of humor and foster an environment that is fun, for both you and your employees.

Invite your employees to a potluck at the office, an informal get-together at a local lunch spot, or a barbecue at your home. Surprise them with special awards, such as the strangest tie or the most creative workstation. Joke with your employees. Be playful.

When managers retire, they usually aren't remembered for the fantastic job they did in creating department budgets or disciplining employees. Instead, people remember that someone who didn't take work so seriously and knew how to have fun brightened their days or made their work more tolerable. Don't be a stick in the mud. Live every day as if it were your last.

Chapter 21

Ten Tips for New Managers

*N*o matter how much experience a manager has under the belt, every manager was once a *new* manager. When you're new to management, you may find it difficult to know what tasks are important and what tasks can wait (or what tasks you can ignore altogether). However, becoming an effective manager requires you to separate the should-dos from the don't-have-to-dos. In this chapter, we consider ten tasks that every new manager should do.

Set Clear Goals and Expectations

Your job as a manager is to get big things done in your organization by leveraging the talents, abilities, and brain and muscle power of your employees. In short, to get much of your work done as a manager, you must delegate a lot of work, and you have to be able to rely on the people to whom you delegate it.

When you delegate work to an employee, however, it's not enough to simply make an assignment and hope for the best. You must also set clear goals and expectations for your employees. When employees aren't sure what exactly they're supposed to do and when they're supposed to do it, they can't meet your expectations — whatever they may be. However, when you're crystal clear about what you want your employees to do and when you want it done, your employees can prioritize their own work to ensure that they meet your deadlines. This approach provides a great learning opportunity for them to take on new or different projects, too.

Work with your employees in setting goals and expectations. Goals must be realistic, and you must ensure that your employees have bought into them and committed to achieving them. By making your employees a part of the goal-setting process, you not only get their vital input on the goals (for example, you may not be aware of a conflict that interferes with a deadline), but you also increase employee engagement (we discuss the importance of this in Chapter 4).

Don't Play Favorites

Think back to your school years. Was someone in your class the teacher's pet? If you were the teacher's pet, you probably enjoyed the position. However, if you didn't hold that coveted position, you probably weren't happy that your teacher played favorites with one or more of your classmates — especially if the favoritism meant someone was forgiven for transgressions that other students were punished for, or was given a better test score than others who performed just as well.

The same is true in the workplace. No one likes a manager who plays favorites with certain employees. Of course, people naturally like some people better than others — interpersonal chemistry simply favors some relationships over others. However, as a manager, your job is to be as impartial and fair as you possibly can in how you treat your employees. You can't punish an employee you don't like so much and then excuse the same behavior in an employee you do like. And you can't give favored employees raises, time off, bonuses, and other rewards when employees you don't favor exhibit the same performance or achieve the same goals or milestones.

Employees know when a manager is playing favorites — they can sense it a mile away. Our advice is to simply treat all your employees the same as the ones you like best.

Set a Good Example

Research shows that the most important relationship at work is between an employee (at any level) and the direct supervisor or manager. As a manager, you set the example for all the employees who work for you, and you influence the behavior of your peers and colleagues. The example you set sends a clear message about the kinds of behavior you personally find acceptable in the workplace. If you're chronically late to work, your employees will assume that being late for work is okay, and they'll be late, too. If you aren't ethical in your business dealings with customers, clients, and vendors, your employees will assume that they also don't have to behave ethically.

Model the behavior you want from your employees, and they'll reflect that behavior right back to you.

Remember That You Get What You Reward

Managers are often surprised when an employee exhibits a particular behavior or achieves a particular goal that's completely different from what they intended. When that's the case, you need to take a close look at exactly what behavior you are rewarding. For example, you may tell your employees that you want them to submit suggestions for cutting costs. However, when an employee submits an idea, you either ignore it completely or chew him out in front of his peers for having such a "stupid idea." In this case, instead of rewarding employees for submitting ideas, you're punishing them for it. You can bet that employees will think twice before they ever again think of submitting an idea to you for consideration.

Catch your employees doing something right. This approach works particularly well for managers who like to focus on getting things done. Just add the names of the people who report to you to your weekly to-do list. Then cross them off when you're able to praise those employees — because you catch them "doing something right" in accordance with their performance goals.

Although money is important to employees, what tends to motivate them to perform — and to perform at higher levels — is the thoughtful, personal kind of recognition that signifies true appreciation for a job well done. This recognition also builds trust and a collaborative relationship, which leads to higher levels of employee engagement. (We cover employee engagement in Chapter 4.)

Get to Know Your People

Back in ancient times, when we were new managers in large corporate settings, we were warned not to get too close to the people we supervised. We were told that doing so would undermine our authority and make it harder for us to make our employees do what we wanted them to do. This old-style management philosophy is now officially obsolete.

Using raw authority to make employees do what you want them to do is out. Instead, you involve employees in decision making and get them engaged in their jobs. When you do that, they *want* to achieve the goals that you set together.

You may not be inviting your employees to your house for Christmas, but there's nothing wrong with getting to know them as people. In fact, you stand to gain a lot by having normal relationships with your employees. These benefits may include increased levels of trust and loyalty, better communication, and higher performance.

Learn How to Delegate

Delegation is perhaps the most powerful tool at the disposal of any manager — it's the way managers get work done. Delegation is a win-win activity. When you delegate, others do much of the day-to-day work of the organization, freeing you up to manage, plan, and take on more complex work, with the potential for earning a higher salary. As your employees develop a broader range of skills, they'll be ready to move up with you. This partnership builds trust, enhances your career potential, and improves the health of your organization.

 Effective delegating involves more than asking someone to do something. It includes mutual consultation and agreement between the manager and team members. Solicit team members' reactions and ideas, thereby bringing trust, support, and open communication to the process.

Find a Good Mentor, Be a Good Mentor

Mentors serve as one of the best sources of the feedback you need as a manager. At work, two major mentor relationships exist: upward and downward. In an upward mentor relationship, a boss or higher-level executive in the organization agrees to give you career guidance and feedback. In a downward mentor relationship, you mentor a lower-ranking employee. If your company doesn't offer some way to pair up with a mentoring partner, check within your industry to find someone who may benefit you in such an arrangement.

Especially for a new manager, a good mentor can give you the kind of guidance and feedback that's hard to find anywhere else. Your mentor mixes experience with candid assessments of your performance to help nudge you in the right direction. Similarly, you do a great service to employees you mentor by mixing your experience with candid feedback. In every good mentor relationship, both the mentor and the person who is mentored can learn and grow from the experience.

Encourage Teamwork

Smart managers realize that they can get far more out of their organizations when employees cooperate with one another than if they compete against one another. Many tasks now get done through teamwork, and organizations are changing the way they do business. Organizations no longer measure employees only by their individual contributions; they also take into account how effective employees are as contributing members of their work teams.

As a manager, you want to encourage teamwork in your organization. Carefully assess work assignments and decide whether it makes more sense to assign them to individuals or to teams of employees. Reward your employees when they exhibit good teamwork skills — every business needs more of these skills.

Communicate, Communicate, Communicate

Good managers are skilled at communicating with their employees, and they do it often and through every means at their disposal. As a new manager, set aside some time each day to communicate with your employees. Walk through the work area to casually meet with employees and discuss current projects or customers. Keep in touch with employees through e-mail messages or telephone calls. Have regular staff meetings to discuss current opportunities and issues and to keep employees updated on the latest company happenings. Create a department blog or Facebook fan page to enable discussions within your organization.

When in doubt, err on the side of overcommunicating.

Be a Coach

A good coach helps employees perform at a higher level, in the same way that a baseball, football, or soccer coach helps athletes perform at a higher level. Coaches do this by offering advice on how to perform better, giving valuable feedback, and supporting the people they coach. They help employees gain confidence, and they applaud their efforts when employees make progress toward completing a goal. As a manager, you're in the perfect position to coach the people in your department or other organizational unit. Let them see that you're a human being; if you're approachable (and not perceived as perfect), your employees will find you more genuine, resulting in a better working relationship.

Chapter 22

Ten Tips for Maintaining Your Work–Life Balance

*I*n all the hustle and bustle of a typical day at the office — another rush order to get out, meetings stacked back to back, the computer network down, the latest crisis *du jour* — you can easily get caught up in work. There's nothing wrong with getting caught up in your work, but when work begins to intrude on your personal life a bit too far and a bit too often, you have a problem.

No matter how high up in the organization you are, or how important your job is, or how much you're getting paid, you have to take care of yourself first. When you take care of yourself, you stay in top form and you're a more valuable asset to your organization, your customers, and your employees. You also have a much better chance of surviving to retirement and enjoying the fruits of all your hard work. Doesn't that sound nice?

Life is all about balance, both at work and in your personal life. This chapter gives you ten easy ways to keep your work and life in balance, which makes you a better manager in the long run.

Make the Case for a More Flexible Workplace

You know that you and your employees need ways to move the balance of your lives more to the personal side and less to the work side. How exactly are you going to convince the powers-that-be that, first, this idea is good to implement and, second, company policies should be modified to make it happen?

You have to develop a business case for creating a flexible workplace, clearly spelling out the benefits to your organization for making the changes. Suggest that the change first be made as an experiment or pilot program that can be permanently implemented if it's successful. As you move through the process, consider the impact of alternative work arrangements on your customers, as well as on meetings and other ongoing company events. In many cases, flexible work schedules can directly benefit your customers by extending the hours of service available to them.

Avoid Workaholism

As the old saying goes, everything works in moderation. Unfortunately, regarding work, many people (both managers and workers alike) don't achieve much moderation. You're in overdrive from the moment you arrive early in the morning until you go home, often late at night. You normally work long hours and accept them as a part of today's workplace. Work takes over your life, leaving precious little time to spend with friends or family, or to pursue the kinds of physical or leisure activities that help you unwind after a hard day's work.

When overwork becomes more than an occasional event and you often push aside everything that isn't related to your job, you have a classic case of *workaholism.* And workaholism isn't good. Not only can workaholism lead you to neglect your family and social life, but it also can make you less productive and less efficient. The good news is that you can cure yourself of this obsessive addiction to work by following these tips:

- ✔ Work fewer hours. Commit to a 40-hour-a-week schedule and stick to it.
- ✔ Leave your work at the office when you go home every day.
- ✔ Spend more time with friends and family.
- ✔ Slow down. Take time to really relate to your co-workers, clients, customers, suppliers, and other people you encounter during the course of your business day.

✔ Take vacations, and don't take your work with you or check in with the office before your vacation is over.

✔ Set up a regular exercise schedule and stick to it.

✔ Take time for lunch, and get outside the office as often as possible to eat it.

Make the time now to take positive steps to ditch your work addiction. You can do it if you try. We guarantee that you'll be a changed person if you simply let go. Go ahead — what do you have to lose (besides an aggravated ulcer or two)?

Manage Your Stress

Have you ever wondered why so many organizations make such a big deal about stress-management training? Organizations must deal with stress because when employees allow stress to overcome them, they lose their effectiveness. And when employees lose their effectiveness, the organization loses its edge.

Most stress-management training focuses on treating the symptoms of stress, not on curing the root causes within the organization. We see a problem with this approach. The training programs teach workers relaxation techniques to decrease their level of stress, but top management isn't forced to make better and faster decisions. The training shows employees how to use positive affirmations to reinforce their feelings of self-worth, but the lousy phone system that cuts off customers midsentence isn't fixed. The program instructs the staff in better time management, but poor planning still leads to repeat organizational crises.

You can't wait for someone else to do something to reduce your stress for you. Find out how to manage stress yourself. Fortunately, managing stress isn't as hard as you may think. Effective stress management boils down to this: Change what you can change and accept what you can't change.

Change What You Can Change

You can take several steps right now to change your work environment and decrease your stress. If these steps sound familiar, you've probably thought about doing them before but maybe just couldn't get around to it. Well, now is the time to get serious about decreasing your stress. Don't delay and put it off until tomorrow — the life you save may be your own!

- ✔ **Get healthy.** You know that regular, vigorous exercise is one of the best activities you can do for yourself. Not only do you strengthen your mind and body, but you also work off tons of frustration and stress. And when you're under stress, your body quickly depletes its store of certain vitamins and minerals. Eat right. Don't forget your fruit and veggies! Particularly follow this advice when you're on the road; don't forgo exercise and proper diet because you're making a business trip.

- ✔ **Learn how to say no.** What's the old saying? "You can please some of the people some of the time, but you can't please all the people all the time." Recognize that you can't do everything. When you *do* try to do everything, usually nothing gets done well. When you already have a full plate of work to do and someone tries to give you more, say no.

- ✔ **Manage your schedule.** If you don't manage your own schedule, it will quickly find a way to manage you. Get a personal planner, desk calendar, or electronic schedule planner, and take charge of the meetings you attend and the appointments you keep.

- ✔ **Streamline.** Why make your job harder than it has to be? As a manager, you're in the perfect position to look for ways to improve your organization's work processes and systems. Be brutal in reviewing everything your department does, and remove needless steps. Simplify, shorten, and condense. Fewer steps in a process translates into a workforce that expends less effort, fewer problems, and, ultimately, less stress for you. And less stress is good!

- ✔ **Look for silver linings.** Be an optimist. Look for the good in everything you do and everyone you meet. You'll be amazed by how much better you'll feel about your job, your co-workers, and yourself. You'll also be amazed by how much better your co-workers feel about you when they can depend on you to lift their spirits. Be an ambassador of optimism. You can decrease your own stress and the stress of those employees around you, too.

Accept What You Can't Change

You just can't change certain things, no matter how hard you try. Instead of changing the unchangeable, you only end up stressed, defeated, or ill. When you can't change the unchangeable, you have one choice left: Change yourself.

✔ **Surrender to change.** Stop fighting change. Continuing the fight simply increases your stress level — along with your blood pressure and the number of bottles of antacid you need to quell the fire in your stomach. Instead of trying to row against the swift currents of change, let go and drift with them.

✔ **Don't take change personally.** Change doesn't affect just you. Everyone has to deal with change and its effects on the working environment. But the question isn't how everyone else responds to change; the question is how you respond to change. Do you retreat into your shell? Do you get frustrated and angry? Or do you take charge?

✔ **Adjust your attitude.** Losing perspective is sometimes easy to do. When you've worked at a job for a few years, you can start to get visions of grandeur. You may think, "How would this place survive without me?" Instead, think, "How long could I survive if I lost my job?" And don't be so sure that your organization will never experience a layoff or workforce reduction. Who do you think would be let go first, employees who willingly do whatever they can to get the job done or employees who think they're above all that? If you picked the former, you may be due for a major attitude adjustment.

✔ **Don't be a victim.** If you're a victim of change, you've stopped fighting change (which is good), but you've also stopped responding at all to the changes going on around you (which is bad). Don't give up and unplug yourself from the organization. Refuse to be a victim of change; instead, become its biggest fan. And if you absolutely can't stand your organization any longer, find another one.

✔ **Control your anger.** Getting mad when your job doesn't go your way may be expressive, but showing anger isn't a productive use of your time and energy. Getting angry about something you can do nothing to change saps your energy and distracts you from accomplishing the tasks that you *can* do something about.

Don't Sweat the Small Stuff

Much of what happens during the course of a normal business day is small stuff — filling out forms, pulling messages off your voice-mail system, poking at a few buttons on your computer keyboard. You may spend 80 percent of your time getting 20 percent of your results. The point is, most of what you do is small stuff, so don't sweat the small stuff! If you're going to worry, at least save it for something that's really important.

Use Positive Affirmations

Crowd the negatives out of your life with positive affirmations such as, "Gee, I really have this customer's needs figured out," or "I did a great job on that last assignment. I can't wait for another one so I can do a great job on that one, too." Get positive. The more positive your life is, the less stress you experience. (Plus, you're a lot more fun to be around than those naysayers you have to work with.)

Relax!

Relaxation is an extremely important part of any stress-management program. When you relax, you give your brain a break and give yourself a needed opportunity to recharge your batteries before going back into overdrive.

Every minute counts. Do you remember what breaks are? You may not have taken one for a while, so you may be a little rusty. When you take a break to relax, make it a real break from your routine. Get up from your desk and go someplace where you can remove yourself from the day-to-day business at hand. If you stay at your desk, chances are good that someone will call and you'll feel compelled to answer the phone, or someone will barge into your office and need your immediate attention. Go for a walk outside your building. Smell some flowers. Listen to the birds. Relax!

Take a Mental Vacation

Imagination is a powerful tool. No matter where you are, you can take a vacation anywhere you want, anytime you want. When the crowd at your door is five deep, your phone is ringing off the hook, everyone has a problem instead of a solution, and your blood pressure erupts like Krakatoa east of Java, a mental vacation is definitely in order.

Close your door, forward your phone to the operator or to voice mail, turn down your lights, kick your ergonomic chair back into its full relax mode, and let your mind float downstream. Picture yourself in a boat on a river with the sun shining and the birds chirping. Take yourself far away from the challenges of the day.

Have Fun

You're going to spend roughly a fourth to a third of your adult life at work. Sure, you need the money, and you need the psychological satisfaction that doing a good job brings with it, but don't ever take work so seriously that you can't have fun with your job and your co-workers.

Having fun with your job and with your co-workers is an important way to reduce stress on the job. Don't forget the saying, "All work and no play makes Johnny a very boring guy." Not only does a good laugh give you a great way to release stress, but it also reminds you that life is more than work. Right?

Index

• **Z** •

Business/Accounting & Bookkeeping

Bookkeeping For Dummies
978-0-7645-9848-7

eBay Business
All-in-One For Dummies,
2nd Edition
978-0-470-38536-4

Job Interviews
For Dummies,
3rd Edition
978-0-470-17748-8

Resumes For Dummies,
5th Edition
978-0-470-08037-5

Stock Investing
For Dummies,
3rd Edition
978-0-470-40114-9

Successful Time
Management
For Dummies
978-0-470-29034-7

Computer Hardware

BlackBerry For Dummies,
3rd Edition
978-0-470-45762-7

Computers For Seniors
For Dummies
978-0-470-24055-7

iPhone For Dummies,
2nd Edition
978-0-470-42342-4

Laptops For Dummies,
3rd Edition
978-0-470-27759-1

Macs For Dummies,
10th Edition
978-0-470-27817-8

Cooking & Entertaining

Cooking Basics
For Dummies,
3rd Edition
978-0-7645-7206-7

Wine For Dummies,
4th Edition
978-0-470-04579-4

Diet & Nutrition

Dieting For Dummies,
2nd Edition
978-0-7645-4149-0

Nutrition For Dummies,
4th Edition
978-0-471-79868-2

Weight Training
For Dummies,
3rd Edition
978-0-471-76845-6

Digital Photography

Digital Photography
For Dummies,
6th Edition
978-0-470-25074-7

Photoshop Elements 7
For Dummies
978-0-470-39700-8

Gardening

Gardening Basics
For Dummies
978-0-470-03749-2

Organic Gardening
For Dummies,
2nd Edition
978-0-470-43067-5

Green/Sustainable

Green Building
& Remodeling
For Dummies
978-0-470-17559-0

Green Cleaning
For Dummies
978-0-470-39106-8

Green IT For Dummies
978-0-470-38688-0

Health

Diabetes For Dummies,
3rd Edition
978-0-470-27086-8

Food Allergies
For Dummies
978-0-470-09584-3

Living Gluten-Free
For Dummies
978-0-471-77383-2

Hobbies/General

Chess For Dummies,
2nd Edition
978-0-7645-8404-6

Drawing For Dummies
978-0-7645-5476-6

Knitting For Dummies,
2nd Edition
978-0-470-28747-7

Organizing For Dummies
978-0-7645-5300-4

SuDoku For Dummies
978-0-470-01892-7

Home Improvement

Energy Efficient Homes
For Dummies
978-0-470-37602-7

Home Theater
For Dummies,
3rd Edition
978-0-470-41189-6

Living the Country Lifestyle
All-in-One For Dummies
978-0-470-43061-3

Solar Power Your Home
For Dummies
978-0-470-17569-9

Available wherever books are sold. For more information or to order direct: U.S. customers visit www.dummies.com or call 1-877-762-2974.
U.K. customers visit www.wileyeurope.com or call (0) 1243 843291. Canadian customers visit www.wiley.ca or call 1-800-567-4797.

Internet
Blogging For Dummies,
2nd Edition
978-0-470-23017-6

eBay For Dummies,
6th Edition
978-0-470-49741-8

Facebook For Dummies
978-0-470-26273-3

Google Blogger
For Dummies
978-0-470-40742-4

Web Marketing
For Dummies,
2nd Edition
978-0-470-37181-7

WordPress For Dummies,
2nd Edition
978-0-470-40296-2

Language & Foreign Language
French For Dummies
978-0-7645-5193-2

Italian Phrases
For Dummies
978-0-7645-7203-6

Spanish For Dummies
978-0-7645-5194-9

Spanish For Dummies,
Audio Set
978-0-470-09585-0

Macintosh
Mac OS X Snow Leopard
For Dummies
978-0-470-43543-4

Math & Science
Algebra I For Dummies,
2nd Edition
978-0-470-55964-2

Biology For Dummies
978-0-7645-5326-4

Calculus For Dummies
978-0-7645-2498-1

Chemistry For Dummies
978-0-7645-5430-8

Microsoft Office
Excel 2007 For Dummies
978-0-470-03737-9

Office 2007 All-in-One
Desk Reference
For Dummies
978-0-471-78279-7

Music
Guitar For Dummies,
2nd Edition
978-0-7645-9904-0

iPod & iTunes
For Dummies,
6th Edition
978-0-470-39062-7

Piano Exercises
For Dummies
978-0-470-38765-8

Parenting & Education
Parenting For Dummies,
2nd Edition
978-0-7645-5418-6

Type 1 Diabetes
For Dummies
978-0-470-17811-9

Pets
Cats For Dummies,
2nd Edition
978-0-7645-5275-5

Dog Training For Dummies,
2nd Edition
978-0-7645-8418-3

Puppies For Dummies,
2nd Edition
978-0-470-03717-1

Religion & Inspiration
The Bible For Dummies
978-0-7645-5296-0

Catholicism For Dummies
978-0-7645-5391-2

Women in the Bible
For Dummies
978-0-7645-8475-6

Self-Help & Relationship
Anger Management
For Dummies
978-0-470-03715-7

Overcoming Anxiety
For Dummies
978-0-7645-5447-6

Sports
Baseball For Dummies,
3rd Edition
978-0-7645-7537-2

Basketball For Dummies,
2nd Edition
978-0-7645-5248-9

Golf For Dummies,
3rd Edition
978-0-471-76871-5

Web Development
Web Design All-in-One
For Dummies
978-0-470-41796-6

Windows Vista
Windows Vista
For Dummies
978-0-471-75421-3

Available wherever books are sold. For more information or to order direct: U.S. customers visit www.dummies.com or call 1-877-762-2974.
U.K. customers visit www.wileyeurope.com or call (0) 1243 843291. Canadian customers visit www.wiley.ca or call 1-800-567-4797.

DUMMIES.COM®

How-to?
How Easy.

From hooking up a modem to cooking up a casserole, knitting a scarf to navigating an iPod, you can trust Dummies.com to show you how to get things done the easy way.

Go to www.Dummies.com

Visit us at Dummies.com

Dummies products make life easier!

DVDs • Music • Games •
DIY • Consumer Electronics •
Software • Crafts • Hobbies •
Cookware • and more!

For more information, go to
Dummies.com® and search
the store by category.

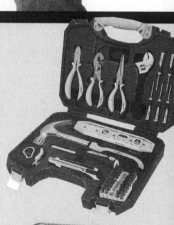

Making everything easier!™

Notes

Notes

Notes

Notes

Notes

Notes

Notes

Notes